RESILIENCE

RESIL

IENCE

FAITH, FOCUS, TRIUMPH

ALONZO MOURNING

WITH DAN WETZEL

BALLANTINE BOOKS   NEW YORK

Resilience is a work of nonfiction. Some names and identifying details have been changed.

The medical information imparted in this book is specific to Alonzo Mourning's unique situation. Kidney disease is a serious ailment, and any treatment should be conducted under the supervision of a physician.

Published in the United States by Ballantine Books, an imprint of The Random House Publishing Group, a division of Random House, Inc., New York.

BALLANTINE and colophon are registered trademarks of Random House, Inc.

Grateful acknowledgment is made to *The Washington Post* for permission to reprint an excerpt from an article that appeared on November 23, 1989, copyright © 1989 by The Washington Post. All rights reserved. Used by permission and protected by the Copyright Laws of the United States. The printing, copying, redistribution, or retransmission of the material without express written permission is prohibited.

All photos, unless otherwise credited, are from the personal collection of the author.

Library of Congress Cataloging-in-Publication Data

Mourning, Alonzo
Resilience : faith, focus, triumph / Alonzo Mourning with Dan Wetzel.
p. cm.
ISBN 978-0-345-50701-3 (hardcover : alk. paper)
1. Mourning, Alonzo, 1970– 2. African American basketball players—Biography.
3. Basketball players—United States—Biography. I. Wetzel, Dan. II. Title.

GV884.M65A3 2009
796.323092—dc22 2008026626
[B]

Printed in the United States of America on acid-free paper

www.ballantinebooks.com

9 8 7 6 5 4 3 2 1

First Edition

Book design by Karin Batten

This book is for my mother and father, who were always there for me no matter what; Mrs. Threet, who taught me so much about life, spirituality, and the importance of giving; my wife, Tracy, the love of my life; my children, Trey and Myka, the greatest gifts a man could hope for; my friend and agent, Jeff Wechsler; my coaches, Bill Lassiter, John Thompson, and Pat Riley, not only for my development on the court but for teaching me how to be a man, a professional, and a student of the game; my teammates through the years; all of my doctors and nurses at Columbia Presbyterian and in Miami; Jason Cooper, the man who saved my life; the Reverend Willie Alfonso, a guiding light; the entire staff of Alonzo Mourning Charities, which works so dilligently to enhance the lives of children and families; my sponsors; and all the survivors of organ transplants and their families and friends.

Command those who are rich in this present world not to be arrogant nor to put their hope in wealth, which is so uncertain, but to put their hope in God, who richly provides us with everything for our enjoyment. Command them to do good, to be rich in good deeds, and to be generous and willing to share. In this way they will lay up treasure for themselves as a firm foundation for the coming age, so that they may take hold of the life that is truly life.

—TIMOTHY 6:17–19

CONTENTS

1. THE WAKE-UP CALL   3

2. TIDEWATER   19

3. TRANSITION GAME   33

4. GEORGETOWN LESSONS   52

5. CHARLOTTE   69

6. MIAMI   89

7. THE BATTLE BACK   108

8. THE SEARCH FOR A DONOR   125

9. THE SURGERY   143

10. SURVIVORSHIP   158

11. THE COMEBACK   172

12. HOLISTIC MEDICINE   184

13. OVERTOWN   198

14. THE TITLE   211

    EPILOGUE   229

RESILIENCE

1

THE WAKE-UP CALL

The kid wouldn't eat. Not a bite. There was nothing his father could do. Doctors, nurses, and even fellow patients tried and got nowhere. For almost two weeks, no food. "I think he was giving up," said Brian Mossbarger of his ten-year-old son, Zach. Of all the setbacks in a lifetime of setbacks, this was the most crushing for the father to watch.

And this from a dad who found Zach unresponsive at the tender age of three weeks old, rushed him to a small-town Ohio hospital, had doctors set up a medical helicopter to a bigger facility in Toledo, and was told, brutally, "Don't expect him to survive the airlift."

Zach did survive, but his was a difficult life. He was in and out of hospitals, doctor after doctor, treatment after treatment, surgery after surgery, infection after infection. One thing and then another; every solution brought a new problem. He suffered from chronic kidney failure, and by the age of eight the self-conscious boy had scars all over his body and two six-inch tubes coming out of his neck to serve as a temporary catheter; then, at nine, he started regular dialysis. The schoolkids were predictably cruel.

Eventually doctors settled on a transplant. Brian, thirty-five, a tough machine repairman at an aluminum factory, was a perfect match. The transplant took place on Valentine's Day, 2007, at the University of Michigan hospital. For nine days, the kidney worked. Then it didn't. Vascular rejection, the doctors said; the worst possible kind.

And so Zach stopped eating. Doctors had to tube-feed him. "He thought the transplant would be it for him," Brian said. "When it didn't happen, he was really depressed."

No one knew what to do, what to say. In a small-world way, they found someone who might. Brian's older brother worked with a guy who knew another man whose mother, Shari Rochester, was Alonzo Mourning's assistant. The story got to Shari and she told Alonzo, told him about the vascular rejection, about the not eating. Alonzo said, "I have to meet this kid."

The Miami Heat were scheduled to play at the Detroit Pistons in a few days. Alonzo set it up so Zach, who hadn't left the hospital in six weeks, and Brian could visit him at the game. A doctor came along, just in case. On April 1, outside the Detroit visitors' locker room just before the game, they wheeled small, frail Zach in front of big, strong Alonzo, two transplant survivors, two kidney patients sharing a look of mutual understanding and respect. Then Alonzo knelt down and flexed one of his massive biceps at the awestruck kid.

"You want some of these, you've got to start eating," Alonzo said. "I had a transplant too, and look at me."

They talked some more. Took pictures, signed autographs, and exchanged phone numbers. Then Zach got wheeled out to courtside seats and stunned everyone.

He asked his dad for a hot dog.

A hot dog? Yes, the boy needed to eat, but something as nutritiously empty as a stadium hot dog? The doctor shrugged. "Go for it. It's something." Brian got Zach a hot dog. Then a half hour later Zach asked for nachos. A large order, no less. Brian got Zach nachos.

Back at the hospital everything seemed to change. The kid ate. The kid smiled. The kid started thinking positive. "He had been so down," Brian said. "Then it all changed."

Three weeks later, doctors tested his creatinine level—the key stat for all kidney patients, where the lower the number the better. Zach had been hanging around a too-high 2.1. The test came in at 1.6, an incredible improvement. Unbelievable, really. So they tested again. The creatinine was 1.6. Again. Over a month after rejection, was this kidney finally working?

Dumbfounded, the doctors huddled and decided to push the issue. They took Zach off dialysis, just to see. The next day he registered a 1.1. The next 0.8, normal for him. No one knew how it could have happened. Within days, Zach was out of the hospital.

"I'm not real religious," Brian said. "But one of the things Alonzo kept saying was 'Pray for it and everything will come out the right way.'

"How do you thank a guy like that, who has no clue who you are but steps into your life and helps out, calls, prays, offers advice and hope? What can I say about him?"

Brian said this from the side of a fishing hole in northwest Ohio, his old kidney going strong in his son's body. Dusk was coming fast and father and son were having a long, carefree time. The ten-year-old boy looked like any ten-year-old boy, laughing and jumping around as he caught a bass.

"You just have to stay positive and believe and never lose hope," Brian said. "That's what I'd tell other parents. That's what Alonzo kept telling me."

With that he went and unhooked his son's fish.

Your life can change in a single instant, at the most unexpected time in the most routine manner. One second you have a list of concerns and challenges and plans to deal with. The next second that all seems trivial and God is laying down a challenge—a challenge you never saw coming.

Mine came courtesy of a ringing telephone while I was asleep. I was taking a rare midday nap. Unless it was a game day, I was the last guy to spend the afternoon sleeping, especially with another NBA season to prepare for. But I was exhausted, suffering from what I believed was a combination of a lingering flu and extreme jet lag.

At my doctor's suggestion I had gone in for some medical tests, a precautionary biopsy, but I didn't believe anything serious was wrong, maybe a thyroid condition, or a virus. Maybe I was just ignoring the signs, but I really wasn't very concerned. At worst, I figured, I'd take some pills and get back to getting ready for the fast-approaching NBA season, one in which I had my eyes on winning the championship. After all, I was the healthiest person I knew—thirty years old, six foot ten, 255 pounds with just six percent body fat. I benched over three hundred pounds with ease. I worked out with hundred-pound dumbbells. I was a professional athlete, coming off a season where I was first team All NBA, a runner-up for NBA Most Valuable Player. That summer I had been named USA Basketball Player of the Year after we won gold at the Sydney Olympics. With defense as my specialty, my reputation as a player was as perhaps the toughest and hardest-working one in the entire league.

At that point, in September of 2000, I felt invincible, like I could leap tall buildings. Nothing ever fazed me. I kept telling myself, even after my doctor had suggested those tests, that I was just under the weather, the understandable fallout of recent events in my life. A grueling NBA season had led straight into summer with the Olympic team. With Dream Team IV, I had toured Asia before hitting Australia for the Olympics. At the same time, life at home was blessed but hectic.

My wife, Tracy, was pregnant with our second child, and part of the deal I made with her was that I could fulfill my dream of being an Olympian as long as I promised to make it back for the birth. I tend to push things and believe everything will work out, so we had looked at the Olympic basketball schedule, found a couple of open days and decided to have the labor induced on a Saturday right in the middle of the games. That way, I could fly back to Miami with my mother-in-law and my first son, Trey, be at the birth, and then fly back to Australia and not miss a single game. USA Basketball was on board with the plan and NBC was even going to send a camera crew along. Nothing makes for great television like a new baby. It was all set.

But two days before the induction, the baby decided to come anyway. My wife started feeling labor pains and was in the shower singing to her, "Baby girl, wait for Daddy. Wait for Nana and your big brother." By the time she got out of the shower, though, she knew she couldn't wait. She called me and said, "Look, it's time; it's coming." I dropped everything. We grabbed the next flight from Sydney to Los Angeles—fourteen hours in the air—and then jumped on a plane from L.A. to Miami, which is six more hours. The trip from L.A. came on the private jet of the owner of the Miami Heat; if he hadn't been so gracious, we probably wouldn't have made it.

That trip seemed to take forever. The last few hours, my wife was in the delivery room still singing to the baby to "wait for Daddy, wait for Daddy," but it was getting close. Tracy's sister, Lisa, was at the hospital, and in between contractions she was staring out the window looking for us to pull up. She finally said, "I see a limo, they're here!" I went racing up and my wife was just bawling because she couldn't believe we had made it, and within half an hour Myka Sydney—named after the town hosting the Olympics—was born. It was one of the greatest moments of my life, holding this little baby girl in my big hands and gaining that immediate love that only being a parent can provide. I was so overwhelmed I forgot to even be tired.

Talk about a whirlwind. I have so much faith in God, I never worried that I would miss the birth. It seemed perfectly reasonable to me that I arrived from the other side of the world, camera crew in tow, with twenty-five minutes to spare. That's the mentality I had, the trust I had in God. We all spent a great night together and then, less than twenty-four hours after reaching Tracy, I headed back to Australia where I arrived just in time for the medal rounds. I was exhausted but managed to play well. We won the gold, and my lifelong dream was fulfilled.

I returned to Miami and a house with a newborn, which isn't conducive to sleeping off jet lag. All things considered, I kept telling myself, I had every right to be tired.

I was being naïve, of course. This was more than jet lag. The truth is I had been fatigued all summer. I was fidgety and my muscles were taking on more water than usual. One day at the Olympics I was getting stretched out and my leg looked swollen. I pushed into the leg and

Trey, Myka, and me right after the Olympics

it left an indentation. I said to the trainer, "What the heck is this?" He told me I needed to get it checked out. But still, I was so unconcerned I never even told Tracy about it. She was busy with the baby, anyway, and I just thought, *this is nothing.*

Back in Miami, I wasn't feeling any better. I decided I just needed a good workout. This is how I had always attacked the problems in my life. Whatever obstacle was in front of me, I would work right through it. I would just train harder or push harder until I beat it. I had been injured countless times as a professional basketball player and this approach had always worked for me. I went to the Miami Heat facility and put in a grueling four hours. I lifted weights, ran sprints, did a whole bunch of stuff. I thought, "I just need to sweat it out." I thought whatever was wrong would be just another thing I could ice down and wrap up. Of course, the workout only made me sicker, because my immune system was shot.

Later that day, on the way to the hospital for the tests—my agent, Jeff Wechsler, was driving me—I passed out in the passenger seat. I had a temperature of 104. I was very weak and depleted. But it still didn't dawn on me how sick I was. I wouldn't allow myself to admit it. I had training camp coming up and I knew the physical challenges ahead would be brutal. Which is why the voice of my doctor, Victor Richards, on the phone the next day made me sit up in my darkened bedroom. He said he had my test results and without hesitation he unloaded it on me.

"Alonzo, your creatinine level is pretty high," he said. Before I could even remember whether that was a good or bad thing (I thought it was bad), he said, "You have a rare disease called focal glomerulosclerosis."

I was stunned. I didn't understand what he was saying except that something with as many syllables as "focal glomerulosclerosis" couldn't be good. Having played competitive basketball since I was a teenager, I had spent years around doctors and trainers, and I'd either experienced, or seen teammates experience, countless surgeries, medical treatments, injuries, and general ailments. Never had I heard of focal glomerulosclerosis.

"What did you say?" I asked. "What do I have?"

"You have a kidney disease called focal glomerulosclerosis," Dr. Richards said. I was completely awake now.

"Am I going to die?" I asked.

"You're going to be okay."

"Well, will I be able to play basketball again?"

"That's up to you."

"There's a cure for this, isn't there?"

"No."

He might as well have hit me with a baseball bat. *No cure?* What did that mean? I remember dropping my head into my hands; I was trying to grasp it all. Had Richards really just said there was no cure for this disease I had never heard of? If there was no cure, how was it up to me to play basketball? What would I tell my wife? What would I tell my son? What would I tell my baby girl? Would I ever be able to play with them and watch them grow up? And how could—of all things—my body, my strength, my health, the one thing that never let me down, now be called into question?

At the same time, everything was moving so fast and so slow; my mind was racing while my stomach was churning.

"You're going to need a kidney transplant," Dr. Richards continued.

This guy was incredible. He just kept coming with the bad news. A transplant?

"Ten to twelve months you'll be on dialysis and you'll be up for transplantation." At this point, I didn't even know what Dr. Richards was going to say next; he was just lobbing SCUD missiles in on me, and I was just taking them. One minute ago I had been convinced I had the flu; I thought I just needed a long nap.

"Dialysis?" I said. "What is dialysis?" I was just freaking out. Dialysis seemed like something for old people. Victor was trying to explain but all I could think was *Transplant? Did he say 'transplant'?*

Dr. Richards said, "Well, you know we're probably going to have to interview some family members and you might need another kidney."

Another kidney? Obviously that is what a transplant entails, but it takes on a completely new meaning when you hear it said about your own body. Another kidney? Someone else's kidney? In me?

I didn't know what to say to Dr. Richards. I didn't even try. He had just laid it out, painfully honest. I actually appreciated that; I'd rather know up front. He finally said he wanted me to come in and discuss the situation further. I thanked him, hung up, and put my head back in my hands. I had a whole bunch of stuff going through my head now. I didn't cry, not one tear, although little did I know tears would come in buckets as this process played out.

Instead I just sat there thinking. This was so out of nowhere, so impossible to imagine. I thought the biggest challenge that coming year would be juggling the sleepless nights that come with a newborn while battling Shaquille O'Neal and Tim Duncan and pushing the Miami Heat to the NBA Championship.

Now points and rebounds were about to become secondary to hemofiltration and leukocyte antigens. Not that I knew those words yet.

Less than a minute after I hung up the phone, Tracy came to check in, and after one look at me sitting on the edge of the bed with my head down she knew something was terribly wrong. I had probably never sat that way in my entire life. I was the kind of person who attacked everything head on. All great athletes are—no secret there. When challenged, you fight. When that isn't enough, you fight harder.

When I was growing up, my family and I lived in a rural section of Chesapeake, Virginia; I was an only child until I was eleven, when my sister was born. We were working class. My father was a machinist at a local shipyard, and my mother worked a number of different jobs. When I was ten, my parents' marriage began to deteriorate, and eventually they divorced. In the interim, life at home became very difficult, very emotional.

It wasn't the worst situation in the world, and my parents were both great people, but the atmosphere was not good for me. Emotionally, I began acting out. I wasn't normally a bad kid; I was actually a good kid. But all of a sudden I was in trouble all the time, and it was obvious, even to me, why that was happening. My parents and I went to a counseling session at the department of social services and that's when I asked to be put into a group home for a while. My parents reluctantly agreed.

Once I was in the group home, I saw kids with real problems, the kind that made mine seem like nothing. The place actually had a room with padded walls. There was a restraining chair and I witnessed hauntingly disturbing outbursts. But I still didn't want to go home. So I asked the state to put me into foster care, as crazy as that sounds. Just because I wasn't in the worst situation didn't mean my parents' place was a good one. In the end, I got very lucky: I wound up with a woman named Fannie Threet, a local hero who as a foster mom helped raise forty-nine kids in Chesapeake. I was one of those children. Although things with my parents calmed down and with split custody they did a fine job raising my sister, Tamara, I never left foster care and never returned to live with either of them. Despite my youth, I knew Mrs. Threet's house was the best place for me.

I am close with both my parents to this day, but I still call Ms. Threet "Mom" too. As an adult and a parent, I look back and realize it was a courageous thing for a ten-year-old to do, to realize that I needed a change, seek it out, and then make a leap of faith that it would work, but that was just me. That's how I approached everything in life, with the attitude that there is a solution to every problem as long as you don't fear the path to the solution.

That mentality has helped me my entire life. It got me out of that home environment and eventually out of Chesapeake. By maximizing my athletic abilities, by assuring that I used basketball rather than having basketball use me, I earned a full scholarship to Georgetown University. And once I was there, that drive got me academically through one of the elite schools in the country.

I wasn't your typical Georgetown student. Most of the kids came from upper-class families; I came from foster care. Most of my classmates had attended fancy college prep schools; I just went to regular public school in Chesapeake. Most of them had two parents who graduated from college, if not graduate school. I was the first person in my entire family to get a diploma. I just wasn't as prepared as they were. But as long as I worked on my studies, I could succeed also. At one point at Georgetown I was coasting, concentrating on basketball a little too much, and my coach, John Thompson, challenged me. It wasn't that I was failing or anything; my grades were good. But he called me out on my effort, said I was more intelligent than I was showing people, which is a shameful way for a young man to act. He was correct. So I buckled down and made the dean's list that semester. Just work harder, that was always my solution.

It's also the way I play basketball. I am a big man by general standards, but in the NBA, I often gave up four or five inches and sometimes fifty to seventy pounds to other players, guys like Shaquille O'Neal, my seven-foot-one, 350-pound chief rival and later teammate, and the man who was picked first in the 1992 NBA draft, one spot ahead of me. Throughout my career I have prided myself on being an undersized center who can beat players bigger and stronger than me. I wasn't the most naturally gifted player, and there were guys my size who had offensive skills I didn't, so I needed to outwork them.

There were times when as soon as the game was over, rather than go home or out with the guys, I'd head directly for the weight room. I'd still have my game jersey on as I lifted weights and pushed myself. I always knew that I had to stay one step ahead of the competition in order to compete. I had to work just that much harder. They have a lot of rules in basketball and in life, but there is no rule that prohibits preparation. No one ever says you can't work harder to be better prepared.

The result wasn't just physical, either. It was mental. When you've prepared harder than everyone else, it instills confidence. I developed a psyche that said, *You know what, they're not here after the game lifting extra weights. They're going to shower up and go home, but I'm going to go in and put in another hour.*

That *just get it done* mentality was something I established at a young age, and like a wave it's carried me all the way through. Whatever difficulty I met, I always believed if I faced it with a certain level of intensity and focus and determination, I would come out on top. Strength is not just physical, it is mental. And if you are mentally strong you can accomplish anything.

So when Tracy saw me like that—silent, worried, head down—she knew there was a major, major problem. She knew this was not me, that I must have just been hit with something greater than I had ever confronted. I told her what Dr. Richards had said. No cure. Dialysis. Transplant. Retirement. Understandably, she started crying. She described her immediate reaction as being like a wounded animal's. She just assumed the worst: that I was going to die. I don't blame her—the poor woman had just given birth, and now *this* comes along? Although I understood, crying was the last thing I wanted. My entire life, I never wanted people making a big deal about me.

When there was something wrong with me, some challenge, I always wanted to take it on myself. I'm the most independent person in the world. As a husband and a father, I am very protective of my family. I am the one who helps them, who protects them and worries about them. I can't handle being on the other side.

As I sat on the edge of that bed, my wife standing over me crying, I

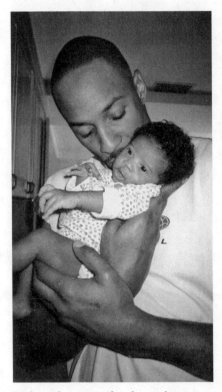

Myka and me soon after she was born

leaned in, put my head on her stomach and we hugged for a minute. I was supporting her as much as she was supporting me, which is the only way families can get through things like this. Serious illness doesn't just affect the afflicted.

I got Tracy to stop crying and asked her to be positive and strong for me. And she did. I decided right then and there that there would be no more feeling bad about the situation, because that wasn't going to help solve the problem. Tracy also had an incredible life growing up; she was raised by a single mother who dealt with major racial discrimination. Later, when she asked her mother what to do, her mom just said, "What would have happened to us if I had felt bad about things and given up?"

We were immediately determined to win this battle. That was the only way to approach it. There are often doubts in life, but you have to stand up and attack what is attacking you. Meet force with force. You have to learn as much as you can, come up with a plan, and be positive. "Hey," I started to tell everyone, "I'm lucky. We have money and resources, the best health care options in the world. We're blessed. I have a strong wife, a strong family, and strong faith. If anyone can handle this, we can. God always has a plan, and if this is his plan then let's go."

Focal glomerulosclerosis, I decided then and there, was going to somehow become the best thing that ever happened to me. God wouldn't have given it to me if he didn't want it to be that way. I just had to figure out how to make it so.

I said to Tracy, "Right now, we have to think about Plan B. We have to take this head-on." I called my agent, Jeff, who doubles as one of my best friends, and told him the news, only to have him break down and start crying, too. Great, just what I didn't need. I said, "Jeff, please. Come on, listen, we've already moved past this and we've got to think about our next step."

Once Jeff had gathered himself, he said, "Well, first of all, we have to find the best kidney doctor in the world." Now, *that* was the kind of stuff I was looking for. I said, "Let's do it. Let's go to him. Let's find the best kidney doctor in the world." So he mentioned that his father-in-law, Norman Braman, who was the former owner of the Philadelphia Eagles, knew someone who sat on the board of New York–Presbyterian Hospital. Jeff called Norman and Norman called his friend and his friend said that Dr. Gerald Appel in New York City was the guy considered to be the best, the most respected and most renowned in the world. We called him that day and it turned out he was about to head to Toronto to attend a convention with more than a thousand nephrologists. He told us to send him all my information and test results, and he would bring them to the convention. It was a true blessing, because the best nephrologists in the entire world were attending this convention, and when that box arrived the next morning Dr. Appel showed the case to them. God has a way with timing sometimes.

With focal glomerulosclerosis, once you rule out all of the possible causes such as HIV, drug abuse, and steroid abuse—which the doctors did—it is labeled a genetic disorder. They call it idiopathic, meaning they don't know the cause. That's part of the challenge. After seeing my lab results, Dr. Appel said he would come to Miami in a couple of days.

It was a crazy time. Word was leaking out that I was sick, and the newspapers were reporting all sorts of stuff. I was sure to retire. I was facing death. I had no chance of a normal life. So much of that wasn't true. But we couldn't control the media.

We set up a meeting at my house. I didn't just want to rely on my doctors. I wanted a lot of bright people around who cared about me. So in addition to Dr. Appel, I asked Tracy, Jeff, Jeff's colleague David Falk, Georgetown coach John Thompson, and my current coach with the

Heat, Pat Riley, to attend. We all sat down around my dining room table so Dr. Appel could lay it out.

Dr. Appel is a very intelligent-looking guy. You know how some people just look intelligent? He is a little guy, with a mustache—he kind of looks like one of the Super Mario Brothers, from the video game. But he commands a lot of respect. So even though there were a lot of powerful people at the table, everyone sat still and listened to him. He was in charge. He said it flat-out: "Alonzo has to retire right now to deal with this." He said I was carrying about twenty pounds of water weight and that my cholesterol measure was between 500 and 600. He couldn't figure out how I managed to play basketball, let alone compete for an Olympic gold medal.

He said there were some positives, though. He thought there were ways to treat the condition that Dr. Richards hadn't initially seen. He said, "There are certain new medicines that you could possibly respond to, so I'm going to try this particular regimen and we're going to see how we can combat this. Maybe, just maybe, you won't need a transplant. But you definitely have to retire right now."

Even though he was saying I had to retire, I saw great hope in that diagnosis. That's why it is so critical to get a second and third opinion. Less than a week earlier, Dr. Richards had said I would certainly need a transplant. That was a tough road for a number of reasons, not the least of which is that for a transplanted organ to work you generally need someone of similar height, stature, and weight. I'm almost six ten, and I weigh 255 pounds. You don't just find people that size walking down the street. So the odds were already against me. For Dr. Appel to say that I might be able to live with my kidney was a real boost. For him to give me that little light at the end of the tunnel, for him to give me a little hope rather than just saying, "Hey, it's over, you don't have a chance of ever playing again," meant everything.

After that initial moment of doubt in my bedroom, my attitude had never wavered. I was going to beat this. That was my only mentality. I had spent hours and hours on the Internet, learning everything I possibly could about kidney disease. I talked to every expert I could get on the phone. I began looking into holistic treatments—which I would later use—and natural cures. My entire focus was now on beating the disease, and I felt that if I put my mind to it, I would succeed. That was the attitude that had always worked for me, and that was what was going to get me through this. *Resilience.* I would be even more resilient than ever.

So that glimmer of hope was all I felt that I needed. I'm not sure if anyone else at the table was even aware of it—they were probably focused on the negative, the "Alonzo has to retire" part. But I was aware. I heard the message loud and clear. I just needed a chance. I was ready to do everything remotely possible to get myself physically right and make it happen.

It was a somber meeting, of course. Immediate retirement—that hurt, coming right in the prime of my career and on the eve of a season where an NBA Championship seemed possible. We agreed we should schedule a press conference, tell the world about my illness, and that I then should work toward either getting better or getting a transplant. It was a very matter-of-fact situation. These were the people who had always been there for me, who always had my best interests at heart, the ones I could trust. I had the best wife, the best agents, the best coaches, and the best doctor. Everyone agreed that this was the best path for me. And everyone agreed that my career was over.

Everyone, except, deep down, me.

Most people aren't aware that I'm a very spiritual person. In general, I keep it to myself. For many people the name "Alonzo Mourning" conjures a big, scowling black man, a guy who grunts and hustles, blocks shots and grabs rebounds. It's not a bad way to comport myself on the basketball court. My coaches and fans wouldn't have been too happy if I turned the other cheek or paused for prayer every time Hakeem Olajuwon posted me up. Once or twice, it might have crossed my mind, though.

My faith is something that has sustained me through the highs and lows, through the mistakes I've made and even through some of the triumphs. There have been a fair share of both, but there was only one time in my life—during my illness—when that faith came into question.

As a professional athlete, I'd trained myself to power through, to never question my will to succeed. Resilience was a trait that served me well. But in the darkest days of this battle against kidney disease, it was tested like never before. I was still a large man in stature, but at times I was as weak and helpless as my newborn baby. That wasn't a situation I could easily accept, and it rocked my faith in a way that, to me, was almost unimaginable.

But in the days, weeks, months, and years since then, that crushing moment became a sort of wake-up call, and I now realize how grateful I am for it. I had to come to terms with my faith in ways that I never would have, had I not gotten kidney disease. I had to take the deepest possible look at my life, acknowledge each and every weakness, each and every mistake, and come to the realization that just because faith is in your head, doesn't mean it is in your heart.

I have been blessed with great teachers along the way. Family members, educators, coaches, doctors, and the Reverend Willie Alfonso served to restore that faith during my recovery. And there were others, too, who you'll read about. God certainly works in mysterious ways. He puts you in situations to test your faith, and it can only grow stronger as you overcome these hurdles. From faith comes resilience.

Faith makes things possible.

But it doesn't make them easy.

2

TIDEWATER

The long, lanky kid was coiled up on the floor, huddled over a Monopoly game that he was, as always, way too wrapped up in. He was the car, of course. He always had to be the car. And he always had to get Boardwalk and he always had to win. That was just the way it was.

Alonzo Mourning was about seven, taking on his aunt while his mother, Julia, sat on a couch nearby and started snapping pictures of her son, one every couple minutes. Eventually she burned through an entire roll.

Later, when she developed the pictures, they showed a roller coaster of emotions—elation at the start, when things were good; a combination of disappointment, anger, and powerful focus as the game broke bad on him late. By the end of the roll of film, as his money pile dwindled, as his aunt refused to play along and let him win, this looked like a miserable kid.

"He was not happy." Julia laughs now. "He was losing. And my son hates to lose. Absolutely hates to lose."

Alonzo's parents were stunned as they watched their little boy grow seemingly by the night, running through shoe sizes in a matter of months. People wondered if he was mentally handicapped when they saw him playing little-kid games with friends who looked five years younger than he, although they were actually the same age. Doctors predicted a height that would push seven feet.

But they were just as surprised at this child's ferocious focus and competitiveness. He did not like to lose. At anything. If he played any game and lost, he'd burst into incontrollable tears. Checkers with his dad, pool with his friends. It didn't matter.

"I would always tell him, 'Look, someone has to lose. It may not be you all the time, but sometimes it is,' " Julia said. "I don't think he agreed with that."

So he tried to ensure that he never lost.

"At school one time, they took him on a fishing trip," said his father, Alonzo Senior. "And sure enough, here he comes back with the blue ribbon for the biggest fish. I just laughed. Nothing was just a game to him."

But it wasn't just games that Alonzo was concerned with winning. He had his eye on the prize in every pursuit, especially the most important one of all—his future.

When he was ten years old, his whole world turned confusing and angry because of his parents' deteriorating marriage. Life at home was bad. Emotions were raw, times tough, and Alonzo handled none of it well. So he surveyed the game of life, focused harder, and decided to change the outcome, no matter how painful or difficult his plan needed to be. Even if that meant, at age ten, breaking free from his family and all but striking out into the world on his own.

"When he's got his mind made up, he isn't changing," Alonzo Senior said. "He's very stubborn. When he thinks he is right, that's it. I don't care what you tell him. He's always been that way, and he's broke my heart because of it."

When a basketball caroms off a rim, the result of a missed shot, any player can grab it. There is no rule that says any one player has to get it. It is a 50–50 ball, anyone's to seize. You can sit back and wait for it to come to you, hopeful that everything will work out, or you can assert yourself and move toward the ball. That's about all there is to it. Wait and hope, or go make it happen.

Even then, there are degrees. You can assert yourself somewhat, mostly, or completely, the latter being to assert yourself to the point where you impose your own will on the situation, pushing all other obstacles and opponents aside to absolutely assure success.

That's how I play basketball. I don't sit back and hope. I go take things without apology. I try to guarantee victory, no matter who I have to shove out of the way. You don't worry about hurt feelings when a rebound is to be had.

My mother and father were both nineteen when I was born. They were just two overwhelmed teen parents from the projects of Norfolk, Virginia, hoping it would all work out. All they could afford was a small home off in a rural section of Chesapeake called Deep Creek, hard by the Great Dismal Swamp. If you line that up for a child and calculate the odds of everything working out fine, sitting back and waiting for success isn't advisable. It might happen—but don't count on it. It's best to go grab success, to knock your way into the best possible position no matter who gets run over in the process.

My parents married because of me. As long as I lived with them I was an only child, although I had so many cousins that sometimes it didn't feel that way. My mom was one of eleven kids, five sisters and five brothers. Whenever we all got together at one of my grandparents' houses there were so many relatives running around, I never felt alone. Chesapeake is part of the Tidewater or Hampton Roads area of Virginia, which includes cities such as Norfolk, Newport News, Hampton, and Virginia Beach. It's a blue-collar area, a big military region with a number of Navy bases and some of the biggest shipyards in the entire world. It's one of the oldest settled parts of the country, not far from Jamestown and Williamsburg, Virginia, some of

Christmas 1971

the nation's first white settlements.

Most of our family was in Norfolk, about ten miles north. As far back as I can remember, I'd get dropped off at one of my grandparents' and hook up with my cousins to go fishing, play kids' games, barbecue, ride bikes, and run around outside long after the sun had set. With my father having steady work as a machinist in a shipyard and holding positions as a reservist in both the Navy and the Marines, my parents managed to overcome the long odds of teen parenthood. I had a carefree childhood. I wanted for nothing.

At least, until I was ten years old and my parents' marriage fell apart. The entire ordeal rocked me, not just because of what it was doing to our family but also because of how it was happening. Out of respect for my parents, I don't want to delve into too much detail. It's enough to say they were having their own issues, and that those issues had quite a bit of an effect on me. I started going through some serious emotional problems. I didn't accept the situation, and the tension in the household was not helping. It was just tough for me to adapt to.

I wasn't abused or anything like that, but I was acting out all of a sudden. I became a very rebellious kid. I would cause some mayhem at school, get punished there, have the teacher send home a note, which I would just crumple up and throw in the closet, only to have my parents find it. Eventually, I'd catch myself in more trouble because of it. It was a bad cycle. The more trouble I caused, the more I got punished. The more I got punished, the more rebellious I became, and the more trouble I caused.

I was always the biggest kid in school, five foot eight when I was ten years old. So I stood out. And the thing about being so big at such a young age is people see you as being older than you are; they expect a level of maturity from you that isn't consistent with your age.

Mostly, though, I was reacting to the negative family atmosphere that I was involved in. It got to the point where my parents sought some professional help for all of us. One day as we sat in a counseling session at a place in Norfolk, I came to understand that even though I loved my mom and my dad, I needed to find a new living situation, whatever that might be.

Looking back, I can say I was a very self-aware young man. I don't know why. I don't know how. But I was. I looked at the situation at home, I looked at how it was affecting me and how it was a potential threat to me succeeding in life and I knew, I just knew, in my ten-year-old mind, that I needed to do something for myself.

The place where we had our family therapy sessions had a group home connected to it. At some point during the counseling, the psychiatrist offered me the option of not going back with my parents. The offer was, basically, "Leave him with us for a little while and let us have some more time with him."

I was at the point where I knew I wasn't crazy. I knew I wasn't comfortable in the environment I was in at home. I was very angry. It wasn't like I needed to be admitted or anything, but I decided that a real and serious change might be preferable, that I'd rather try living by myself in the group home and adapt from there. I decided to assert myself. I didn't know where it would lead and I didn't even understand what I was getting into. At that age, you don't have a lot of long-term perspective. But I knew there had to be something better, that somehow I might be able to find a better way. I had a lot of love for my parents, but even at that very young age I knew that my future would be best if I took it into my own hands.

I know this doesn't seem possible, especially these days. But this was the option I was given by the State of Virginia. My parents were against it, of course. They begged me to reconsider and later petitioned to get me back. But the way the social services system in Virginia worked then, the decision was mine. They would ask the child what he wanted to do and often they would honor that wish. If a child wasn't comfortable at home, then he or she didn't have to go home. The idea was to not put a child in an environment if they weren't comfortable being in that environment; and with the issues that we were dealing with at home, I was not comfortable. They actually listened to the child and catered to the wishes and the needs of the child.

As I look back on it, I can't believe I did it. But I did. And I did it for me. That moment felt like a real tipping point in my life. I was ready to take a leap of faith. I had the self-confidence that I would make it work. This wasn't a full break from my parents; they could still visit and be a part of my life. And it wasn't necessarily permanent, although, deep down, I thought it might turn out that way. Mostly, I didn't want to act out anymore. I didn't want to rebel. I wanted a new start. I wanted to make something of myself. I was ready to chase the possibility of better rather than settle for the reality of worse. If I failed, it wouldn't be because I didn't try to assert my will in the situation. That was a very conscious decision on my part.

At the time, I had little concern for my parents' feelings. I know now that my decision inflicted considerable pain on them. I realized that when I became a parent myself. Just the thought of having one of my children live away from me, in a state-run group home no less, makes my heart sink. The pain, anguish, and embarrassment it caused them must have been considerable. But I didn't worry about anyone other than myself back then. Ten-year-olds aren't supposed to.

Life in the group home made me realize very quickly that I didn't have it nearly as bad as I thought. This was a heavy-duty reality check, and maybe it gave me the perspective I needed. The group home had a couple dozen kids living there and I'd look at how they behaved and the issues they were dealing with and I'd say, *You know what? These kids have got some* serious *problems.*

Kids were very angry, violent, and had emotional and psychological problems. Sometimes they had to be restrained to stop them from hurting other people or themselves. They would be strapped down onto chairs or put in a padded room. It was some sad, shocking stuff. The padded room they called "the quiet room." It was like solitary confinement. It had a little window and I would look in there and see some scary stuff, some disturbing moments, things that were no joke. I saw stuff you don't want to see, especially at that age.

I remember lying in bed one night telling myself, *You know what? I am not there. I'm not at that point. It's not that deep. I've never had to go through anything like that. I've never needed to be restrained. And I'm not going to get to that point.* At the same time, I began building a wall between myself and other people. I was very guarded in the group home, and for good reason. People could hurt you there, as much emotionally as physically. I learned that trust was a luxury and that the best way to assure success was to be wary of everyone. It was a personality trait that I carried for years, and in many ways it defined the public's perception of me deep into my playing career, a personality failure that I continue to fight to this day. Between the situation with my parents and the group home, I learned to trust only what was consistently trustworthy—and that was myself and nothing else. That was how I survived.

In 1980, my parents' marriage appeared to be over. They actually reconciled later for a while and had my sister, Tamara, but divorced for good in 1983. One thing I knew was if my parents divorced and I decided to leave the group home, I was expected to choose to live with one or the other. That was another thing they used to do at the time, they made kids choose a parent. But out of love for both my parents I didn't want to show any favoritism. And I still felt the environment I would return to would be unhealthy for me.

By that time, the tension had gotten a little bit further along between my mom and dad. A lot of it is hard for everyone to share at this point, and it's very private. Families all over the world have problems. It doesn't matter how much money you have, what race you are, where you live, what kind of education you have—everyone has problems. So my family was no different. And in the end, my parents were able to be friends. They jointly raised Tamara into a great young woman. And they continued to play a big part in helping me to grow and live a very productive and, I think, successful life. Our family isn't any different than a lot of families.

Me, in Chesapeake, Virginia

But back then, let's just say it was bad enough that even as my initial time in the group home was supposed to end, I still felt that living with kids who sometimes had to get locked in a padded room was the best option for me. That felt like the place I would be less likely to take the wrong turn in life and continue to rebel, get in trouble, rebel some more, get in more trouble, and, well, eventually rebel too far and get in real trouble, where it was no longer just kid stuff.

My father began petitioning the Commonwealth of Virginia to get me back, but I kept telling everyone I didn't want to go. Finally I was required to go to family court and stand in front of a judge and ask to be placed full-time into social services. My knees were practically shaking as I stood and looked up at him, full of power in his black robe.

"Where do you want to live?" he asked, staring down from the bench.

I paused for a second, not because I didn't know what to say, but because I could barely breathe enough to say it. I finally found a way to muster something out.

"I want to go into foster care, sir."

The judge nodded and gave me my wish. I guess he figured if I was willing to go through all of that, I was serious. I don't know if they would do that today, but they did back then. And I'm forever grateful they did.

I stayed in the group home for over a year. For a while, both my mom and my dad came back for therapy sessions and to visit me and everything, and every time they saw me they would ask me if I'd like to come home, and I would tell them no. Eventually my mother got fed up with the group home—she disagreed with the way it was being run—and I didn't see her for a brief stretch. It was a hard time all around for the family.

The way the system worked, you stayed in the group home, but there were periods of time where you would go and visit foster homes with the possibility that you might join one. You got to take a look at foster homes and foster families before making a decision.

The first foster home I visited made me very uncomfortable. I had a very strong intuition, a kid's intuition, that this was not the place. It didn't feel safe. It didn't feel like an improvement over even the group home. So I said no and waited.

The second home I went to was a well-kept split-level ranch in a pleasant middle-class neighborhood of Chesapeake, in an area called West Munden, although a lot of the kids called it Strawberry Lane. It was owned by a woman named Fannie Threet, who was in her late fifties at the time; over the course of her life she raised forty-nine kids, most of them foster kids. She adopted some and had some of her own, but she was a mother to anyone who came into her home.

The love that I felt when I walked in the door overwhelmed me. I was almost twelve by then, and I felt like this, at last, was home. Mrs. Threet was taking care of three other kids at the time, but it immediately felt like a family. Once I walked in, I never wanted to walk out. And I didn't. That's where I lived until I went off to college.

Mrs. Threet is such a motherly person, it was impossible to tell who were her biological children, her adopted children, and her foster children. She treated each and every one of us with so much love and respect that I think there were times when a lot of us forgot we weren't blood with her. I meant no disrespect to my own mother when I called Mrs. Threet "Mom." That was just the case; she made everyone feel that way.

Within a few weeks, Mrs. Threet called my mother and told her she could come over and visit me anytime she wanted. My mother learned to love Mrs. Threet too—she could be a mother even to mothers—and my mother would come over and cook or just sit at the kitchen table and the two of them would talk. Sometimes I would come running in from outside and yell, "Hey, Mom!" and both of them would turn their heads. But my mother said she was never jealous of that. Mrs. Threet had a way of making everyone feel better.

Entering a foster home can be a very traumatic thing for a kid. You have great hope, but experience has tempered you to expect disappointment. You are reaching out for the best, but are trained to expect the worst. It is a very uncertain time and for a young child there is nothing worse than uncertainty. I felt very uncertain at times.

What made Mrs. Threet a great foster mother was her ability to get right to the source of what was happening in a person's life. She just has that gift about her. I think it's her connection with God. She's very rooted in church and in God and she instilled that in all of us. Her father was a pastor in North Carolina, and nearly every day there would be some form of work with the Bible or a very open discussion about the importance of prayer. She always said that through good times and bad times, the main thing that connects you with God is prayer. And she said that when no one else will be with you, God will. It was a very easy way to bring religion into the life of all these kids who at some level felt very much abandoned. Faith was first and foremost in her home. Second was education. We prayed a lot.

Mrs. Threet used to sit down with each new arrival and sternly but calmly explain the rules, the responsibilities, and the expectations of the house. She was a great combination of soft and stern. She set the tone and that was why she managed to have very little trouble. The forty-nine she raised to adulthood doesn't even count the hundreds who spent maybe ten days or two weeks with her before moving on to another situation, maybe off to a relative or back with their parents. And there is no telling how many kids she took in from the area in the years before she became a licensed foster mother. She helped so many kids that no one even knows how many lives she touched. Mrs. Threet was the last safety net for a generation of youth in Chesapeake, a real angel. Today, at age eighty-nine, she lives in the finest retirement home in Chesapeake, Virginia.

When I first came to the house, I was quiet and reserved. I was eager to live there, but as a foster kid you never know if you really belong, so I took my time to feel out how I might be received. Once I realized there was nothing but love in the home, I began opening up. Mrs. Threet ran a tight ship: we had chores and we were expected to do them right the first time; schoolwork was a priority; and if we wanted money, we were to go find a job. I started my own lawn-cutting business in the neighborhood.

I was a big kid at that point, standing over five foot ten and wearing a size 12 shoe. The first time I met my foster brother Bud Threet, I was sitting on the couch with Mrs. Threet. She introduced us and I stood up and we were eye to eye. Bud was seventeen at the time. Within a few months, I shot up to six foot two and soon was the tallest person in junior high, teachers included. Not long after that, I grew so tall I no longer fit in my bed. Mrs. Threet had seen a lot of kids come through her home, but this was a new one. She got the bed sawed apart, had two feet added to it and then glued it back together. She kept that bed for years, a reminder of me.

My first love was football. The Washington Redskins teams of the mid-1970s were my teams, and when I was young I had Redskins everything in my room, from the trash can to the curtains to posters on the wall. Everyone in the area plays football; Allen Iverson is from Hampton and he was as good at football as he was at basketball, although he finally settled on hoops in college. That's just the way it is there; it is a football-mad area. When I got to Indian River Middle School that fall, they saw my size and immediately put me at defensive end. But they had no cleats to fit me, so I was out there in size 14 Chuck Taylors, sliding around and jumping off sides all the time. It was pretty comical. Obviously I wasn't going to be a football player.

I was a pretty good eater, though, and I had a legendary appetite. I would sit down for breakfast and eat Cap'n Crunch until the roof of my mouth was raw. Sometimes Mrs. Threet would cook pancakes for Bud and me. I would knock down about fifteen of them and she would throw her hands up and say, "If y'all want to eat that many pancakes, y'all going to have to get up here and cook them yourself." She had raised all these kids and said she had never seen an appetite like mine.

Even with all that eating, I was still skinny because I was so active. Football was a disaster, but everyone kept saying I should try basketball. When I was about nine, my dad had put me in a rec league back in Deep Creek, but I was so much taller than the other kids that it wasn't fair. The other parents used to complain and my father had to keep arguing it wasn't my fault I was so tall.

Just after I moved in with Mrs. Threet, my dad enrolled me in a summer basketball camp at Old Dominion University in Norfolk, which is a Division I program that has had some pretty good teams. He'd pick me up and drive me over there, and I found out right then how basketball would change my life. At the time, the Old Dominion coach was Paul Webb. He took one look at me when I walked into camp, found out I was just twelve, and immediately waived the fee. Then he started recruiting me for college. Whatever some of the col-

My dad and me

lege players got, I did too. They gave me a pair of baby blue, old leather, Converse Dr. J shoes that were about the most beautiful thing I had ever seen. I rocked those all over town thinking, *Wow, I'm getting free shoes!* I needed the shoes, too. There was a stretch where I was growing a full shoe size every six months. I didn't wear shoes out, I just outgrew them.

I might have been the youngest boy in NCAA history to be highly recruited by a Division 1 school. And it almost worked, too. I loved Paul Webb and for a while there, I was telling everyone I was going to be an ODU Monarch. That camp helped me to become a better player. By the time I was in eighth grade, I was playing on the high school junior varsity.

You can't go it alone. No matter how much you think you can, every one of us is influenced by how we interact with others. How someone treats us can shape our entire life, either in a positive or negative manner. We are all a product of how others have treated us. That's the power of influence. And no one can avoid it. In the group home, I thought I could. I thought I could just run away from my problems at home, withdraw and be just fine. I thought I could protect myself that way.

It wasn't until I was reaching out to Bud and Mrs. Threet, among others in my new home, that I realized the impossibility of going it alone. I was desperate for a family. I was desperate for people I could count on emotionally. I was desperate for positive influences. Bud became much more than an older brother to me. He influenced me in profound ways. To this day, he is the one who can call me up and tell me when I need to shape up; he can be completely honest with me.

I do not believe in coincidences. I think God has a plan for all of us and certain things happen for a reason. Those things may not make sense at the time, but they will in the end. How else can I explain finding the strength to enter the foster care system, except that God wanted me to meet Fannie Threet, be taught by Fannie Threet, and mostly, to be loved by Fannie Threet?

God had a plan for me to do things with my talents and I knew that I was on the brink of straying from it. So he sent me to this woman. If not for that, who knows what would have happened with me? Countless careers have been derailed by even a single mistake.

My decision to go into foster care and then remain with Mrs. Threet hurt my parents. I understand that now. Both of them stayed involved in my life, and I would still go and visit my grandparents and cousins over in Norfolk. My parents would come to visit me, and my father, even though he was often working a great deal, missed just one of my basketball games growing up. I always knew I could look up in the stands and see him there. My father says it was embarrassing that his son wasn't living with either parent. He'd try to avoid telling people. For a while he kept petitioning the court to get me back, but in time he realized there was no way I was ever leaving Mrs. Threet's house and that was the best place for me. He knew I was never going back.

These days, both my parents thank the Threets. Everyone now acknowledges this was God's plan all along. My father and Bud are even great friends. "Bud and Mrs. Threet changed his life," my dad said. "I don't think he would have been the same person if he stayed with me and his mother. I don't think we could have given him what they gave him. I think they had a lot to do with how he turned out.

"You know, God works in mysterious ways."

3

TRANSITION GAME

Having become a father when he was just nineteen, practically a kid himself, Alonzo Mourning, Sr., didn't know a whole lot about children. When his son ran around the house nonstop, an endless ball of energy, bouncing off the walls until he finally collapsed out of exhaustion, he figured it was normal.

At age six, though, Alonzo Junior went to school. After the second day of class his frantic teacher called home declaring there was no way she could contain this kid. "He's hyperactive," she said. "He won't stop moving and it's hard for a child to learn anything when he can't stop moving."

The Mournings got Alonzo checked out and the doctor agreed. They put him on Ritalin, a prescription drug used to treat hyperactivity. It only helped a little. Alonzo was too big and too strong for even that. He still wouldn't stop. Rather than upping the dosage to absurd levels, they decided to just take him off the medication and find another way to corral that energy. Alonzo Senior steered his son to sports.

He tried boxing, but no one Alonzo's age was willing to fight him. His father brought him down to a youth football team, only to find out that Alonzo Junior, at age seven, was too young for the league. He had to be eight, the coaches said. When they went back the next year, the coach looked at this massive child in size 8 adult shoes, put him on a scale, and shook his head.

"Well, he's too big. He's over the weight limit. He can't play."

"I thought, 'There's always a situation with this one,'" Alonzo Senior, said.

Basketball seemed like a good idea. In a local rec league, the coaches were more than willing to take a player who towered over the others.

"He was so big he was just standing over the top of the other kids," Alonzo Senior said. "It was like a teenager out there playing with eight-year-olds. He would just walk up to them and take the ball right out of their hands."

Finally they had found something to burn that energy. Alonzo could play basketball all day, for all his father cared. He needed to do something. This was perfect—at least, until one day when he took a seat in the stands and overheard a bunch of parents of kids on the other team discussing his son.

"They didn't know I was Alonzo's father. But I could hear them complaining because he was running around with these little kids. He was the same age as them, but the parents were acting like he was older.

"They were saying, 'Look at that big kid, it's not fair they're playing with him.' Everyone was angry. I wasn't trying to make anyone angry; I just wanted my son to play. I just shook my head and said, 'Oh, my God, I can't win.'"

Later, when Alonzo was in eighth grade, he was such a promising prospect that the coaches at the local high school plucked him out of junior high and put him on the junior varsity. Better at the game than any older kid they had, he started dominating players who were three years older.

Alonzo Senior came to every game. He was a proud father, happy to see his son excel, until he heard about a plan by opposing coaches to ban Alonzo from playing on the junior varsity: "They said it wasn't right for a boy from junior high to play with the high school kids. They decided there ought to be a rule against it. Zo was so dominant, the only way they could stop him was to find a way to ban him from playing."

But this time his son wasn't going to stop playing. Since when should rules be enacted to save high school kids from junior high school kids?

"I just laughed at that one. It was like, 'Well, these coaches better learn how to deal with it because he isn't quitting basketball now.' "

God does work in mysterious ways. And other times his path is clear right from the start. For all the times in my life where I fell into the trap of self-pity, for all the moments when I questioned why I'd been singled out for this or that bit of trouble before eventually understanding his genius, there are other times when God's plan couldn't have been more obvious.

There wasn't a whole lot of doubt about the direction I was headed as I sprang up inch by inch as a teenager. I was six two, then six four, then six seven, and eventually six foot ten, even though no one in my family was within seven inches of that height. My size was so unexpected that when I was little and a doctor told my father I might reach seven feet, my dad figured the doc had mixed up the records with those of someone else's son. He thought it was impossible.

I wasn't just tall, either. With each growth spurt there was a corresponding advance in my coordination, giving me preternatural athletic ability. I had big hands, long arms, and light feet. I was slightly awkward in the seventh grade, when a guy named James Reap started over me for half a season, but by the end of the year I had caught up. I never fell behind again.

There was no doubting my ability to play basketball. And as a young man I was blessed with two great coaches: my junior varsity coach, Freddie Spellman, who's now the athletic director at Indian River High School, and my varsity coach, Bill Lassiter, who patiently and relentlessly worked on my fundamentals.

The game came easy to me back then. I could dunk in the eighth grade. I could block almost every shot, grab almost every rebound. At Indian River I teamed up with some guys who got to be lifelong friends—Greg Ford, Vinnie Nichols, Sean Bell, Gary Robinson, and Keith Easley—and we kept winning and winning, from junior high right through to a state title. We'd even cruise around the playgrounds, looking for games against older guys.

One time in high school, we got access to the Norfolk Naval Base and went to the gym to try to play some sailors, grown men. We were crushing them when I tried to dunk the ball and wound up shattering the glass backboard. I landed on my back, still holding the rim, as glass crashed all around me, scattering across the floor. Everyone in the gym just stopped and looked at me. I thought I was in a lot of trouble, this being a military base, but the sailors all started cheering and laughing. A couple of years later, I brought down another glass backboard, this one in an actual game against Norcom High School in Portsmouth. The crowd went nuts—people ran out on the court to grab pieces of glass as souvenirs. That one made the newspapers.

I was making the papers a great deal then, in the late '80s. They don't have professional or major college sports in Hampton Roads, but many of the 1.7 million residents are sports fanatics, so the attention falls on the high schools. A ton of great athletes have come out of that area—Iverson, Michael Vick, Pernell Whitaker, Bruce Smith, and so on.

I knew I was one of the best players locally, but I had no idea how I measured up in the big picture until I hooked up with a guy named Boo Williams. He was an AAU coach who was trying to put together a team to take out on a national summer schedule. Today Boo's one of the most respected guys in amateur basketball. He opened up a huge multisport complex in Hampton that hosts all sorts of tournaments year-round. But back then he was just starting out and was a hustler. Boo had this Dodge Diplomat that he'd pile all the players into and we'd drive around to games and camps during the summer.

Boo knew a lot of people in basketball and got me into the prestigious Five Star camp, which was run by a man named Howard Garfinkel each summer in the Pocono Mountains. They had these regimented skill stations which helped you work on your game, but the reason every player wanted to go was to face the best competition across the country in competitive games played each night. Driving up there I didn't realize how big a deal Five Star was. Then I saw the other players, guys like Billy Owens from Pennsylvania, Sean Kemp from Indiana, Christian Laettner from Buffalo, and so on.

Everyone who was anyone went to this camp. To add to the pressure, all the best college coaches would stand around and scout you. So you'd be in a tough game and notice Dean Smith, Mike Krzyzewski, or John Thompson watching. Maybe all three would be there, scrutinizing every play.

Before the Internet, information about top players was kind of spotty. There were a few basketball magazines. And there were some recruiting newsletters, the most important of which was run by a man named Bob Gibbons. He was an insurance agent from Lenoir, North Carolina, who used to spend the summer traveling around watching high school players. Each fall he would put out a list ranking the best players according to class. It was at Five Star after my freshman year that I first met Bob Gibbons.

In the face of a great challenge, nerves can be your toughest opponent. Nervousness breeds timidity, and timidity stands in the way of maximum performance. I was only fifteen when I went to my first Five Star camp, and a lot of the best players were a couple of years older than me. But rather than be nervous, I decided right away I would not back down no matter how good the competition or how many famous coaches were standing there scribbling scouting notes on a clipboard.

I let my game speak for itself. I was raw, mostly just running and jumping and trying not to be out of control or overly aggressive. I had a great shooting touch for a big guy, but a lot of what I was doing was just playing harder than my opponents. People always talk about talent, but your desire to outwork the player in front of you comes from within. It can make up for deficiencies in other areas. Coach Lassiter had instilled a defensive mindset in me, and defense was what I concentrated on. There was an AAU game later that summer where I blocked twenty shots against a team from Arkansas.

I knew I had played well at Five Star and during some of the AAU tournaments with Boo Williams, but I didn't know how well I'd done until I returned home. Back at school, Coach Lassiter pulled out a big box full of mail he had received while I was gone: hundreds of notes, media guides, and information packets about college basketball programs. I sat down and started reading. There were handwritten notes from Jim Boeheim, Dean Smith, Larry Brown, and all the biggest names in college coaching. All of a sudden everyone was recruiting me.

Reading them, I was filled with both confidence and humility. I knew I was going to have a chance to go to college for free, but only if I lived up to the promise these coaches saw in me. Still, as awed as I was, it didn't take long before I realized that all the letters pretty much said the same thing, and eventually I stopped reading most of them. Coach Lassiter started throwing them out unopened.

At the start of my sophomore year, though, Lassiter handed me a piece of mail he knew I'd be interested in. It was Bob Gibbons's newsletter, the one with the national ranking of players. At the top of his list of the hundred best high school sophomores was my name. I was the No. 1 basketball player my age in the entire United States. That was a feeling I could get used to.

After my sophomore year of high school, *Sports Illustrated* flew me to New York City for a photo shoot. Like Gibbons, the magazine had declared me the nation's best player in my class. Soon after that, *USA Today* featured me on its front page. That's when it really hit me that there was more to this than just me loving the game.

All the publicity put a bull's-eye on my back. Everyone wanted to measure themselves against me, maybe make a name for themselves by blocking my shot or dunking on me. It didn't matter if it was a local high school game, or if I was at a playground or at Five Star or the Nike All American Camp in New Jersey. Guys would try to take it to me. But I saw that No. 1 ranking as my possession and I would not allow anyone to take it away from me. No matter how hard you work you have to remember there is someone out there working just as hard. That thought alone pushed me. If they were going to use playing against me as motivation, then I would flip it around and use their drive to motivate myself. If someone was going to get the better of me, it would only be after a serious struggle. And no one did—at least, not consistently. Three years later, after my senior year of high school, I was still Bob Gibbons's No. 1 ranked player.

Boo Williams helped me out in a number of ways, but the best thing he ever did for me was bring me to an AAU tournament in 1987 run by Nike's Sonny Vaccaro in Las Vegas. I was between my junior and senior years, just having fun playing a team from New York in a small auxiliary gym at the University of Nevada, Las Vegas. I came running down the court at one point and noticed a girl standing behind one of the baskets. I was supposed to be concentrating on winning the game, but she turned my head and I couldn't help myself. Then every time I went down to that end, I couldn't stop looking at her. She wasn't just tall and beautiful; she had an intelligence that radiated and a smile that slayed me. I had never seen a girl like that before and I thought, *You know what? I can't let her get away. I've got to meet her.*

When the game ended, I was talking to a friend of mine who played on the New York team, Cornelius Muller, and trying to find the girl in the crowd. But I had lost track of her. Suddenly Cornelius's friend Rubina walked up to him. Rubina was from Vegas—and who should be walking up right next to her but the girl I'd seen under the basket. She was friends with Rubina. Her name was Tracy Wilson, she was going to be a senior at Clark High School in Las Vegas, and after a little small talk a group of us decided to go out to dinner.

We all went to the Denny's inside the old Dunes Casino, so at least I know my wife wasn't after me for my money—she even drove. At least I was willing to spring for the Grand Slam. We all had a good time that night. It was obvious she was very intelligent and driven. As she tells it now, I made a point to mention, or have Cornelius mention, that I was the No. 1 rated player in the country and had been in *USA Today*. Obviously, I was pulling out all the stops—but she claims she was most impressed by how respectful I was.

After dinner we exchanged phone numbers and addresses, and that was it. The tournament was about to end; she lived in Las Vegas and I lived in Virginia, so our relationship was going to have to be long distance. There was no e-mail or Facebook back then. We were pen pals that entire year; we'd send letters and pictures and things like that. She was the first and last woman I ever wrote a letter to. I look back on it now and I can't even believe I wrote all those letters to her, especially when I had no idea where it might lead.

I had a big decision to make during my senior year: where to go to college. The process for me was a little different than it is for the normal high school senior. For one, most high school kids don't announce their college plans at a press conference. I was not just a McDonald's All American but the first player to sweep the national player of the year awards: the Naismith, USA Today, Gatorade, and Parade magazine. There was never any doubt that I would attend college, it was a matter of which of the more than two hundred offering a scholarship I wanted to choose.

The recruiting process was something I had been looking forward to. I'd heard a lot about it as a player and I was eager to make this decision which would affect my life forever. The hardest part was paring down the list. All the schools had positive aspects, and the coaches all said the right things on the phone. Everyone was trying to get to me. One day I was home at Mrs. Threet's house when the phone rang and Magic Johnson was on the line. I couldn't believe it. He was trying to get me to visit UCLA, claiming we could play pickup ball together in the summer. I listened, but I didn't want to go all the way out west.

I finally settled on five schools—Maryland, Syracuse, Virginia, Georgia Tech, and Georgetown. My main criterion was that I wanted to play for a big-time team, get a great education, and get away from home, but not too far away. One thing about recruiting, everyone has an opinion on where you should go. Your friends, your teachers, guys you just met on the street. But their motives may not be in your best interest, so you have to lock everyone out. The only people I wanted to hear an opinion from were Coach Lassiter, who I really trusted, and Mrs. Threet, who I knew would be able to spot a phony a mile away. That was it. Not even my parents were involved; they didn't know my decision until they read about it in the newspaper.

The recruiting process was really wild, and the campus visits may have been the wildest part. Forget about seeing the library or the chem lab or anything academic like that. These coaches knew how to spin the head of an impressionable seventeen-year-old. By the time it was over, I had been involved in more than one NCAA violation (at Maryland) and part of one of the wilder recruiting rides of all time.

I took a trip to Maryland where Bob Wade was the coach. The thing that appealed to me about Maryland was Len Bias, who had been a star six-eight forward for the Terrapins during the mid-1980s. I idolized Len. Bud and I used to watch him on television every chance we could. He was the kind of player I wanted to be: he would battle inside but had a face-up game and great athletic ability. He played with so much energy—every play meant the world to him. He blocked shots, rebounded, did all the things on the defensive end. He wasn't just a scorer. He was a legend in the Atlantic Coast Conference and was someone I looked up to a great deal. Len Bias was also a tragedy. After an All-American career at Maryland he was drafted with the second overall pick in the 1986 draft by the Boston Celtics. To celebrate, he and some guys had a party on campus and Len overdosed on cocaine. He was twenty-two when he died, just as his entire life was opening up in front of him.

I'll never forget that spring day in 1986 when I heard the news. I was still a sophomore in high school and I worked at a car dealership, Parkway Pontiac, that was owned by a man named Tommy Gibbs. It was right across the street from school. I was a lot attendant, washing and prepping cars. When they sold a car, they'd bring it back to the attendants and we'd get it ready and then return it to the front of the dealership lot.

We had a radio on, right there in the wash area. The news came on and it was announced that Len Bias had died. I dropped the bucket and scrub brush I was carrying in shock. I couldn't understand how that could happen. Even though we weren't close, I felt a real connection with Len, perhaps because I hoped my career would follow his.

His death really scared me. It made me scared of any kind of drugs.

I sat there and thought, *If drugs could take down a guy like that, if drugs could end Len Bias's life, then they could take me down, too.* That's why I was never around anybody who did that stuff. Never. I wasn't perfect—I drank alcohol. But I would never allow any drugs like that near me. I didn't even want my friends near them because, when you think about it, those guys who gave the coke to Len, he thought they were his friends. Instead, they killed him.

My love of Len Bias convinced me to visit Maryland. His death had prompted the firing of Lefty Driesell, the longtime coach there. They had brought in Bob Wade, who was a big-time high school coach at Baltimore Dunbar, where he once coached a team that was so good, future Celtics star Reggie Lewis was the *sixth* man.

It didn't take long to understand my campus visit wouldn't be like that of the normal prospective student. The first thing they did was drive me up to Cole Field House where this enormous banner was draped that read: "Welcome Alonzo Mourning." It was so big you could have put it on the side of the Empire State Building. I was pretty impressed with that. Then they led me inside, lowered the lights, and played over the loudspeaker a fake radio call of me being introduced as a starter and then beating North Carolina on a dunk at the buzzer. It was pretty exciting.

My entire trip to Maryland was great, except that the NCAA eventually caught Wade in eighteen recruiting violations and my name even appeared in the NCAA report for one of them. Maryland wound up banned from the NCAA tournament for two seasons and Wade lost his job.

The main violation involving me was when they took me to the student bookstore and told me to take whatever I wanted. I was like, "Are you serious?" And they said, Take as much as you want, go for it. Well, I did. I grabbed clothes, lettermen jackets, bags, all sorts of stuff. I had tons of stuff. I cleaned the place out. I brought all of it back to Chesapeake for all my boys.

I was excited about visiting Syracuse, even though I'm not a fan of cold weather. But they had the program rolling back then with Derrick Coleman, Sherman Douglas, and Rony Seikaly and were putting

30,000 fans into the Carrier Dome. Plus the Big East was a big deal at the time and I thought it would fit my style of play.

The one thing I remember about that trip was Jim Boeheim, the coach, took us all out to a big dinner. Derrick was there, Sherm, a whole bunch of people. I was sitting right next to Boeheim when the bill came. They put it down in front of him and with all of the people it was probably a three- or four-hundred-dollar bill. But to pay it, rather than use a credit card, Boeheim pulled out this huge, softball-sized wad of money, with hundreds showing. He had thousands of dollars in that wad and he peeled off whatever he needed to pay the bill and then rolled that wad of cash back up right in front of me and put it away. It was obvious to me at that moment that there was a lot of money behind college basketball.

At the University of Virginia, Terry Holland was the coach and he had helped develop big man Ralph Sampson in the early 1980s. This was my in-state school and it had great academics, so it was a natural for me. The campus is only about a three-hour drive from my home, but for reasons I never understood they decided to fly me to Charlottesville for the weekend. I guess they thought I would be impressed with a private plane coming to get me. The problem was, they sent this tiny propeller plane into Norfolk. It didn't impress me; instead, it scared me to death. It was my first time ever on a little plane like that, and I thought we were going to crash the entire flight.

John Johnson, who was a great player at Virginia, was my host for the weekend. He took me out and we went to a bunch of parties. It was a complete party weekend. I had lived a pretty sheltered life because Mrs. Threet's home was so disciplined, and now I tried to make up for lost time. Saturday night we went all around campus, party after party. John introduced me to girls and the two of us just had a great time. I drank so much that night that I could barely stand.

The problem was, Sunday morning I was scheduled to have breakfast with Terry Holland and his family over at their house. I was so hung-over I could barely speak. But Terry was putting the full sales job on me, talking and trying to make it a big upbeat thing. Why in the world they even scheduled that breakfast, I don't know. They must have told John to take me out on Saturday and show me a good time, so wouldn't they expect me to be a little rocky the next day? I'm at the head coach's house trying to be cordial, but my head was throbbing, my stomach spinning, and I couldn't eat a bite, I was so sick. I just kept saying, "Oh, no, I don't want too much to eat." I was just dying. Then after breakfast, still completely hung over, I had to fly back on that bouncy little plane.

I visited Georgia Tech, which was a big-time team then under coach Bobby Cremins. One of the things I remember about Cremins was he mentioned to me that if I was worried about moving all the way to Atlanta and being too far away from my family, they could arrange some things and have them come with me. He said they could help with the relocation and get the family set up professionally.

This was funny to me because it completely misread Mrs. Threet. She was a foster mother; there was no way she was ever leaving Chesapeake. I don't even know how you'd think someone would move their foster care home, like it was just any old job. This woman raised hundreds of children for almost no financial reward, so I don't think she was going to suddenly do something for the money. These coaches get a lot of credit for being great recruiters, but sometimes I think they did strange things.

Then again, during my visit at Georgia Tech I was all but ready to commit. My host was a future NBA star and this was the craziest visit of them all. I'm not even sure if we went to the campus. I was taken out into Atlanta and the first place we went was Freedman Shoes, a famous shoe store where I still shop. At the time, I had never had a good pair of dress shoes. It was very difficult to find any that fit me, and the ones that did cost way too much. I was wearing penny loafers. I was a size 17 and, just as I am now, I was very into fashion and looking good. So to take a seventeen-year-old like that to Freedman's for the very first time was a powerful experience. I remember looking around at the selection, looking at all these designer shoes from around the world and saying, "All these shoes fit me?"

My host said, "Pick out a couple of pairs." So I picked out a couple of pairs. I was so excited. We just walked out with the shoes. No one asked me for any money. After that, he took me to this fancy dinner, and we had a blast. Then he said we were going to a concert. We go into this place and it was Anita Baker and we had first-row seats. I was so thrilled, I had never experienced anything like that. When the show ended he said, "Come on." We go backstage and meet Anita. She was hot then. I could barely speak—my jaw was just on the floor. It was too much.

But it wasn't over. After hanging with Anita, I was taken to a strip club, Magic City, which was a famous place. That was the first time I had ever been in a strip club. I wasn't even legally old enough to go, I wasn't old enough to drink, but in Atlanta back then, if you were a Georgia Tech basketball player, that didn't matter. I know this stuff shouldn't determine something as important as a college choice, but I was young and if they had thrown a letter of intent on the table inside Magic City, I would have signed on the dotted line. New shoes, an incredible dinner, Anita Baker, and then this strip club? Georgia Tech didn't waste any time showing me the library or anything. In the end, Cremins did know what he was doing and it almost worked.

But not quite. No matter what happened on the recruiting visits, my decision was going to be based on what the coaches said when they visited me in my home. They all had to come into Mrs. Threet's living room and meet her and Coach Lassiter and explain to them why I should attend their school.

Four of them, Wade, Boeheim, Holland and Cremins, came in and told us what I was going to get. It was all "He's going to start, he'll get this, we'll give him all these things, he'll score twenty points a game." None of the coaches were offering specifics when it came to money and things like that, but it was just "You don't have to worry about anything, you'll be taken care of." Everyone understood I could have gotten money at any of these places. The message was sent.

But then Big John Thompson of Georgetown came in and it was just completely different. He stands six ten and is just a huge man, big shoulders, hands, and legs. As big as he is physically, he is even bigger in personality. He has such a commanding presence and was a man that we all looked up to. It was an honor just to have him there in our house. I was intimidated by him immediately and I remember trying to listen carefully when out of the corner of my eye and down the hallway I see my brother Bud waving at me, making faces, trying to get me to laugh. No one could see him but me, and I didn't want to laugh because of my immediate respect for Coach Thompson.

Georgetown's entire recruiting approach was different from the other schools'. When I went on my trip there, I was expecting the same wild times as I'd had at Georgia Tech. I thought we'd get out and around Washington, D.C., and have the run of the city. Instead, they had me meet with academic counselors, and for fun we just hung out in the dorms. It was fine, but it wasn't a party like everywhere else.

When Big John came to my house, it was the same thing. He sat there and was very direct. When it came to how I would fit in as a player, he said, "I'm not promising him anything. I'm not promising that he'll even get any playing time."

Coach Lassiter, Mrs. Threet, and I kind of looked at each other. This was new.

"He's going to have to work to get into the starting lineup or get any time on the court. I have no idea if he'll be good enough."

Coach Lassiter loved that. He and Coach Thompson had the same defensive mentality. Coach Lassiter had learned the game from John B. McLendon, who is in the Hall of Fame and was a pioneer of basketball, the first black professional coach and a legend in the NAIA. Coach McLendon had learned the game from no less than James Naismith, when he was the coach at Kansas. So the entire thing seemed perfect.

Then he turned and looked directly into Mrs. Threet's eyes.

"The only thing I'm going to promise you, Mrs. Threet, is if he wants to get an education, he'll get one. I'll make sure he gets an education."

That was his pitch. None of the other coaches had even mentioned education or me getting a degree. It never came up. It was all basketball. With Coach Thompson, it was all education.

"Mrs. Threet, if he goes to class he's going to get an education."

The thing with Coach Thompson was, he had all the graduation statistics to back it up. Almost every one of his players graduated. You knew what he was saying was true. And since Georgetown is one of the elite academic institutions in the country, that degree was going to mean something.

By the time John Thompson left, my recruiting process was all but over. I was going to Georgetown. John Thompson had appealed to Coach Lassiter by refusing to promise me playing time and he had appealed to Mrs. Threet by promising me an education—and he had appealed to me with both things. I announced a few days later.

While Coach Thompson was the most serious of the coaches, it's not that he didn't know how to recruit. He knew that I really looked up to Patrick Ewing, who had led Georgetown to three Final Fours and a national title before being the No. 1 pick of the New York Knicks. Later in life, we became great friends even as we were heated rivals. But I didn't know him until the summer before my senior year of high school. I was at the Nike All American Camp in Princeton, New Jersey, sitting down on the court stretching. All of a sudden who appeared over me but Patrick, who was already a star with the Knicks. He reached out

I announce that I will attend Georgetown.

a hand, introduced himself, and made some small talk. I was in awe. Then he left, walked up into the stands, and took a seat next to none other than John Thompson.

See, Coach Thompson couldn't speak to me at that camp, because of NCAA rules, but Patrick could. I got the point even before I noticed who was seated on the other side of Coach Thompson: Bill Russell. Coach Thompson was Russell's backup on the Celtics. So now here was Russell, the best center of all time, a man who had won eleven NBA titles; and here was Ewing, the best young center in the game, and the two of them were sitting as bookends to the coach who wanted to coach me, the best high school center in the country. That was an impressive visual. I got that message loud and clear.

One of the things that appealed to me about playing for John Thompson at Georgetown was I knew I was joining something special. It was a real fraternity. To this day, when you tell someone you were a Georgetown player, it means something. It means hard work, getting a real education, and being a good citizen. That isn't the case with every school. Coach Thompson's son, John Thompson III, is the coach there now and he has the Hoyas back as a national power, so the tradition just keeps going.

The only downside to Georgetown was that it was a long way from Tracy. She said she was going to attend Pepperdine, in Malibu, California, and I had crossed UCLA off my list. I couldn't get her out of my mind, but I really had no idea what the future held.

In Las Vegas, the father of one of Tracy's friends worked in the entertainment industry and knew Bill Cosby. One night he got Tracy and her friend tickets to Cosby's comedy show, and after the show they went backstage to meet him. Cosby asked Tracy where she was going to college and she said, "Pepperdine." He was like, "Oh, really? That's great. Do you have a scholarship?" She said, "No." He then asked what Tracy's parents did for work and Tracy said that she and her sister, Lisa, were raised by a single mother who cleaned houses. Cosby knew how much Pepperdine cost, so he wondered how a house cleaner could afford the bill. Tracy decided to tell him about her mother.

Hannah Jean Wilson is an incredible woman. Everyone calls her Nana now, even people who aren't in her family. She is white and grew up in rural Kentucky. She got married young, to a white man, and they had three children before things fell apart and the two got divorced. Nana had custody of the children and was commuting to Cincinnati for work to support them when she met Tracy's father, a black man. They fell in love and got married. In 1964 she got pregnant with Tracy's older sister, Lisa. When her first husband, the white one, heard about this, he took her to court. At that time it was against the law in Kentucky for a white woman to marry a Negro. Nana was breaking the law. So the judge gave the first husband custody of the three kids.

The thing was, the first husband didn't want custody of the kids. He told the judge, "I just didn't want *her* to have it." The entire thing was terrible. Finally, Nana's parents stood up and told the judge that they would take the three children. The judge agreed. Later, the parents told Nana that she could have the kids back—on one condition: she would have to divorce Tracy's father and either have an abortion or put the baby up for adoption. They wanted no part of a black son-in-law or a mixed-race granddaughter.

Nana would have none of it, of course. She and her second husband moved to Miami, where they had Lisa. Tracy was born a couple of years later. But the marriage didn't work out, and times were very tough. After the divorce, Tracy's father abandoned the family and as a result Tracy grew up very poor in a dangerous neighborhood. There were nights when she hid from gunfire under her bed, dreaming of a better life.

People were cruel, too. Back then, not many people accepted biracial children. Compounding this, Nana was white and her daughters looked black. The white community didn't accept them because the kids were black. The black community judged them because Nana was white. They had nowhere to turn. There was an incredible amount of hate and prejudice directed at them.

Nana had a choice at that point. She could have crumbled and given up, or she could have turned every drop of evil directed at her

A better life: Nana with Myka

and her girls into fuel to drive them to a better life. She not only chose the latter, she instilled that mind-set in her girls. No one was going to allow the Wilson family to break.

One of Nana's children from her first marriage, Donna, lived in Vegas and had been stricken with cancer. Nana wanted to be there to help. They packed up and moved to Las Vegas, driven by the desire to help Donna and by the promise of a fresh start that brings so many people out there. Nana began cleaning houses. She cleaned so many houses that she was able to scratch out not just a living for her children but the promise of college tuition. The strength of this woman is awe-inspiring.

It even inspired Bill Cosby. In the late 1980s, he was perhaps the biggest star in the world. But he sat there quietly and listened as this teenage girl gave this entire testimonial about her mother. At the end he said, "I've got to meet her."

Nana is a firecracker of a personality. If you think anger should have consumed her, you've got it all wrong. She's a tell-it-like-it-is, fun-seeking, larger-than-life figure. These days she plays poker with our landscapers, tells dirty jokes to our friends, and cusses so well she'd embarrass a trucker. She recently had a seventy-fifth birthday party up in Kentucky and it didn't end until three days and four cases of bourbon had been used up.

So when Tracy got her mother on the phone with Bill Cosby, Nana busted his chops and acted like they were old friends. He loved it. The two of them hit it off immediately. Cosby was completely taken by her honesty, her toughness, and her sense of humor. He even hired a screenwriter, Kathleen McGee-Anderson, to write a play about Nana, called *Mothers*. It eventually played at the Crossroads Theatre in New York. And from that day on, Bill Cosby told Nana not to worry about the cost of college for her daughters; Tracy was now on the Bill Cosby scholarship plan.

There was one big catch, though, Mr. Cosby said. If he was paying for the college, he was picking the college. Pepperdine was out. He wanted Tracy to attend Howard, a historically black university with world-renowned academics.

Tracy did as Mr. Cosby said. And it was just my luck. Howard is in Washington, D.C., just three miles from Georgetown.

4

GEORGETOWN LESSONS

The air is thick and warm, even though it is past midnight. It's July in South Beach, and Alonzo and Tracy Mourning are standing outside the Forge nightclub, waiting for their car. They have just hosted a small party at the conclusion of their annual Zo Summer's Groove charity weekend.

The crowds notice the two of them, both tall, radiant, and famous. But while Tracy smiles at each person who approaches or calls out their name, Alonzo stands to the side, holding her shoulder, with an intense look on his face, scanning the crowd with serious intent.

That this isn't an obviously dangerous group doesn't matter. Alonzo's eyes dart like a Secret Service agent's. His initial reaction is to not trust. If that puts a few people off, so be it. Through all these years as a celebrity, dating even back to high school when people wanted to be around a phenom, he's learned that not every person's intent is always positive.

"I think he was taught to not open up to people because everybody wants something," said his agent, Jeff Wechsler. "It comes with the territory."

The contrast is striking. One of the most generous professional athletes in America, the one arguably most committed to humanitarian efforts, has a reputation for being one of the least approachable stars.

Wechsler has witnessed numerous scenes like this one, Alonzo staring everyone down so only the most courageous would even dare approach him. He's also gotten the early-morning phone calls that go like this:

Alonzo has just finished reading the paper. "Jeff, let's go."

"Zo, where are we going?"

"We're going to this kid's house."

"What are you talking about?"

"Did you read in the paper about the kid who was raising money for his basketball team? They were out collecting and he got hit by a car. They need fifteen thousand bucks for their team, their traveling team. But since he got hit by the car, he can't raise the money. C'mon, we're going."

Alonzo has already gotten the kid's address. Soon enough the two are knocking on his door, offering a check to his stunned parents with a single caveat: Don't tell the newspapers about it.

"That's the thing with Alonzo," Jeff said. "If he sees someone trying to better himself or his community and he hears about it, then he'll do anything.

"It's not just money, either. He'll hear about someone getting injured and send his personal trainer to help with rehab. He'll go to someone's house unannounced with something they need. He's always starting charities, trying to raise money for a gun buy-back program, trying to do something. He never stops.

"But if you just approach him, it's different."

Alonzo has worked hard through the years to lighten up. He's mostly succeeded. He isn't the brooding guy he once was. But there are limits. He doesn't even realize the look he so often throws around in public.

But there are reasons why such a generous, caring, even emotional soul is concealed behind the hardest of exteriors.

"The thing is, I was once naïve and trusted everyone," Alonzo says. "And it almost cost me everything."

W hen a person who is open to guidance finds a mentor willing to dispense wisdom, great things can happen. When I arrived at Georgetown University, I knew John Thompson was that wise and willing mentor. I thought I was that young man open to guidance. I even played my part.

But it is like a man's relationship with God: There is listening with your ears and listening with your heart. There is saying the word and living the word. From the outside, no one can tell the difference. From the inside, if you're honest, it's clear to see.

To be committed at a level that only you personally can recognize, to truly live the right way when no one else is capable of calling you on it, to do what's right even when no one is looking is the most difficult thing for a person to do. Anyone can act the part. Anyone can pretend they are living the right way, that they are walking hand in hand with God. And that was me as a freshman at Georgetown. I was trying to fool everyone. I was trying to fool myself. I thought I had all the answers; pretty quickly though, God taught me the questions.

The summer before my freshman year, the world opened up for me. John Thompson had been selected to coach the 1988 U.S. Olympic team. This was back when only amateur players—college guys—could play for USA Basketball. That changed in 1992 with the creation of the Dream Team, featuring Michael Jordan, Larry Bird, and Magic Johnson. The 1988 U.S. Olympic Team was really the last of the old-time college teams to represent our country. The games were held that September in Korea, and even though no high school player had ever made our Olympic team, I was extended an invitation to try out.

At the first part of our training camp, in Colorado Springs, I was just tearing it up the whole time. I may have just gotten out of high school and I may have been playing against guys three and four years older than me, established college players, but I had no fear. I just played my game, didn't overextend myself, and kept telling myself that I wasn't trying to steal the last spot on the team, everyone else was trying to steal my spot.

Just before we broke camp we played an exhibition game in Denver and I was one of the leading scorers, which was big news with the national media. A lot of people thought I was playing better than Rony Seikaly, who had just completed his senior year at Syracuse and appeared to be my main competition. The Olympics looked like a reality.

One thing I couldn't count on was any favors from Coach Thompson. I may have been his prize recruit, but he was just as relentlessly on me as he was on everyone else. After Colorado, the team went to Washington to practice before a brief European tour that would precede the final cuts. We had a practice scheduled for the same day as my high school graduation, and Coach Thompson said I could go back to Chesapeake for the ceremony. But he also told me I needed to be back in time for practice. It was an exciting day for me, spending time with my family and friends, and I ended up returning late for the practice. The team was already working at McDonough Gym, the old facility on the Georgetown campus, as I came strolling in.

I thought, "Hey, I'm excused, it's okay. Coach knows I was graduating, he won't do anything to me."

But as I walked across the floor, Coach stopped practice and threw one of those heart-stopping glares at me.

"What do you think you're doing?"

I was like a deer in the headlights. There is just nothing quite like Big John Thompson's voice when he's angry. It booms like a cannon; it just goes right through you. I defy any man not to live in fear of it. John Thompson is not someone you want to mess with, and now I'd done so for the first time.

I couldn't even speak. I was just thinking, Yo, what, what, what? He just boomed again. "Get your butt up there and get in your practice gear. You're late!"

I was scared now. So much for favoritism, so much for even the slightest bending of the rules. He'd told me to be on time and I wasn't—there would be no discussion as to why. I had gotten my ankles taped but I wasn't dressed and I had to run and get my shoes. But to do that I had to run up a flight of stadium stairs that were made of polished cement and were very slippery. All while wearing my socks.

I was scrambling so fast, I slipped. Bam! I banged my knee. To this day, I still have a little dent; I can still feel the spot in my knee where I hit it on the corner of the step. All that did was make Coach Thompson even angrier. My knee swelled up immediately but I practiced that day. My leg would have had to have fallen off for me to skip practice.

The team went on a tour of Finland and Austria, where we played a series of exhibition games. It was just an incredible trip for me. Just a few weeks earlier, I had been living in foster care. Now I was traveling Europe, representing my country, playing alongside guys such as David Robinson and Danny Manning.

I was absolutely on top of the world. For an eighteen-year-old, I don't know what could be better, except maybe to make the Olympic team and win gold in Seoul. I was certain that was going to happen because, based on my play, I thought I was a lock to make the team.

I was the final cut. There was no explanation. I didn't dare ask, because I knew there would be no sense in doing so. Big John was not going to discuss personnel decisions with me.

I was crushed. This was a dream I thought was about to happen and now it was done. Years later the assistant on that team, George Raveling, who was the coach of Southern California and a close friend of Thompson's, told me that I was left behind because Coach didn't want me to start my time at Georgetown by missing three weeks of classes. The assistants had argued passionately that I should be on the team, but Thompson wouldn't budge. Much later, when I was long gone from college, I worked up the nerve to ask Coach about his decision and he confirmed what George had said.

Coach Thompson knew that with my background I would be tested by the academic demands of Georgetown, and he thought the Olympics would really set me back. "I just couldn't let you fall behind," he told me. Today I appreciate what he did, because it was a difficult adjustment for me, competing academically with some of the brightest and best-trained students in the country.

His gesture took on extra meaning because, unfortunately, we failed to win the gold in Seoul. Our bronze medal was our first non-gold since the disputed 1972 Olympics, when the refs basically stole the game for the Soviets. Coach Thompson took a lot of heat for that Olympic "loss." So he sacrificed having his best possible team for my academics. This was how he graduated so many players at Georgetown.

He selflessly put my interests ahead of his own. And to repay him, I selfishly put mine in front of everyone's.

With all the free time college provides and with Coach Thompson off in Asia, I decided to embrace my newfound stardom. In Washington, D.C., Georgetown basketball was a big deal, not just on campus but all over the city. Everybody loved the Hoyas and in a lot of ways we were treated like a pro team. As the No. 1 recruit in the nation, the high schooler who almost made the Olympic team, I instantly had the run of the city.

I first met Rayful Edmond through my teammate John Turner. They were both from D.C. and had been friends for years. JT was a six-foot-seven forward, a real tough guy, who had spent a couple of years at junior college before coming to Georgetown. He was new to the team, but in the city he knew everyone. JT was my road dog. He took me out, showed me around, brought me to some different places, and got me familiarized with the city. I was able to meet a lot of his friends.

That August was amazing. I was in D.C. but didn't have a lot to do. School hadn't started, there was no practice, and Coach was preoccupied with the Olympics. Tracy was still in Las Vegas, since Howard hadn't started up yet. I didn't know when she was coming, so I started calling the Howard freshman dorms all the time and leaving her messages with my new number. I guess I went a little overboard trying to get hold of her, because by the time she finally moved in, her new roommate took one look at her and in a less than pleasant tone said, "Oh, you're Tracy?" Then she handed her a big stack of messages from me.

But until Tracy arrived, I was out on the town with JT and his friends. Rayful was about twenty-three, twenty-four, and just seemed like a nice, smart guy. He was kind of low-key, he wasn't a flamboyant dresser or anything, didn't have jewelry or tattoos. He was stylish, but it wasn't anything out of the ordinary. When we were introduced, we had kind of a casual conversation, just, "Hey, what's up." He told me he was a big Georgetown fan, said he was looking forward to the season. I didn't know what his occupation was. I just took him to be a nice guy.

It turned out Rayful Edmond was the drug kingpin of Washington D.C. He wasn't just *some guy*: he was running an operation that was clearing a million dollars a week. Eventually federal prosecutors alleged that he was the person who brought crack cocaine to D.C., although I don't know if that is true or not. I knew none of this at the time, though. I was way more naïve than I realized, just a kid from Chesapeake who thought he could handle whatever was thrown at him. I didn't even realize I was an easy mark for a guy like him.

That summer I began playing for Rayful's playground basketball team, where we'd compete in games against other teams made up of college players from Maryland, George Washington, and other area schools, low-level pros, guys who played in the CBA or Europe, and local street ball legends who might not have made it but had skills. These were big-time games, real high-level stuff. I was just playing, thinking I was getting in some good competition, but it turned out Rayful and the other drug dealers in town all had teams and bet big money on the games.

Those drug dealers were making so much money they couldn't do anything with it. You make a million dollars a week illegally and you can't just put it in the bank. You can't even buy anything. You have to put houses and cars in other people's names, try to launder the money, things like that. And there is just no way to move that kind of money— you're talking maybe $50 million a year. They had money to burn, so much money they would form teams and then gamble heavily on who could win. It was like a mini NBA.

I really was naïve back then. I look back with embarrassment at just how naïve I was. But I was eighteen, thought I was indestructible, and I had come from Mrs. Threet's house, where I had only just begun to learn how not to be skeptical of everything and everyone. I guess I had lost that edge I had in the group home.

To me, Rayful was just a cool guy. There were so many red flags I should have paid attention to, but I didn't. He had a bunch of homes out in Maryland that he'd let us use. And he had guys around him all the time. One night I was coming out of a nightclub with Rayful and a bunch of his guys. I was kind of in the back of the group but I could see over everyone, and I noticed this white van skidding right at us across the parking lot. As it turned in front of us, the side door slid open and a bunch of flashbulbs went off. Then the door closed and the van took off. It must have been the FBI, taking our picture. I found out later that I was in government photos with Rayful. At the time I just shrugged it off, I was young and not really thinking, just enjoying my life.

The time I really started wondering about Rayful was when JT and I were over at his aunt's house. Rayful and some of his crew were there getting their hair cut. They used to go to a barbershop up off Benning Road until one time a guy came in and tried to assassinate one of his boys, this guy called Little Nut. He was a little tiny dude, but he carried a gun about as big as himself. It wasn't that big of a thing to me, because growing up I knew lots of guys who carried guns. And again, I wanted to belong, I wanted everyone to think I was tough and cool. I wanted to keep it real, or what I stupidly thought was real. So I didn't blink at the gun. And I didn't think twice when I heard Nut had gotten shot and wound up in a wheelchair. No one did. Rayful just stopped going to the barbershop. It was too dangerous. The barber, Dusty, started coming to the aunt's house to cut everyone's hair.

I knew that wasn't good. But I wasn't going to start asking a lot of questions. I just tried to play it cool because no one else seemed to be surprised by it. I wanted to fit in. I pretended this was normal stuff for me. I thought I could handle it.

John Thompson grew up in D.C., went to high school at Archbishop Carroll, coached high school ball at nearby St. Anthony's, and then took over at Georgetown in 1972. He knew everyone in Washington and everyone knew him, from presidents on down. He had the city wired, which meant it was just a matter of time before he found out I was associating with a drug dealer, especially one with the stature of Rayful Edmond.

A high school friend of Coach Thompson's worked in the Drug Enforcement Agency. Right in the heart of the season, he called Coach up and told him the situation. I wasn't doing anything illegal, but I certainly wasn't doing anything right, either.

Rather than confront me directly, Coach set me up the next day at practice. We were going along as normal when two DEA agents walked into the gym, and said, "Coach, we need to talk to one of your players." Then they pointed at me.

I tried to play innocent. "What is going on? I didn't do anything!"

Coach told me to go up to his office. A minute after I sat down, he and the DEA agents came in. They all pretended not to know each other. Then the agents started grilling me, questioning me about my affiliation with Rayful.

"Yeah," I said, "I know the guy."

"Do you know he's under surveillance? Do you know he's a drug kingpin?"

The truth was, I didn't know. Maybe I had begun to suspect Rayful wasn't the most innocent guy, but this was stunning news to me. I was floored. I felt like throwing up. I just kept telling the agents, "I didn't know. I didn't know. I've got nothing to do with it, with drugs, with anything."

I shot a glance over at Coach Thompson. He was standing there, his big arms folded across his chest, looking down on me. He was so angry he could have ripped me limb from limb. I had just brought heat on his program, two DEA agents were in his office, and there was no excuse.

Eventually the agents left and Coach Thompson started in on me. Within a minute, he had me in tears.

"You're an embarrassment to the school and to the program," he bellowed at me. "Son, I will take your scholarship from you. I brought your butt here and I will send your butt home."

I was terrified. I thought he was going to throw me out of school. I thought it would cost me my career. How would I explain this to anyone? To Mrs. Threet? To Bud? To my parents, Coach Lassiter, Tracy? Who would believe me?

"I don't want you around these individuals," he said. "You're not only hurting yourself, you're hurting this program. You're hurting every player who ever came here and built this program with their blood, sweat, and tears. You're hurting me. You're hurting everybody else around you. You're hurting your family."

And that's when I just broke down and cried, because I had no malicious intent whatsoever. I wasn't out to hurt anybody. I was just living my life recklessly without even thinking of the consequences and the repercussions behind it. I thought I was on a roll, man. I was just playing ball and having fun. I hadn't thought about how anything might impact or reflect on me, my family, Coach Thompson, or Georgetown. Really, the only thing I did that was close to being wrong was drinking. I drank a lot of alcohol when I was a freshman. I used to drink a lot of beer, so much I would pass out. But I never did drugs. I wasn't dealing drugs.

None of that mattered to Coach Thompson.

And while Big John didn't like us drinking alcohol, he knew we did it. You couldn't put anything past that man. He used to send his assistant, Ed Spriggs, up to the dorms to pay us surprise visits. Spriggs would come in and snoop around, check the refrigerator and anywhere else he cared to look. Ed would even show up in classroom doorways to make sure we arrived on time. We lived in these dorms that were like an apartment; there were four of us in each one. One time Ed came in and saw all this beer in our refrigerator.

Coach didn't saying anything to us about it—but the next day in practice, he ran us into the ground. I mean, ran us and ran us and ran us. No one knew exactly why. And he wouldn't give us a water break. It was a brutal practice. Finally he gave us a water break. Everybody had their own personal bottle, labeled with their number, that was filled with Gatorade. We went over to get our bottles and he's sitting across the way, arms folded, leaning back watching us.

We all started chugging from the bottles and it just hit me. It wasn't Gatorade in there, it was beer. One of my roommates spat it out, but I just kept right on drinking it. I tried to play it off, pretend it wasn't beer. Big John just looked at us.

"I told you all I didn't want beer in the dorms," he shouted. "When I tell you I don't want any beer and I don't want any women in the dorms, that means I don't want any beer and I don't want any women in the dorms. Let this be the last time."

He never cracked a smile but he later told me that he and Ed Spriggs laughed for a while at that one. Even we knew that, while he was dead serious, it was funny.

But hanging out with Rayful was much bigger than having some beer in the dorm. I now realized the impact that I had on the program. I realized all of the individuals that I represented and how I had this family legacy to carry on. I realized the decisions that I made could affect so many other people's lives. What if this news got out? The stories wouldn't just be about me associating with drug dealers, they would be about *John Thompson's player* associating with drug dealers, *Georgetown player* associating with drug dealers. The entire program would take a hit.

That day with the DEA agents was a huge day in my life; if Coach Thompson's plan was to scare me straight, he succeeded. He didn't pull my scholarship. He let me return to the team. But I knew I was on the thinnest of ice.

From then on, I was conscious of making the right decisions, so much more alert and much more aware of my surroundings and the things that I did. Years went by before I found out the DEA agents were a setup. But that didn't matter. What they said was the truth, and I needed to hear the truth in its rawest form.

"I wanted to make it as clear as possible to Alonzo who he was involved with and how high the stakes were," Coach says now. "I asked them to come because I thought that would be more effective than just having me do it."

John Thompson is a genius, of course. It couldn't have worked any better. I changed my life immediately—I changed the way I lived my life. I was done with Rayful and all of that. My only problem was that, by that time, I had befriended a whole clique of guys who were in the game, truly in the drug game.

Now I had to make a clean break from them; I had to distance myself. But these weren't regular people. You don't know what they are going to do if they think you are big-timing them or abandoning them. These were the sort of issues I had never contemplated, the problems I had gotten myself into. Now I had to keep my distance. I was friendly with them, but I kept my distance. They actually understood that and were good about it.

I also didn't know at the time that Coach Thompson had put word out on the street that he wanted Rayful to come visit him. He was going to work both angles to protect his players and his program.

If you want to know the power and the respect that John Thompson commanded in Washington back in the 1980s, this was it. Not only was he able to get word to Rayful, but the drug kingpin of the city, a guy running an intercontinental narcotics operation that had made him a millionaire many times over, one of the most dangerous men on the entire East Coast, went to the Georgetown campus by himself and sat down in John Thompson's office for a talk.

These days Coach Thompson won't tell anyone, not even me, what he said to Rayful. He did say on *Nightline* once that he told Rayful in no uncertain terms to stay away from his players, especially me, and that he needed some help making sure none of us would get hurt because of our mistakes. Ray supposedly listened intently and agreed. All I know is that was the end of it between the two of us. Ray never tried to talk to me again.

At that point, I thought the entire ordeal would blow over. I spent the rest of the season concentrating on basketball, class, following every order from Coach, and hanging out with her. I spent so much time over at Howard, people thought I was a student there. But I knew I wasn't going to get in any trouble with Tracy. That was where I was supposed to be, spending time with her, not out on the streets.

Things looked promising until April. Just after my freshman season, the news broke. In a major organized crime sweep, Rayful Edmond and his entire operation got busted. The feds locked everyone up, the case was going to trial, and now, all of a sudden, my association with Rayful was public. Not just in the local papers, but everywhere. Now my embarrassment was national news. There was no hiding it, no way for Coach Thompson to protect me. I had shamed him and the program, and there was no way to unring that bell.

To make matters worse, when they put Ray away, the streets completely dried up. He'd been the chief supplier; with no crack on the streets, the violence—which was already very heavy in East Coast inner cities—was even greater. Now I was scared that someone would come after me, thinking I had something to do with putting Ray away, that I was a snitch. Every day I began to realize how deep a hole I had put myself into.

United States v. Rayful Edmond III was one of the most famous criminal cases in the history of Washington, D.C. Everyone was riveted by the details and the trial was front-page news every day. Because of death threats, the jurors were kept anonymous and there was bulletproof glass set up between the courtroom spectators and the participants, just in case someone wanted to try something against Ray or anyone else involved in the case. The precautions were taken for good reason, too. One possible witness was shot in the leg before the trial and decided not to testify, while the mother of another prosecution witness had her home firebombed. Rayful was considered such a prime target that, rather than keep him in regular jail—even in solitary—they housed him at the Quantico Marine base in Virginia and flew him to court in a helicopter each day. That was the only way they could assure his safety.

I was brought in to testify, even though there was no good reason for doing so. I think the U.S. attorneys just wanted the extra publicity of having a Georgetown basketball star on the witness stand. Rayful never brought me around any drugs, I never took any drugs, and he was never *on* drugs. He was smart. He was *so* smart. I never realized the depth of his intelligence and the extent of his power in the drug industry until Ted Koppel and *Nightline* did a big story on the case.

For me, it was just a daily nightmare. It was the most nerve-racking time in my life. I could barely sleep, I could never relax, not even over at Tracy's. I was supposed to be a college student, not a witness in a drug trial. I had been partying too much and hanging out with the wrong people, but really I was a good person. I had never been in any serious trouble. But now I knew everyone at Georgetown was looking at me differently. The professors, the other students, everyone knew about it. It was even posted in *The Hoya*, our school newspaper. I was living up to their worst stereotypes. I remember the newspaper sketched a picture of me sitting on the stand having to testify against Rayful. Who wants the world to see that?

The day I had to walk into that courtroom, it felt like the weight of the world was on top of me and I was just trying to get it off. I was just trying to get to the very last question so I could step off that stand. It was clear to me that I had walked the wrong path. That was a very uncomfortable realization. I could see Ray out of the corner of my eye when I first walked in. He didn't give me any type of look, no smile, nothing. But I caught his eye. When I sat on the stand, I just looked at the attorney.

They asked me all of these questions—"Have you ever seen this? Have you ever seen that?" They were talking about drugs and things like that. They were hoping I had eyewitness evidence, I guess.

My first thought was about my life, number one, because I knew Ray still had connections in the street. I know all I was supposed to think about was telling the truth, but it isn't that easy. That bulletproof glass was nice inside the courtroom, but what about outside of it?

But I didn't have any answers for the questions, anyway. I hadn't seen any drugs. I didn't know anything. I wasn't a part of anything. I didn't have to lie. It was all "No," "No," "No." You don't give any lengthy answers in court. So I just told the truth. I just wanted to get out of there. I just wanted to get on with the rest of my life. Ray got sent to federal prison for the rest of his life. So I was lucky, man. If you can't learn from that experience, then you're a fool.

Michael Wilbon was a young columnist for *The Washington Post* then. He's all over ESPN now, but he covered my day as a witness and wrote a couple of pointed sentences about it.

Over and over, people in Courtroom 10 looked at Mourning—
6 feet 10, clean-cut, well-dressed in his black double-breasted
blazer and slate-gray slacks, a man who eventually will earn millions of dollars. They looked at him and whispered to each
other, "Isn't it stupid that he would associate with these
guys? . . ."

The lesson Mourning has to learn from all this is that at 6-10,
friendly, dashing and soon-to-be rich, he's going to attract a
crowd for the rest of his life. The people who want to watch him,
hang out after games with him, won't always be lawyers and doctors and sportswriters. He's got to be exceptionally careful about
the people he associates with. Thompson was a safety net this
time, but he won't always be. If Mourning doesn't learn from
this mistake, next time it could be a lot more serious than an-
swering a few questions behind bulletproof glass.

I couldn't have agreed more, then or now. I learned from that experience. In hindsight, I think it was one of the best things that ever happened to me in my career because it just made me so much more
aware of my surroundings. While I didn't ask for a résumé from everybody who came into my life, I made sure I watched how I picked my
friends. You can't just trust anyone. Ray didn't look like a drug kingpin,
but there were plenty of warning signs that said *Stay away* that I ig-
nored.

I've watched a lot of athletes, not just basketball players, get taken
down by their friends. They put themselves in bad situations, get used
by negative people, and lose everything. And that could have been me.
When they arrested Rayful, they arrested his mother, all his aunts, his
cousins, because all of them were affiliated. They were either launder-
ing the money or involved in some way. They got *everybody. Everybody*
did time.

A great athlete who grew up near me was Michael Vick. He's from Newport News, which is the next town over from Chesapeake. I've always liked Mike, he was such an exciting football player. But Mike lost his career, $100 million in contracts, and his freedom because he was hanging around people who didn't have his best interests at heart. They were running a dogfighting ring in his name, on his property. He was into it, too. I don't deny that fact. But he obviously wasn't associating with the best people. And it cost him.

I learned to channel my energies toward surrounding myself with the right people. I've always tried to do that. Unfortunately, people often say when they first meet me that I am very serious, that I can be very unapproachable. This was especially true during the rest of my time at Georgetown and the early part of my career.

My reputation was that I was mean, standoffish, and even rude. I can't necessarily argue with that, either—I probably was. I may have swung too far the other way, but that was the only way to take control of the situation and assure that I was in charge of my future.

There is a lot of pressure on athletes, especially ones from disadvantaged backgrounds, to "keep it real." But keeping it real is keeping your best interests at heart. It is protecting yourself and your family, the ones doing right by you, not holding on to some misguided sense of loyalty. There is nothing "keeping it real" about taking an incredible opportunity and blowing it, about refusing to learn and mature and grow.

And there is nothing "keeping it real" about turning your back on the people who are trying to show you the way. I was pretending to be one thing and acting the other. I was just playing the role of responsible, dedicated student, athlete, boyfriend, protégé. Really, I was dishonoring all those things by also pretending to be cool with everything Ray and his crew were doing.

Rayful Edmond was a blessing for me, an experience sent by God. Back on that witness stand, I never thought I would say such a thing. Back in Coach Thompson's office, crying and begging for my scholarship, I never imagined there was a single positive about that humiliating situation. But I was flying too high before I got cut from the Olympic team. God brought me crashing down to earth and humbled me. Life's experiences have a way of reminding you of your blessings.

Rayful Edmond assured that for my remaining three years at Georgetown, I would concentrate almost exclusively, even fanatically, on basketball, education, and Tracy.

5

CHARLOTTE

On November 9, 1989, the Georgetown basketball team was, not surprisingly, at practice. The session was physically and mentally demanding. John Thompson towered over every small detail of the game. Then, for no apparent reason, he sent his players to the sideline bleachers. No one was sure what was up.

Thompson is a serious and intimidating man, who for decades made college players cower. It was no different that day, as he made eye contact with his players.

"Can somebody tell me what happened today?" he barked.

None of the players knew what he was talking about. Did he mean what happened in practice? Had someone screwed up off the court? No one said a word.

Thompson pressed on, feigning surprise.

"No one? Who read the paper today? Raise your hand if you read the *paper today." None of the players raised his hand; none had read a newspaper. Thompson wasn't happy.*

"Can somebody at least tell me what happened on the headlines today—something of historical significance? Did any of you even bother to glance at the headlines?"

Still no one had any idea what Thompson was talking about. Finally one of the student trainers, Markhum Stansbury, raised his hand.

"Coach, they tore down the Berlin Wall."

"Right," Big John said. "They tore down the Berlin Wall."

Then he turned to his team, almost all black kids, most from poor backgrounds, all receiving the opportunity of a lifetime to attend one of the elite institutes of higher education in this country. He shook his head.

"That's a shame. You guys go to Georgetown University, a prestigious, world-renowned university, and not a single one of you can keep up with current events?" Then his voice got louder, turned into that powerful blast that Thompson was famous for.

"The damn world could be at war, and you wouldn't even know about it."

The players were humiliated, which was the point. Thompson was relentless in pushing his players off the court. But it was about more than just earning diplomas, which virtually all of them did during his nearly three decades at the school. It was about making them grow intellectually, socially, and spiritually. It was about setting up the habits that would continue that growth through the rest of their life.

It was about pushing them, maturing them, and making them aware of the big world outside of basketball. Thompson just could not tolerate anything less. There are no small lessons with him—just lessons.

Not knowing what was on the front page was no more acceptable than failing a class or not trying for a rebound. It might seem minor to many (plenty of college kids are blissfully unaware of the world at large), but it wasn't to Thompson. There was no excuse for an educated adult not to know that the Berlin Wall had been knocked down, so he sure wasn't going to accept such ignorance from his players.

"The next day," Alonzo Mourning said, "I went to Wisemiller's, a little deli store just off campus where everyone went, and I bought The Washington Post. *And every day after that if I didn't buy it, I at least read all the headlines.*

"Even today, I pick up the newspaper and at least read the front page or, at the very least, look at the headlines."

Two decades later, the smallest of John Thompson's lessons was still important.

"Just in case Coach Thompson ever asks me again what happened today." Mourning laughed. "This time I'll have the answer."

The first priority of wealthy parents in this country is to get their children the very best education possible. That's the No. 1 concern. They pay for it, push for it, preach for it. You don't have to be wealthy, or even be educated, to have those goals for your children, but every single parent who has enjoyed success absolutely demands that their children have that base, that safety net. It's like an insurance policy. And yet in many of our poorer communities, education is dismissed as nonessential, or a luxury.

Worse yet, the wealthy in the country who care so much about the education of their own children, who put it first for their sons and daughters, drop it deep on the list of priorities for other people's kids. We have the wealthiest nation in the world and we can look in every city and see an educational system that excels in some schools and fails in others. And there is no real consensus, no real determination to fix it. Instead, we watch generations of kids languish for years in a way we would not tolerate for our own children.

John Thompson stood at the crossroads of America's education system. He coached at one of the most competitive schools in America, a place that produced doctors, lawyers, CEOs, and even presidents. The nonathletes who attend Georgetown are driven and gifted students, the best of the best, and mostly from very privileged backgrounds.

The players Coach Thompson recruited were among the best athletes in the country, but often we were from disadvantaged backgrounds, lousy schools, broken homes. We grew up in situations where the chief priority was simple survival, not some far-off idea of education. To add to the mix, the regular students were overwhelmingly white; the Hoya basketball team was overwhelmingly black.

For this to work, for the two sides to come together and work together, required a man of incredible talent and dedication. Coach Thompson was not naïve about the situation; and he understood both sides of the coin. He pushed for understanding and compassion at the school as well as with the NCAA and the national media. There was simply no way the players could make up for all that lost academic time, quality of teaching, and life habits. We couldn't just step into real classes and get straight As. It had to be a process. There were bound to be setbacks. But Thompson promised the school he would guide us through, and he put his reputation on the line for us.

But he also demanded we rise to the challenge. One could not work without the other. There would be and could be no shortcuts or excuses. He constantly reminded us that the way we performed in the classroom—not just on tests, but in our demeanor—reflected solely on him. We were nobodies; he was the face of this program. He was on us about how we acted, dressed, and behaved. He had spies all over campus and if we were screwing around at all, even just normal college kid stuff, he heard about it. We'd argue that we were just doing what a regular student was doing and he'd bark, "You're not a regular student."

It wasn't just about getting a diploma; it was about getting an education. It was about opening our eyes to a lifetime of learning, of intellectual curiosity, of challenging ourselves outside our comfort zones. It was about embracing this incredible environment we were in, just blocks from the White House, a school where classes were taught by world-class professors and where we were surrounded by students who would assuredly go on to success. If we didn't try to connect with the talented people on campus and off, then it was all a waste, diploma or not. No, we weren't all going to magically get 4.0s. But that didn't mean we couldn't maximize our potential. This was the opportunity of a lifetime for us. I thought I appreciated it at the time, but it's now, as an adult and a parent, that I fully understand. My son is eleven and he has already toured the Georgetown campus.

We were not allowed to skip class. That's probably the case with most college programs, although there are far too many that don't care much about the education of the players. But we also weren't allowed to just show up and slump in the back row. We were expected to sit attentively and participate. Then, each night, all the freshmen had a scheduled time to call our academic adviser, Ms. Mary Fenlon, and she would grill us on what had happened in class that day and discuss the lecture with us. It was like going to class twice.

Ms. Fenlon was a short, smart, middle-aged white woman. You've never seen so many big black guys so scared of someone like that. Every night it was, "Did you call Ms. Fenlon? Oh man, I've got to get ready for Ms. Fenlon." She was one of Coach Thompson's closest advisers, maybe even closer to him than his assistant coaches. She even traveled to road games with us and sat on our bench. She knew all the classes we were taking, all the professors, so she knew what had been taught that day. And if we didn't match her understanding of the lesson, if it was clear we hadn't paid attention or were slipping, she would tell Big John and all hell would break loose.

And you never, ever wanted that.

So we kept our eyes open, and in turn, had them opened even more.

In terms of basketball, Coach Thompson was also an ideal teacher for me; I only wish I had won him a national championship during my time at Georgetown. We never even made the Final Four.

Thompson took over the program in 1972, after a 3–23 season, and soon transformed it into a national power. Before his retirement, he won 596 games and reached the postseason 24 consecutive seasons, including 20 in the NCAA tournament. From 1979 to 1992, when I was a senior, he reached the NCAAs every March, advancing to three Final Fours and winning the NCAA title in 1984. With that, he became the first African-American coach to ever win the NCAA men's basketball championship, an accomplishment that made him a legend to many around the country.

Before that, he was a great player, and won two NBA championships with the Boston Celtics as a backup to Bill Russell, the greatest winner in the history of the game. Thompson learned defensive basketball not just from the Celtics' great coach, Red Auerbach, but by playing day in and day out against Russell. He knew everything about the center position and he taught me all of it. Russell was just six foot nine—an undersized center like me. His rival was Wilt Chamberlain, who was bigger (seven foot one) and superior offensively (he once scored 100 points in a single game). But Russell knew how to dominate the game defensively, and as a result his Celtics always defeated Chamberlain's teams in Philadelphia and Los Angeles.

I was a Bill Russell–type player. In the NBA, one of my chief rivals would be Shaquille O'Neal, who was more like Wilt Chamberlain. I scored a lot of points, but I played the game with a defensive mentality. I always prided myself on stopping people. Coach Thompson measured his teams by their ability to stop people. It was perfect. We shared a personality trait, too: we hated to lose even more than we loved to win. It was fear of failure that drove us, not the pursuit of glory. The result was an intense commitment to preparation.

A team is most successful when individuality is not the concern. In basketball, it is only acceptable to be selfish in rebounding and defense. You can't hurt your team by trying to grab too many rebounds or stopping too many shots. This was my mind-set and I never got discouraged or concerned about individual statistics, even though I annually put up very big numbers. In truth, they didn't matter. Winning did. There are no shutouts in basketball. Not in college, not in the NBA. As a result, there are many false or empty offensive stat lines. Even the worst team in the league is going to score some points, so someone on that team is going to have a nice average. But it's worthless if you're not winning games.

Even though I was a 20-point-a-game scorer in both college and the NBA, I never got discouraged by a bad game on offense because I knew that even if no one passed me the ball, I was still going to have an impact on the game. Each shot I stopped, each turnover I created, each shot I blocked was a basket also. It's not about being the first team to 100. It is about which team has one more point than the other at the end of the game. This sounds simple. Having an entire team execute that plan is what's difficult.

The best team I played on at Georgetown was my freshman season. We went 29–5, winning the Big East Conference regular season and tournament championships. We were a great team, blowing just about everyone out by 20. I adapted well to the college game, averaging 13.1 points and 7.3 rebounds and blocking a crazy 4.9 shots a game, a single season school record. We advanced in the NCAA tournament until we got to the Elite Eight, where Duke knocked us off. That especially hurt, because in the Final Four they lost to a Seton Hall team we had beaten twice with ease during the regular season. We watched that Duke–Seton Hall game back in the dorms and thought we had blown our chance. And we had. The next two seasons we lost in the second round of the NCAA tournament, and despite so many memorable games—especially against Big East opponents like Syracuse, Connecticut, and St. John's—it felt like we hadn't accomplished what we were capable of.

After my junior year at Georgetown, I almost declared hardship and turned pro. This was 1991, back when players rarely left college before exhausting all four years of eligibility. The NBA actually prohibited a player from leaving early, although you could petition the league on the basis of economic need, which was known as "declaring hardship." Some players were beginning to make that jump, usually after their junior year, and I certainly would have qualified.

There was a lot of appeal to jumping to the NBA. This was before Commissioner David Stern was able to get rookie contracts slotted and capped. Back then rookies had a great deal of power and could negotiate their initial salary. They could even hold out to make that salary happen. Now it is all predetermined. The first pick is guaranteed X amount of money; the second pick slightly less, the third slightly less than that, and so on. Now there really isn't that much of a difference between being the fifteenth pick and the fifth pick. They call it the rookie scale.

The old system gave rookies too much power but it actually helped push me back to college. Since draft position meant so much in negotiations, I had an incentive to stay in college in order to try to move up as high as possible. There was a real value in being a top two or three pick because you could try to earn a bigger first contract. There were millions at stake if I stayed in school. I talked to Coach Thompson about the draft and his advice was that my draft position would be higher after my senior year than my junior year. If I went out and had a great senior year, I could make up some of the difference of not being paid for the previous season.

I thought about the importance of finishing my education and being the first in my family to graduate from college. I knew it would mean a great deal to my parents and to Mrs. Threet if I could earn not just a diploma, but one from Georgetown. Also, within the program and with former players, our team's high graduation rate was a point of pride, something that set us apart from so many other teams that were just about basketball. I knew I wanted to contribute to the Georgetown legacy.

So I returned for my senior year and went out and had my best season, upping my averages to 21.3 points and 10.7 rebounds a game and earning All America honors.

Dikembe Mutombo and me

What made my level of play jump was that the previous summer all I did was work on my body and work on my game. I shot a lot, lifted a lot of weights, just concentrated on basketball. It was the true start of my fanatical workout regimes—that summer I saw the results of being selfish when it came to individual development.

The summer before, 1990, I had played for USA Basketball in the World Championships. That's the tournament that runs every four years in between the Olympics, and other than the Olympics, it's the biggest competition in international ball. This was the last time the senior men's team was made up of college players; two years later the 1992 Dream Team would usher in the age of the pros.

But that summer it was still college guys. Mike Krzyzewski of Duke was the coach and we had Kenny Anderson of Georgia Tech, Christian Laettner of Duke, Billy Owens of Syracuse, and a bunch of really good college players. The pressure to win the gold was enormous since the 1988 team of college guys, the one I was the last player cut from, fell short in the Olympics. However, we were competing with seasoned professionals, grown men. We had a lot of potential, but lining up against us were guys from other countries who were already playing in the NBA. We played Yugoslavia in the semifinals and I matched up with Vlade Divac of the Los Angeles Lakers. I had 26 points and 11 rebounds while holding him to 7 points and 4 rebounds, but across the board they had so much experience and size that we lost, 99–91. We did manage to salvage a bronze by beating Puerto Rico, but it was still disappointing.

I loved playing for USA Basketball, but when you play on those teams you tailor your game and your workouts for the team. *A team is most successful when individuality is not the concern.* I was shooting jumpers in international ball, which was something I never did at Georgetown.

But to make the NBA was not a team thing, it was an individual thing. It depended on my skills and ability. I needed a summer to just work on my own game, and once I gave myself that time to work and prepare, things took off. Although my career ended with a loss to Syracuse in the finals of the Big East tournament and then an upset to Florida State in the second round of the NCAAs, returning for my senior year is something I've never regretted.

My time at Georgetown was invaluable to my development in every imaginable way. By the late 1990s, the trend in basketball was for top players to skip college altogether and just go to the NBA. If that was the case in 1988, when I was the No. 1 rated high school player, I'm not sure what I would have done. I'm blessed I never had to make that decision, because if I was the same naïve kid, the one who got mixed up with Rayful Edmond, only this time without a disciplinarian such as John Thompson to protect me, what would have happened to me? What would have become of my career? That's why I support the current NBA age limit that requires players to attend school for at least one year.

It was with great pride that I earned my sociology degree from Georgetown in the spring of 1992. Graduation day was special; my families came up from Chesapeake. Tracy, Coach Thompson, and Mary Fenlon were there. So many of my teammates and even professors from the school were there to congratulate me. To be the first in your entire family to earn a college diploma is a special accomplishment, and I was proud I'd done it at Georgetown. That entire day, I couldn't stop smiling—I just kept looking around and thinking, *I did it!* I was very proud. Almost as proud as when, across town, I watched Tracy receive her diploma in broadcast journalism from Howard. It was amazing for us to have done that together.

My gamble to move up in the 1992 NBA draft worked out. I was expected to be the second player taken behind Shaquille O'Neal, who was leaving Louisiana State after his junior year. Naturally I would have liked to be No. 1, but I understood and just buried that inside to push me a little harder. I had decided to sign with David Falk, who was a major agent at the time. He was very connected in the NBA and he assured me I was going to get picked second. The question was where.

David, John Thompson, and I all attended a playoff game in the old Chicago Arena in the spring of 1992. At halftime we went inside to the media room to watch the NBA's annual draft lottery on television. This is where the league uses Ping-Pong balls to determine the draft order.

This was a very strange process to be involved with. Essentially, where those Ping-Pong balls went would determine where I went. It might have been Orlando, Florida, might have been Charlotte, North Carolina, might have been right back in Washington, D.C. I had no idea. It's a fun thing for the fans and really, as a player, you just want to get drafted, so you don't care that much, but I could have been shipped anywhere in America—Milwaukee, Denver, Sacramento. There was no telling. Needless to say, I watched the balls closely, I really didn't want to go anywhere too cold—and Minnesota was in the lottery.

It turned out the Charlotte Hornets, a recent expansion team, won the right to the second pick. The Hornets had drafted Larry Johnson out of UNLV the year before and were trying to build a team with a fun, up-tempo style of play. They also had great fans right in the heart of basketball country. I was getting to stay on the East Coast, it wasn't too far from home, and, of course, it wasn't too cold. I was thrilled.

I had gone through so many obstacles, so many humbling experiences, that I was happy to show my appreciation to the people who were there for me. With the enormous financial rewards of playing in the NBA, I would be able to thank them by giving them a much more comfortable life. But no one asked me for anything. That was the beautiful part— my family didn't expect anything.

My family wasn't poor. They weren't rich, either, but money wasn't an issue. Both of my parents had worked their entire lives; they were fine. And Mrs. Threet never wanted anything. She had dedicated her life to helping kids and wasn't a materialistic person at all. They continued to treat me like they always had. From my mom, to Mrs. Threet, to my foster brothers, it had always been "He's still Alonzo." I wasn't surrounded by a lot of yes-men who would say anything just so they could leech off me.

These were people who had insisted I have a savings account as a child in order to teach me the value of money. Just because they didn't ask for anything didn't mean I wasn't going to give them something. I bought Mrs. Threet a new house in Chesapeake, not far from where she lived, that gave her more space even though she was retiring as a foster parent. I built a house for my mom in Portsmouth and another for my dad in Chesapeake and joked that if they had just stayed together they could have saved me some money. It was a great feeling to do that. To pay back people who never expected to be paid back is a feeling like no other.

I hired an assistant named Shelleye Martin, a sharp woman who, despite working for me, assumed a kind of big sister role where she was never afraid to speak her mind and set me straight. Since then, she's helped other athletes make the transition to the NBA. She also had a fashion influence on me.

Getting my first contract negotiated was difficult and in a lot of ways it set the tone for my time in Charlotte. Charlotte's owner was George Shinn, a man I was never comfortable being around. Shinn was a North Carolina native and a self-made millionaire. He graduated last in his class in high school, and after some odd jobs he enrolled in a small business college and decided he could run it better than the people actually running it. So he bought the school, and then a bunch of other small colleges, and in the 1980s he sold them all for about $30 million. He made additional money in other ventures, and in 1988, he bought the expansion rights to the Hornets for $32.5 million. The team became his chief business.

One problem was that he didn't have enough money to run the team well. A lot of NBA owners are billionaires and the team is just a toy for them; they can spend lavishly on making it competitive. Shinn couldn't afford that, so he was trying to do it on the cheap. The first four Hornets seasons were four losing seasons.

As the summer dragged on and training camp began, we were miles apart on our negotiations, which really frustrated me. The last thing I wanted to do was hold out, but here I was doing just that. Since I couldn't be in Charlotte, I stayed in Washington and worked out at Georgetown.

Every morning I would lift weights, run, and shoot jumpers. In the afternoon I'd go through full practices with the Georgetown team. A lot of things were out of my hands at that point, so I was determined to control what I could, such as my preparedness. I would be in the best possible physical condition when I finally reported to the team. I knew the contract fight would add pressure on me to perform right away. Fans hate contract battles, and I don't blame them.

I caught a lot of heat in the media down in Charlotte, especially as opening night of the season arrived and I remained unsigned. The entire process frustrated me. Finally, Coach Thompson and George Shinn had a conversation, a couple of players on the team reworked their contracts to make mine fit in the NBA salary cap, and after I'd missed the first four games, we got the thing finished off. We agreed on a six-year, $25.2-million-dollar contract that allowed me to become a restricted free agent after four seasons. I also had some endorsement deals, including a big one with Nike that my longtime adviser, Allen Furst, had helped work out.

It was a great relief. I knew I was financially set for life as long as I was conservative with my money. And that wouldn't be a problem, not with Shelleye Martin and Allen Furst analyzing everything I purchased. Not that I was going to live some big lifestyle, I bought a place in a Charlotte suburb and tried to keep it simple. Those first couple of years I ate more meals at the Waffle House, Hooters, and a local soul food spot called Simmons than anywhere else. I may have had a big contract, but I was still a twenty-two-year-old kid. Of course, I was a twenty-two-year-old kid who did treat himself to a burgundy four-door Lexus with gold BBS seventeen-inch wheels. Hey, you've got to have a little fun. Tracy moved with me to Charlotte. We had dated all four years of college, so I knew she was coming with me wherever I was going. It was a fun time for us, a very exciting start to life.

With the contract done, I flew to Charlotte, went through a physical, and then was driven directly to the airport where the team's charter flight to Indianapolis was waiting for me. The Hornets were 2–2 and we had a game the next night in Indiana. They didn't want to waste any time getting me in the rotation.

As we pulled up to the plane I thought, Wow, this is a dream come true. I'm about to walk onto my first NBA plane, my first road trip. I was excited about meeting the team. I was expecting to walk on this plane and have the guys excited for me to be there, expecting them to jump up and say, "Okay, we've got our Number Two draft pick. Let's get it on. This is good."

It wasn't like that. Not only did I not get a positive response, I hardly got any response. I walked on the plane like, "Hey, what's up?" And while some guys extended their hands, that was it. I saw J. R. Reid, Kenny Gattison, Dell Curry, Muggsy Bogues, and Larry Johnson, and I think the only ones who really greeted me like they were excited to see me were Muggs, Kenny Gattison, and Dell Curry, who we called "Gomez." He kind of took me under his wing when I was a rookie. Everybody else was just blasé about it. So I took my seat and didn't know what to think. Clearly, I was no longer in college.

The coach, Allan Bristow, told me I was starting from day one. I hadn't been with the team for twenty-four hours but I was already a starter, they were just throwing me in there. Maybe that was why the guys weren't all that excited to see me. And of course there was the fact some of them took pay cuts to get me on the team. This was a business.

I was extremely nervous before that game. In Indianapolis, we checked into a Hyatt downtown. I was so wired I could barely relax. In college we'd always had a roommate, but in the NBA you get your own room, and unlike college players, who hang out together all the time, most NBA players just go to their room. Most teams have their cliques. A few of them might grab dinner together or something, but it's not the same. Since I didn't know anyone, I was mostly alone and bouncing off the walls. I just hoped that I could ride the emotion into the game. I didn't even know the plays.

To hear my name announced as an NBA starter was incredible. This was a dream I first had playing rec ball in Chesapeake. Now here I was. The downside was, I had to match up against Indiana's big center, Rik Smits, who was seven foot four. The big question was whether I could handle bigger players in the NBA. Smits had five inches and maybe twenty-five pounds on me. We lost the game but I held my own, scoring 12 points, grabbing 3 rebounds, and blocking a shot in just nineteen minutes. I was all adrenaline that night. I just ran the floor, dove after loose balls, and attacked rebounds. Two games later, we won. I got 14 rebounds that night, and the next night I had 34 points, 14 rebounds, and 3 blocks in a victory over Golden State. Right away I knew I could play in the league.

My game was all athletic ability. I was so young and it was so much fun, it was like I was on the playground. Muggsy Bogues was our point guard and he was one of the fastest players to ever play in the NBA. He had to be fast, because he was just five foot three, the shortest player in the league. Muggs was a freak of nature. To be able to make the NBA at that height was incredible, but he was a tough guy from Baltimore (he played high school ball for Bob Wade, who recruited me to Maryland) and was a natural in the open court. He had great court vision and could really make plays.

And when he got the ball, he was gone. He was so fast, he would get down the court and be there all alone and have to wait for the rest of us to catch up. Muggs would always say to me, "Young fella, if you run I'll get it to you for an easy basket." I'd say, "Hey, you don't have to tell me," and I would run to the rim as hard as I could.

Playing in Charlotte was the best. The fans down there were used to college basketball, so 23,000 of them used to pack the arena each night and provide an electric atmosphere. There wasn't another arena in the NBA that could match it. They were really excited because our team started making great strides. With me and Larry Johnson, we had two young guys who were averaging 20 points and 10 rebounds a game. And we played an exciting style. Anytime I might be dragging a little, just walking out of the tunnel into Charlotte Arena pumped me up.

I averaged 21.0 points and 10.3 rebounds a game that year and we went 44–38, to qualify for the playoffs for the first time in franchise history. I've always thought I should have been rookie of the year. Shaq got it instead, but I thought at least we should have been co–rookies of the year. We were both double-double guys and while Shaq averaged 23.4 points and 13.9 rebounds, his team didn't make it to the playoffs.

I also thought I should have made the All-Star team that year but I didn't. They put Larry Nance, a veteran player, on there instead of me. I was really disappointed. My second year, I made it. It was very exciting but my Achilles tendon was hurt so I couldn't play. The game was in Minneapolis and I went anyway, and it was fun just being there. I went to a party that Prince threw at Paisley Park, his recording studio, this huge warehouse building. The party started at two in the morning and went to six or seven A.M. He came out and performed. It was a wild party. He had these nude people with painted-on clothes and they stood in the corner like statues. Every once in a while they'd move and take a new position. All the stars were there. It was really amazing. There were twelve inches of snow on the ground in Minneapolis, but that didn't keep anyone from going out anyway.

I remember sitting there at that All-Star game with Shaq and that was when he and I had our first real good conversations. We had a lot in common, but our competitive nature was always there. Even if we did converse and were friends, it was always there. The thing was, he was a natural, seven foot two, over 300 pounds, and gifted with surprising agility. There was nothing like him in the NBA. He could just dominate when he got the ball. I was barely six ten and at the time I was only 245 pounds. I had to work and work and work to try to maximize what I could.

The highlight of my time in Charlotte came that first year, when we met the Boston Celtics in the first round of the playoffs. The Celtics still had some of the parts from their great teams of the 1980s, including Robert Parish and Kevin McHale, plus a young star named Reggie Lewis. It was a dream for me to compete against guys I grew up watching on television. And there was nothing quite like the Boston Garden, with all the old championship banners hanging up above, the dead spots on the parquet floor, and the smoke that used to rise up and circle the court.

This was Charlotte's first ever trip to the playoffs, so the city was electric. It was a best-of-five series and in Game 4 we had a chance to close them out in front of our fans. I hit a twenty-foot shot at the buzzer to give us a 104–103 victory, one of the best moments of my career. I had come out of nowhere, I was young, I was just playing the game the way I knew how to play the game — and now here I was eliminating the Celtics. There was a picture of me lying on the floor and everybody diving on me to celebrate. I have that photo hanging in my house to this day. We lost the next series to the New York Knicks, but by almost any standard it was a great rookie season for me and a great year for the Hornets. We really thought we were building something positive there.

• • •

After my rookie year, Tracy and I broke up. I just wasn't ready to settle down—I wanted to have fun and concentrate on basketball—and she wasn't the type of woman who was just going to wait around. She wanted to be her own person, not just Alonzo Mourning's girlfriend or Alonzo Mourning's wife. Even now that we're married, her name is Tracy Wilson Mourning. She'd never give up her individuality, and that's what I love about her. But at the time, I just wasn't ready for a serious commitment, so many things were happening in my life. I was just coming into my own, and the NBA lifestyle is not conducive to relationships, especially when you are young and immature.

Tracy moved back to Washington, got an internship with Tony Kornheiser's radio show, and waited tables at the Outback Steakhouse to make money. One of her regular customers was George Michael, who had a nationally syndicated television show called *The Sports Machine*, and it wasn't long before he hired Tracy as a reporter.

One time she was assigned to cover a game I played in. We were dating on and off, but just then we were off, in a rocky patch in fact, and at the time I wasn't a big fan of the media anyway. I had answered some questions from the other reporters when Tracy and her cameraman came up to the pack late and she asked me a question I had already answered. Rather than be a gentleman and repeat my answer, I snapped, right in front of everyone, "Where were you when I answered that the first time?" Let me tell you something, she hasn't forgiven me yet. I'll pay for that one forever.

I still loved Tracy, but I just wasn't ready to be committed. I thought at the time the best thing for both of us was some space. And maybe it was. But she, rightly, wasn't going to wait for me. And after that interview, she barely spoke to me for a while.

In 1994, I was selected to be a part of the Dream Team II, the USA Basketball senior men's national team that was going to play in the World Championships in Toronto. The idea was to build on the success of the Dream Team in 1992.

On the Dream Team (Harry How/Getty Images)

It was an honor for me, and a chance to not just have a lot of fun but also meet a lot of the elite guys in the league. We had an incredible team, including Isiah Thomas, Joe Dumars, and Reggie Miller. Our front line was Shaq, Larry Johnson, Derrick Coleman, Shawn Kemp, and me. We had guys such as Steve Smith and Dominique Wilkins — who was winding down his career so we called him Antique Wilkins — coming off the bench. It was an incredible collection of talent.

The entire summer was just one big party. We held a training camp in Chicago that summer to get ready, but every night we'd go out partying. We had so much more talent than any other team in the world that we knew we could win hungover. That's why our coach, Don Nelson, was so disliked. The way the players saw it, you were supposed to have fun at the World Championships. Dream Team II was beating everyone by 30, 40, even 50 points. There wasn't a team that could play with us. But Nellie tried to suck all the fun out of it. He wouldn't play everyone, even when we were up 30 points, which embarrassed guys. Then, the day after a game we'd watch film and he'd be very critical, ripping apart some missed defensive assignment when the game was out of hand. Everyone just rolled their eyes.

Now I think he was just petrified. It would have been humiliating to lose just one game, even in the early rounds. Even if we came back and won the gold, Nellie'd never live it down. The thing was, we had too much talent on that team for that to happen. The games weren't even competitive. We lived for practice, where we could go against each other.

I mentioned that Derrick Coleman was on that team. I knew DC from his days back at Syracuse, and we'd had some epic battles my first two years at Georgetown. That summer I used to look at his game and think, *Wow, he is so talented.* That's what stood out. Even among all these all-stars, Derrick Coleman may have been the best. He was my size, six ten, yet he was so agile that he could do things I couldn't. He could have been the best player in the league if he really wanted to. Attitude-wise, he was the opposite of Michael Jordan, who had the ability *and* the work ethic. Instead, Derek has the same demeanor as Rasheed Wallace does these days. Rasheed is a seven-foot shooter for the Detroit Pistons who can also play on the block. He can defend, he can pass, and he's smart. If he took care of his body and played with a little more passion, he could do whatever he wanted to do on the court. I see him as a Kevin Garnett with three-point range.

The other countries' teams were not at the level they are now, so the World Championships was just one big blowout. The Yugoslavs and the Russians were our toughest opponents and while they could keep it close for maybe a half, eventually we always crushed them. We cruised to the gold medal.

I returned to Charlotte with confidence and the Hornets really started firing on all cylinders. We wound up winning fifty games for the first time in franchise history, mostly because we started playing much tougher defense. But we drew Chicago and Michael Jordan in the first round of the playoffs, and that was that. We weren't ready yet to beat a team *that* good.

That was the season when my relationship with Larry Johnson began to deteriorate. We were cool the first two seasons. I think we both felt we needed each other, that we were these two young guys building something special with a new franchise. But during my third year it leaked out that I was interested in renegotiating my contract, and maybe Larry started viewing me as a threat.

I had the option of being a restricted free agent after my fourth year, so I wanted to get the negotiations over before it came to that. The media found out and started saying "Zo wants more money than Larry." After the 1992–93 season, Larry had renegotiated his original contract and received a twelve-year, $84 million deal that was the most lucrative in NBA history at the time. So now here I was wanting even more. I think it rubbed him the wrong way. The media made a big deal about it and that didn't help the situation. I hated that our relationship had to come to that—I thought we had played extremely well together on the court and had a good relationship off it. But I guess we were doomed to be rivals.

At the very least, it laid the groundwork for some legendary fireworks.

6

MIAMI

On the worst day of Alonzo Mourning's basketball career, he was sprawled on a giant couch in his house in the Miami suburb of Coconut Grove, barely managing to watch as his Miami Heat lost a decisive game to the New York Knicks in one of their epic late-1990s playoff series.

Alonzo had lost his cool two nights earlier when his former teammate, Larry Johnson, elbowed him in the back. Alonzo threw punches, dragged the Knicks coach, Jeff Van Gundy, around on his leg like a poodle biting his ankle, and wound up suspended for the final game of the series.

Without their best player, the Heat were in trouble. A series lost, a season gone, another opportunity up in smoke. All the hard work, focus, and dedication that Coach Pat Riley demanded of everyone in the organization was for naught—and Alonzo knew he was to blame.

"I let everyone down," he says now.

Though on a bigger scale—Madison Square Garden, national televi-

sion, replays of the fight in a seemingly constant loop on the news—the episode wasn't so different from anyone's screwup at work. The feeling is the same, the introspection as difficult, and the vow to do better as serious.

That day, in a darkened living room, with his agent, Jeff Wechsler, joining him, Alonzo said nothing and thought of everything. He was banned from Miami Arena, so he had gone to services at the New Birth Baptist Church in Miami. After services, he stepped out to find camera crews and newspaper reporters waiting for him. That's how crazy it had gotten.

So now he was on the couch, not looking at the television as the Heat attempted a futile comeback. Wechsler saw change overcome his close friend.

Alonzo could be a handful, and not only for opposing centers seeking a rebound that he had determined was his own. He was so intense, so private, so angry, even, that he often saw little beyond his own small world. He was supposed to be the face of the franchise, and for all he delivered on the court as one of the NBA's best players, he often failed off it.

He wasn't great with the fans. He wasn't great with the media. He was all about winning games, and he believed that that was enough. But on that Sunday he realized that the path he was taking wasn't helping Miami win games. There had to be some flexibility. Maybe he had been too guarded, too standoffish. He was never returning to the group home. Rayful Edmond was a long-ago mistake. Maybe he could trust a little. There had to be some middle ground.

"He used to have what he called 'Zo Days,' " Jeff said. " 'Zo Day' was the one day of the week he would talk to the media. He didn't think it was necessary to do more than that. But you can't be the franchise player and act that way.

"That day, watching the game, I could see him really feeling like, What I did has far greater repercussions than protecting my own self on the court. It hurt my teammates, my coaches, the owners, the fans, and I need to change my ways. I could just sense that. You could just see him almost changing."

Alonzo wouldn't pull a 180, wouldn't become basketball's most approachable athlete overnight, but this was the start of something. When you inevitably veer off the easy path of life—the "Walk with God," he calls it— all you can do is try to get back as quickly as possible.

So he began talking to the media almost every day. When fans approached him for an autograph at an unexpected time, he didn't brush them off. He even smiled occasionally on the court. This was growth.

"From that day on," Jeff said, "he became a more rounded player as far as everything on and off the court. And we started doing more marketing. He got out there. I think he felt he had to make amends for some of the things that happened."

Alonzo just nods at the memory.

"I remember Pat Riley once wrote a note to everybody in our playbook and it said, 'Adversity introduces a man to himself.'

"I've been through that introduction a number of times."

I wanted to stay in Charlotte. I liked the city, liked the fans, liked my teammates, and liked where I thought the franchise was headed. I know I was still very private, protective, and standoffish in public — the Rayful Edmond incident was still ringing in my head — but I was growing more comfortable. I was very active donating money and time to the Thompson Children's Home, which helped at-risk children, especially foster children. Charlotte was becoming home.

The only thing I didn't like was the Hornets' owner, George Shinn. He was a local hero for bringing the NBA to the city. Later, the fans turned against him and he moved the team to New Orleans (a new team, the Bobcats, wound up playing in Charlotte). I think Charlotte saw Shinn's true colors eventually, but when we started negotiating a new contract, he still had a lot of goodwill. It was easy for him to paint me as the bad guy.

I had some reservations about Shinn while I was playing for him — a lot of players were uncomfortable around him and we all used to talk about it. But he was the boss and I was brought up to respect that. I certainly never let it affect how I played for the Hornets. I was always able to separate the business side from the personal side. No one can ever say I didn't give it my all on the court. But the simple fact is that this *was* a business, and I needed to learn the cold reality of the business side of the NBA.

My original contract said I could be a free agent after my fourth season, 1995–96. During my third season we began negotiating a long-term deal.

I'll never forget the phone conversation I had with Shinn in 1994, outside the Hornets' practice facility. The negotiations had stalled a little. He was offering $11.2 million a season, but we were asking for an average of $15 million because David Falk was certain we could get that much in free agency. I just wanted to talk to Shinn man to man and work something out, cut the middle people out of the debate. I was being very honest and I told him that I was willing to stay in Charlotte for less money than I could make in free agency. But he had to move a little also.

"I'm willing to stay here for the rest of my career," I told him. "In the market right now, I can get fifteen million per season. My agent is very confident of that. But I'll stay here for thirteen million. Pay me thirteen and I'll stay here."

He just cut me off.

"Nobody is worth that type of money," he said.

Well, he wasn't wrong—I know that kind of money is ridiculous. But it *is* what top players in the NBA made at the time, and I wasn't the one who set the market. During my three seasons in Charlotte, I averaged over 21 points, 10 rebounds, and 3 blocks a game. I was just beginning a stretch where I became a seven-time all-star, a two-time defensive player of the year, and an annual MVP candidate.

Besides, Shinn was selling out the arena because we were a successful, exciting young team. He was moving hats, T-shirts, popcorn, beer, and everything else. It's not like the owners cut the price of popcorn because a player agrees to take less money. It's just that the owner gets the money, not the player. So while $13 million is crazy in the real world, in the sports and entertainment industry it fits. I thought giving Shinn the "hometown discount" so we could continue building what we had in Charlotte was a good deal for him, too.

But his whole tone was so degrading, just completely derogatory.

The tone was even worse than the words. I was taken aback, and it became a very heated conversation. I thought I was being reasonable, a team guy; I was trying to work things out personally. He thought I was being greedy. He ended up hanging up on me.

I was incensed. I called David Falk right away (Jeff Wechsler worked with David at the time and would later become my agent). I told David that George Shinn wasn't going to budge from $11.2 million.

"David, if you can get me $15 million per season, then let's try free agency."

This was a business, and I had to treat it like a business. David felt my market would be Los Angeles, New York, Boston, or Miami, each one for at least $15 million per season. LA was not in my mix. I was an East Coast guy and I didn't want to be that far from all my family back in Virginia. I didn't want to go to Boston, either—too cold. So it was down to New York and Miami.

I called Coach Thompson and I called Patrick Ewing. They had always helped me with big decisions, and there aren't many people whose opinions I value more. When I talked to Coach and told him my options, he didn't even hesitate. "Go to Miami," he said.

His reasoning was that Pat Riley, who'd taken over in Miami, was just the hard-nosed, defensive-oriented coach that I was born to play for. And he thought Riley was one of the best coaches in the NBA, on the strength of his four titles with the Lakers. Riley had then gone on to build up the Knicks before turning the team over to one of his assistants, Jeff Van Gundy, and he would utilize me best and demand the best of me every day.

"But I heard his practices are really tough," I said.

"You went through my practices and you're worried about practice?" Coach Thompson said, incredulous.

There was more to it, of course. I had really grown comfortable in Charlotte. It was a great place for me and I loved the area. I was having second thoughts. I told Coach that, too.

"Well, keep a home there and come back and visit," he snapped.

Patrick had played for Pat Riley in New York. I asked him about the practices and Patrick, in true Hoya form, echoed Big John. "You're worried about practices after what we had at Georgetown?"

There was still a part of me that wanted to unite with Patrick, a player I watched growing up, and join the Knicks.

"Wouldn't it be great if we could play alongside each other in Madison Square Garden?"

"Yes, but you need your own franchise. Go to Miami."

The most valuable friends tell you what is best for you, not best for them. That was Patrick Ewing. He was looking out for me.

Once I had settled on going to Miami, the Hornets worked out a seven-player trade with the Heat so that Charlotte wouldn't be left getting nothing in return. The fans and media in Charlotte were pretty tough on me for leaving, but it was the best thing for me. The Hornets really played up the fact I was turning down all this money, trying to make me sound greedy. They'd put it out there, "Alonzo Mourning rejected a seven-year, $78.2 million offer."

The average working person who reads that or hears that is going to think negative things about me. He's going to say, "That's not enough for him?" There's no good way for an athlete to combat that. Few understand. And trying to explain it just makes you sound worse. The truth was, if it was just about money then I would never have agreed to take less to stay in Charlotte in the first place. But no one wanted to hear that.

I just couldn't play for George Shinn. Once I had my mind made up that he wasn't someone I wanted to associate with, then I was not going to play for him for any amount of money. Miami gave me a seven-year deal worth $105 million, an average of exactly the $15 million per year David Falk had said I could get. I was the first NBA player to ever sign a $100 million contract. To do that brought me a lot of pride. It also brought me a lot of pressure.

Pat Riley was a coach I had always admired. I was a self-motivated player, but I also like to be pushed—and he is a master motivator. He's extremely hard on his players but he also gets the most out of them. He had already worked with some of the greatest centers in the history of the game, guys like Kareem Abdul-Jabbar and Patrick. As a player, he had been a teammate of Wilt Chamberlain on the 1971–72 Lakers, who won the NBA title. I knew that having him as my coach would only make me better in the long run.

The knowledge that he traded for me so I could be the centerpiece of what he was building in Miami motivated me more. I prepared and worked that off-season like I had never worked before. I wanted to be prepared physically for training camp. What I couldn't prepare myself for was the sudden reality of being the face of the franchise.

Even though I was a first-round draft pick of the Hornets and a key component of the team, I was able to lie low when I wanted to while I was in Charlotte. Larry Johnson was also a face of the franchise and Charlotte is a small market. It was much more manageable than the first few months I experienced in Miami. There's just a different vibe to the city—I guess it has to do with South Beach and all the beautiful people who populate the place.

In Charlotte, I'd eat at Simmons Soul Food restaurant, which reminded me of the dinners that Mrs. Threet or my mom used to make. Maybe I'd eat at some little diner. Regardless, no one would bother me. Even if Tracy and I went out to a nice place, people were pretty reasonable. But in Miami, it was different. They were all watching.

I had signed a massive contract and the numbers were published in the paper. With more money came more problems, and more people with their hands out. Everyone wanted to get a piece of me, especially early on. The real estate agents, in particular, were ridiculous. Everyone wanted to sell me a house. They'd call the team offices, they'd call my agent.

Even now, I see guys hanging out after games in front of the visitors' locker room. They're trying to sell condos to players for when they come into town. Athletes are targets no matter how much they try to avoid it. So everyone's looking for something. You look at the NBA Draft and there are all these jewelry guys and suit guys and who knows what else, all trying to get the players to buy their stuff. That's what it is to be an athlete these days. Coach Riley calls it the "Toy Department of Human Affairs." Pretty funny, but real.

I took all that focus and all that pressure to heart. I felt I owed it to the city and the franchise to live up to the contract. Statistically I had a great year, averaging 23.2 points and 10.4 rebounds per game. I even had a game where I scored 50 points. But I wasn't there just to put up numbers, and when we lost to Michael Jordan and the Bulls in the first round of the playoffs, I sat in the locker room and cried. The pressure to succeed brought so much emotion out of me. I felt like I had let everyone down. I had come to Miami to turn the franchise around, and although we made great strides that first year, losing in the first round was not acceptable. I took losing very hard. Especially when I felt like I had prepared and worked harder than anyone on God's green earth. Being the Franchise player, you take the responsibility of the whole team on your shoulders. If you really care.

The greatest home court advantage in the NBA is South Beach. If they ever put a franchise in Las Vegas, then maybe the Strip becomes the greatest home court advantage; but until then, it's the pulsating clubs, the beautiful women, and the warm, inviting winter nights over on South Beach.

A visiting team comes rolling into town on a January night from, say, Cleveland and there is no way anyone is staying in their room—not when they can smell the salt air, see the models, and hear the club music. In the NBA, you get to a road game the night before. When you're in, say, Milwaukee, there is nothing to do except think about basketball. You grab dinner or a movie. You come to Miami and there is no reason to think about basketball. Players head out on the town, hit the clubs, and some wind up drinking too much and staying out too late. It happens for every game.

If you are a star player, you might even "throw" a party at a club. A local promoter will offer you maybe $10,000 to "host" a party. They'll advertise it on the radio, "Allen Iverson is throwing a party at The Mansion nightclub." The promoters know a star like that will draw a crowd. All the player has to do is show up for an hour—but a lot of them will stay much longer. Meanwhile, I'm home getting eight hours of sleep. I've played against some worn-out cats in Miami.

South Beach is worth a couple of baskets a game for us. Then again, it's also cost us, a few times. We've gotten caught up in parties and in hanging out. Through the years there were times when we got a lot of bad press because guys were getting caught up in negativity. It's one thing to go have dinner with your family after the game at Prime One Twelve, as I do. But it's another to stay out all night. For the most part, we've been smart enough to lay off the partying.

But the visiting teams? They can never get enough.

After my first season in Miami, Tracy and I got back together for good. At that time my son was conceived, and knew she was the only woman I could see spending my life with.

We had continued to see each other on and off after she moved out of Charlotte, but nothing was settled or exclusive. When I got to Miami, I was still focused on basketball. I was trying to live up to my contract, and I was getting used to the city. I misplaced my priorities a bit. I was twenty-five, single, and I had rented a penthouse on the thirty-third floor of a building downtown. I was living it up a little bit, the way I think almost any young man would. I didn't think I was ready for a commitment and it almost cost me.

Tracy had spent New Year's in California, and one of her resolutions was to move on from me. She even wrote me a letter telling me it was over. I wasn't being honest at the time, and she was not interested in going through the motions. She had so much going for her—after ten years of dating I wasn't worth waiting for.

But that entire time she was in California, she felt sick. She was at a girlfriend's house and they decided she should take a pregnancy test. It came back positive. They ran down to the store and bought three more—all positive.

Tracy started to cry because everything was so unsettled. It was my child, there was no question about that, but what kind of father was I ready to become? My actions didn't reflect that I was ready to be serious. Anyway, she called me and broke the news.

I wanted her to move to Miami but Tracy was not interested in doing that. She was going to demand I be a man about this. Miami was out of the question. She got a different apartment in D.C. and after the season I moved up there for the summer. In August our son was born, Alonzo Mourning III; we call him Trey.

It was an incredible experience, holding this little baby in my hands, trying to be gentle with him in a way I didn't know was possible. Watching a part of you come into this world is truly a blessing. Kids are God's gift to all of us. There is nothing like the love you have for your children. Of course, there was nothing like the love I had for Tracy, either, and now I asked her to marry me. I had been in love with her since that summer night in Las Vegas when she first caught my eye. But I really couldn't wrap my arms around that love until I saw my son. It moved me along the maturation process that helped me understand our relationship. Now it was time to settle down. God was sending me a very clear message on this one and I was not going to miss it. I knew we would become every bit the formidable team that we have.

I proposed to Tracy down in Miami. I had dinner set up on the roof deck of our old house in Coconut Grove. We were having a wonderful time, talking and discussing the future, and then I picked the right moment, dropped to my knee, and asked her to marry me. She said yes, and I remember thinking that this was how it was supposed to be. Another thing I remember about that dinner was that it was really windy and we had to keep grabbing and holding down the tablecloth. It was a metaphor for marriage: you're going to have times when the wind blows everything around, and together you have to make sure everything stays down, that everything is stable and on an even keel.

We didn't get married until the next summer but I look at my son as a double blessing. Being around him, especially as he continues to grow into a man, has been one of the joys of my life. And if it weren't for him, I would have lost my partner forever.

The Miami Heat jumped from forty-two victories to sixty-one victories in 1996–97, thanks to some of Pat Riley's off-season additions and a commitment to his defensive style. Riley had really established our team personality at that point, and it was to play defense at a very high level. With defense, you have to be committed—the same way you are

With Trey

passionate about scoring. Everybody wants to score. Not everybody wants to play defense. We were very aggressive and believed in a lot of contact. Even if we were struggling to score, we were able to always keep our games close by assuring our opponent didn't score either. Our goal was to keep opposing teams under 85 points, shooting in the 30 percent range for the game. If we did that, we thought we'd win. It wasn't always aesthetically pleasing, but it was effective.

Great teams need great rivals to bring out the best in them. That's the flavor of sports. That's what makes games worth watching. That year was the first of four consecutive playoff match-ups with our rivals, the New York Knicks.

Those games with the Knicks were like prizefights, or like the Hatfields and the McCoys. There was such a competitive level of dislike. It wasn't just a game, it was personal. There were so many subplots to every game, every series—bad blood, big talk in the papers. The funny part was, Pat Riley had created both monsters. That's why there were never any blowout games.

He did what he did in New York and then came to the Heat and did the exact same thing. Heat versus Knicks was Riley's new players versus his old players, Riley himself versus his old assistants, namely Jeff Van Gundy. We knew how each other ate, breathed, and thought. We had all the personnel down to a T. We knew their tendencies and they knew ours. It was like being married to them.

Our games were entertainment at its best. It felt like every time we played, the world stopped and everyone watched. I've always believed if we packaged the best games of that series into a DVD set, it would be a bestseller. It had everything, even Spike Lee sitting courtside at Madison Square Garden booing me. Spike would always talk junk. That's what he did. Spike and I have a great relationship. But I was Public Enemy No. 1 in New York. I'd walk around Manhattan the morning of a game and guys would slow down their delivery trucks to yell at me.

Needless to say, the media ate it up, especially the ravenous New York tabloids. Each game had this huge buildup surrounding it. Every little story became a huge one. Those playoffs series had as much media as the NBA Finals. It was such an emotional high, with so much at stake. Those games were not regular NBA games. Those particular games featured an intensity that would raise the hair on the back of your neck.

That first year the story lines included a simmering rivalry between Pat Riley and Jeff Van Gundy and my showdown with fellow Hoya and great friend, Patrick Ewing. A lot of the attention was on the fact that Patrick had outplayed me during our regular season meetings. I admit it, he definitely had gotten the best of me, but this was a totally different scenario. It was the playoffs and I was determined to make some adjustments. Patrick is seven years older than I am. No small part of my strategy was going to be to try to wear him down and hope it would start to have an effect on him. I also vowed to try to push him off the box, because the closer he was to the rim, the higher the percentage was that he'd make a shot. I knew I had to make it difficult for him to catch the ball, so I had to try to stay in front of him and make them lob the ball over the top and wait for help from my teammates on defense. We took a lot of pride in our help-defense.

But Patrick was a difficult matchup for me that entire series. I was in foul trouble a lot. He was just a great player. The more heated the games got, the easier it was to forget he was my friend, especially when they took a 3–1 lead heading into a heated Game 5.

This was the moment our rivalry got elevated to a whole new level. We had broken open the game with a late 16–2 run and were cruising to a victory to send the series to a Game 6. With just 1:53 remaining, New York's Charlie Ward got nasty and undercut P. J. Brown so the two fought for position on the free-throw line. Brown retaliated and threw Ward to the floor. Bedlam ensued. It was a pretty wild scene.

The NBA has a rule that you can't leave the bench if there is a fight on the court. The league is adamant about stopping bench-clearing brawls, which can get out of control. But during the mêlée, four Knicks players left the bench—Patrick Ewing, Allan Houston, John Starks, and my old teammate in Charlotte, Larry Johnson.

By doing so, each player earned an automatic one-game suspension. As a result, the fight was a blessing for us. Ward, Ewing, and Houston were gone for Game 6 and Starks and LJ would be for Game 7, if necessary. We only lost P. J. Brown, albeit for both games.

Madison Square Garden was now going to be an even more hostile place to play. The New Yorkers were riled up, but without Patrick in the game, I scored 28 points and grabbed 9 rebounds to lead us to a 95–90 victory and send the series back home for Game 7.

We were trying to become only the sixth team in NBA history to come back from a 3–1 deficit to win a best-of-seven playoff series. We rode the emotion of our crowd to build a 17-point halftime lead and cruise to a 101–90 victory. Tim Hardaway, our star guard, had 38 points for us and I had 22 points and 12 rebounds. Patrick was awesome for the Knicks with 37 points and 17 rebounds, but clearly, the suspension administered by David Stern had a big effect on the outcome of the series. The Knicks' Chris Childs summed up the mood of their team when he punted a ball into the stands in frustration. But the Knicks had no one to blame but themselves—and we were able to move on to face the Bulls in the Eastern Conference Finals, where we managed to win just one game. Jordan and Co. got us again.

We still had a long way to go.

I was injured a great deal in 1997–98. I started the season on the injured list, recovering from knee surgery in late September that was meant to repair a partial tear of the patellar tendon in my left knee. Then I missed two other games with a fractured left cheekbone—afterward, I had to wear a protective mask that many people thought made me look even meaner on the court. The first time I played without the mask came in Game 4 of our opening round, best-of-five series, against the Knicks. It would be one of the most memorable games of my career.

We had put together another great year, fifty-five victories and an Atlantic Division title for the team. I averaged nearly 20 and 10 despite the injuries. As a team, I felt like we had embraced Pat Riley's system completely. This was a stretch when we were one of the best defensive teams in memory, where we were so physical there were times we just broke an opponent's spirit.

The amount of work, focus, and dedication everyone in the Heat organization had at that time was almost unheard-of in the NBA. From trainers and managers, down through the players and up into the front office, everyone just worked and worked. That was the culture Riley demanded, and no one embraced it more than I did. I was a maniac in the weight room and could never prepare enough for games. There were even times after games when I would put in a full workout. I'd hit the gym, still in my uniform, straining and pounding every muscle in my body like I hadn't just played forty-something minutes of basketball.

Practices were demanding, everyone was going all out all the time. Outside practice, we'd work out even more. A few days a week, I'd knock out four- or five-hour sessions in the team gym. Hard work doesn't guarantee you anything, but without it you don't stand a chance. I was obsessed about being the most prepared player in the league. I was a good player, an all-star, but it wasn't because I was as naturally gifted as the other players of that caliber. I couldn't make myself taller. I couldn't suddenly develop the face-up game of other six-ten players. I couldn't even gain that much weight, certainly not the fifty to sixty pounds I was sometimes outweighed by. My game had to come from within, from the heart. I had to want to win more than other players.

So I would try to maximize what I had. That is what all of Riley's players believed about themselves—we all thought that we had to get over that hump. The division title and the fifty-five wins were not what we considered the mark of success. We wanted an NBA title. We wanted to beat the Knicks and advance in the playoffs.

That's what made that Game 4 in Madison Square Garden so disappointing for me. There were only 1.4 seconds remaining in the game and New York was probably going to win (they would eventually, 90–85) and force a decisive Game 5. As I battled under the basket with Larry Johnson, we got tangled up. When he pushed again for rebounding position, he threw an elbow at the back of my head. He'd gone beyond just playing physical basketball and I wasn't going to take that. When someone throws an elbow, you react; it was instinct for me to retaliate. When he threw that elbow at me, my first reaction was to swing. Then he swung, and then we were swinging at each other, and everything had suddenly gone crazy. The funny thing was, despite all that swinging, nothing landed.

With the suspensions from the year before still fresh in everyone's mind, no one left the bench as the fight went on. No one except Jeff Van Gundy. That's where it got a little comical. He tried to restrain me, but kind of got knocked to the ground and wound up wrapped around my left leg as I tried to get at Larry. I didn't even know he was there, and years later I joked with him that it felt like I had a piece of gum on my shoe. Jeff and I have laughed about the incident since then, but at the time, I was just trying to move forward, even with him on my leg. It goes to show you how much my adrenaline was up. Imagine if no one had been holding me back. It could have been really ugly. I didn't know what was going on. I was just in a rage and going after Larry Johnson.

As things finally began to calm down, Pat Riley got a hold of me and he just kept saying to me, "Zo, what did you do? What did you do?" I knew I was going to be suspended for Game 5, which meant that fight would cost us an entire season. Riley couldn't believe I had done that, and neither did I, once I calmed down.

They ejected both LJ and me immediately. I went to the locker room and I was the only one in there because they were still sorting stuff out on the court. I just put my head in my hands and was like, *Wow, what just happened? Damn, I shouldn't have done that.* It's easy for someone on the outside looking in to tell me what they would have done, but it's not so easy in the heat of the moment. That's how many mistakes are made. They aren't planned. Your adrenaline takes over, and you react.

Obviously, I think the strained relationship LJ and I had from our days together in Charlotte affected our reaction to each other. I knew it was Larry who threw that elbow. It wasn't the first time we'd had issues on the court. Earlier that season, on February 1, we had both been assessed technicals after a little skirmish at the Garden. But this was the first time things had escalated to that level, a real fight.

I still remember watching the replay that night. I just sat there at home and watched it over and over. After the game, the media just crushed me. I told them that I'd drawn a line in the sand and that I wasn't going to take it anymore. But I also said that I'd made a mistake and apologized to everyone I could.

If I was in that situation right now, I wouldn't react that way. Now, as I write this, I'm thirty-eight years old and you have a tendency to think a little before you do dumb stuff. The world kind of slows down as you get older. At that particular time, though, I was twenty-eight. I wasn't as savvy in the ways of the world—or the NBA—as I am now. I just wish I had known then what I know now. I just wish I hadn't been so into standing up for myself. But in every adversity there is a seed of equivalent benefit. This was just part of my maturation process.

We had that series won. Even heading back to Miami for the decisive game, I'd felt very confident we would win the series. But because I lost my head when Johnson hit me, it cost us big-time. I was suspended for that next game (so were Johnson and his teammate Chris Mills). We weren't the same team in Game 5. Everyone was flat to start and we trailed by 20 early. Even a huge rally wasn't enough; we faded and lost 98–81 to a Knicks team we were better than.

The LJ fight was one of the lowest moments of my career. I had let down not just every person on the team and in the organization, but the entire city. I had wasted the efforts of so many people.

But like so many moments in my life, this was a humbling, a moment of truth from God, that I probably needed. The truth was I had become too selfish. I had come to believe my little world was the only one that mattered. It wasn't a way I set out to be, but each small step that leads you to selfishness can seem like the most natural thing. And people naturally lose their way at times.

I had. And the result was embarrassing.

In reaction to that fight, I did what you always must do when faced with a truth you aren't willing to acknowledge. I changed. I knew I was a very emotional player, and I knew that when you don't control your emotions you make mistakes. The mistake I'd just made had affected many people's lives. We would have played Indiana, not the Bulls, in the next round, and we had had a lot of success against them. We had a real chance to get to the Finals and I felt I cost the team that opportunity. Now I didn't know if that opportunity would come again, not for me or my team. But for each and every one of us, as painful as our mistakes can be, they can also turn out to be blessings. I don't know how anyone gets better without making mistakes. I think that is the only thing you can take from a mistake—the lesson.

I became a little bit more responsible, both to my teammates and to others around me. I was never going to be the friendliest, most open person. But I began treating the media better, fans better, just everyone better. There was no need for everyone to look at me as this violent guy on the court, getting into these fights. That wasn't who I was. That was just me on the court. I remember Bud Threet calling me up and telling me it was time to start backing down from things like that and thinking about how I could better represent the Lord.

Bud was right, of course. And once again, I felt like I was back at square one.

The next season, 1998–99, was an abbreviated one for the league because a work stoppage caused almost half the season to be canceled. We wound up playing just a fifty-game season but I averaged 20.1 points, 11.0 rebounds, and a career-high 3.91 blocks per game. I was named NBA Defensive Player of the Year and All-Defensive First Team while finishing second in MVP voting, behind Utah's Karl Malone. I was also named All-NBA First Team and led the league in blocked shots. Individually, it may have been my best season ever. I was on top of my game.

We once again won the Atlantic Division title, and once again we faced the Knicks in a first-round, best-of-five series. I wanted to win this series as much as I'd wanted to win anything in my entire life. The disappointment of the year before had burned inside of me, keeping me up at night, pushing me through workouts. I was obsessed with being ready for that one moment when the series seemed to tip. Sure enough we split the first four games and wound up in a decisive Game 5, in Miami. It came down to the final possession. We led 77–76 and needed just one stop to beat the Knicks. Then Allen Houston hit a jumper with 0.8 seconds left to absolutely crush us.

I was so down, even angry, at that result. Regardless of the outcome, I felt we were a better team than they were that season. We didn't want it to end like that, and we'd put in so much time and energy, all our work and dedication, to prepare ourselves for that situation. To have it all come down to one possession and then fall short is one of the most difficult things to accept in basketball.

The following season, I again was named NBA Defensive Player of the Year while averaging 21.7 points (second-best in my career), 9.5 rebounds, and 3.7 blocks per game. That was good enough to finish third in league MVP voting. I hardly cared about any of that. I just wanted to reach the Finals. It was my obsession.

We swept Detroit in the opening round and, of course, there were the Knicks waiting for us in round two, this time in a best of seven. I don't know if there has ever been a harder-fought series in the history of the NBA.

There was never an easy basket, neither team ever took a possession off, and each rebound was fought over like a rare diamond. Only once in the entire series did either team score more than 90 points in a game. The defense was so ferocious on both sides that in Game 3 we won in overtime 77–76. Even with five extra minutes, no one threatened to break 80. Every game was decided by 8 points or less, there were two one-point games, and neither team could get a winning streak going. We went back and forth for the first six games.

The series was tied 3–3. We were back in Miami for Game 7, and the atmosphere was incredible. I was never more ready for a game than

I was for that one, and I wound up with 29 points, 13 rebounds, and 5 blocks. If it was possible to will a team to a victory, I tried. But Patrick Ewing hit a shot with 1:20 left to give the Knicks an 83–82 lead and no one scored again—a telling end to this rivalry. For the second consecutive year, we were knocked out by a single point in the deciding game of a series with the Knicks.

We were furious about a number of calls, including a phantom time-out awarded to the Knicks in the final seconds—that one so enraged us that Jamal Mashburn chased the refs off the court and Tim Hardaway delivered the classic line that veteran ref Dick Bavetta should change his name to Knick Bavetta. I was too depressed for that stuff. I just told the media, "It can't get any worse. It's all misery."

We just couldn't get over the hump against the Knicks in those final three series. Each loss came by the slightest of margins. We lost because of a fight and then we lost two deciding games by a single point. It showed how, to win, you need everyone doing every little thing, how the difference between victory and defeat is so small.

It also is a reminder that sometimes bad things happen. Sometimes you do everything right, you practice hard and play hard and concentrate and follow the plan perfectly, and you come up short. That's life. There are no guarantees. It isn't always fair. But also know that if you prepare to the fullest of your ability, you will always be in the hunt to win it all.

Of course, sometimes you find out what "fair" really means. Going into the summer of 2000, I had nothing to complain about. I had been selected for the U.S. Olympic team and would soon win a gold medal in Sydney. Tracy and I were happily married, growing deep roots in south Florida, and expecting a daughter in August.

If the worst thing in my life was a failure to beat the Knicks, if my greatest challenge was making one more defensive stop, then I was about to find out just how blessed I had been, courtesy of a midday phone call from Dr. Richards.

7

THE BATTLE BACK

Dr. Gerald Appel was seeing patients at New York–Presbyterian Hospital when an urgent call came in. The agent of a famous professional athlete would be calling soon and Appel absolutely had to see this person.

As one of the world's foremost authorities on focal sclerosis and other kidney ailments, Appel was used to these requests. People wanted to see him. He was often a third or fourth referral, getting the most desperate cases and handling situations that would test even his profound knowledge of the disease.

He had plenty of "regular" patients, but often enough, along came a celebrity. So now, there was Jeff Wechsler on the other line, telling him about Alonzo Mourning, promising to get the medical records shipped to New York as soon as possible.

Dr. Appel explained that he was about to speak at a meeting of the American Society of Nephrology, in Toronto. A thousand of the best nephrologists in the world would be there and he would look for input from them. Jeff was excited; this was a great opportunity.

Dr. Appel knew everything about kidneys and almost nothing about the NBA. Not much of a sports fan at the time, he had no idea who Alonzo Mourning was. He called his son, Seth, a basketball fan.

"What kind of a guy is Alonzo Mourning?" Dr. Appel asked.

"Oh, he's been an all-star and a blocking champion. He's from Georgetown." Then Seth rattled off all sorts of info about Alonzo's playing career.

Appel had a different concern: focal sclerosis can be a side effect of some hard living. "Well, do you think he uses drugs or anything?"

Seth laughed. "No. He's one of the cleanest guys in the NBA. All he does is lift weights."

Fine, the doctor thought. Not that he was sure how big a deal this was. On a late flight from LaGuardia, he began reviewing Alonzo's medical records. By the time he got to Toronto, the only place he could find for dinner was a Pizza Hut. He went in, ordered a thin crust, and looked up at the television.

"At the bottom of the screen, on the ticker tape, something caught my eye," Dr. Appel said. "I saw a name I was suddenly familiar with and there it was: 'Alonzo Mourning may not be playing basketball this year due to kidney disease.'

"And I said, 'Well, if it's important enough to get on TV, it's obviously important.'"

I can handle injury. I can handle pain. I practically thrived on pain, embraced it like a test of my manhood. You can't bang and collide with a bunch of physical giants a hundred games a year, not to mention practices, and not get injured, not feel pain.

I've partially torn my calf and completely torn my knee. I've had my cheekbone fractured. I've had plantar fasciitis, which made it feel like I was being stabbed in the heel every time I took a step. I've shredded my patellar tendon in a way that amazed the doctors. I've injured one quad, two ankles, and all ten fingers.

Injuries are nothing, just part of the game. You get one, then you go to rehab, then you get back on the court. Injuries in basketball are as common as time-outs, and that doesn't even count the pain of playing all those games, the mornings I woke with a back so stiff I couldn't move, feet so sore I had to walk on the sides of them, hands so mangled I couldn't hold a spoon for my oatmeal. There were all the neck aches and elbow smashes and chronic headaches that made me feel like an old man. I used to pop anti-inflammatories like Skittles. It's like that in every NBA locker room.

That's the game, and whatever calamity it threw at me, there was always a treatment, ranging from burying myself in ice to going under a surgeon's knife. I never worried. No one wants to be injured, but these days the doctors are so good there aren't many career-ending injuries left.

Until August of 2000, I thought of myself as invincible and nothing could scare me. Whatever was coming next was coming next. I would simply tough right through it and get back onto the court as quickly as humanly possible, if I missed any time at all. It was a point of pride for me. Bring it on. Bring on the pain.

But illness? Disease? Now this was something different. You don't just take some Advil and throw an ice pack on focal glomerulosclerosis. You don't just jump on the fifteen-day disabled list and rest up. Heck, it didn't even hurt. Not the way a bruised Achilles hurts. Kidney disease is annoying, it is uncomfortable, it is unpleasant, and it is frustratingly tedious. But it doesn't really *hurt* the way I had always defined hurt.

You couldn't get a whole lot sicker than I was. My numbers were off the charts for every single test doctors could give me, so high some doctors didn't believe the readings. I was marked for immediate dialysis and a transplant, ASAP. I was essentially in the final stage of the disease.

Yet I was walking around with a new Olympic gold medal around my neck. Yes, I was tired. I had a fever sometimes. I felt terrible. But I didn't feel as bad as I had the time I ripped apart the tendon in my left pinkie going for a rebound. How can you be this ill, have doctors say things this grave, and win the Olympics? My career was over? Heck, I felt like if I just got a good night's sleep I could go out and play the next afternoon.

That's what kept pushing me to find another opinion, find another doctor. But I quickly learned that seeing a doctor wasn't like going to see an auto mechanic. If your radiator is leaking, a good mechanic can find the crack and propose the only solution—a new radiator. Some injuries aren't so different—a torn ligament is a torn ligament. But disease was different, there was so much unknown, so many variables, so many different ideas of how to make things right.

My initial recommendation was for dialysis and transplant. Two very good doctors in Miami looked at my test results and saw that as the solution. But Jeff Wechsler was relentless on my behalf. He found the best in the world, Dr. Gerald Appel, and got him to take me as a patient. And Dr. Appel saw something no one else did.

Gerald Appel is not your run-of-the-mill doctor. He runs Columbia University's Glomerular Institute, which is a place focused on a very forward-thinking effort to foster advances in the study of the disease. He sees patients with glomer all day long. They fly in from all over the country. The doctors at the institute run their own clinical trials on patients and are involved in all the big national ones. They have put together enough scientific knowledge about the disease to allow them to be creative with patients on whom everyone else has given up. Because so many people come to them for a second or third opinion, they spend more time considering, "Well, what did the previous doctor not think of?" Their first consideration is not to find the obvious solution, it's to find the *best* solution. Dr. Appel is not just a genius medically, he is a creative genius as well.

With the knowledge that he has, he's very optimistic that there is a way to cure almost any patient. He was even optimistic about mine. And this pleased me.

I was blessed not just to have Dr. Appel review my situation, but to have him review it at a nephrology convention. He carried my file with him throughout the convention and during slow moments would pull over another doctor or three, lay it all out on a table, and ask them to take a look.

My chemistries were clearly out of whack, so out of whack that some of the doctors were stunned that my numbers could be so high. My creatinine and cholesterol were particularly troublesome. At first glance, almost everyone concluded what Dr. Richards had: I needed a transplant, and the likelihood of me playing basketball again was remote.

In order to understand why I still had a chance, it's important to first understand how a kidney works. According to the National Kidney Foundation:

> There are two kidneys, each about the size of a fist, located on either side of the spine at the lowest level of the rib cage. Each kidney contains up to a million functioning units called nephrons. A nephron consists of a filtering unit of tiny blood vessels called a glomerulus attached to a tubule. When blood enters the glomerulus, it is filtered and the remaining fluid then passes along the tubule. In the tubule, chemicals and water are either added to or removed from this filtered fluid according to the body's needs, the final product being the urine we excrete.
>
> The kidneys perform their life-sustaining job of filtering and returning to the bloodstream about 200 quarts of fluid every 24 hours. About two quarts are removed from the body in the form of urine, and about 198 quarts are recovered. The urine we excrete has been stored in the bladder for anywhere from 1 to 8 hours.

The good news came from the biopsy of my kidney. When you have focal sclerosis, the millions of tiny filters are scarred. "Sclerosis" means scarring. When the filters develop scars, rather than take care of excess protein, they allow the protein to leak into the urine. To make matters worse, the more protein you have in your urine, the more the filters get scarred. So the scarring can accelerate quickly. Once it starts, if it goes untreated it just rapidly gets worse. Since you don't feel very sick at first, early detection can be difficult. Eventually all the filters are damaged and you need either dialysis to do the kidney's job, or a transplant to start anew.

My problem was twofold. One, I was losing a massive amount of protein into the urine, more than most of the doctors had ever seen before. My stats were off the charts. I had 39 grams of protein in my urine. An average level would be 39 milligrams, so I had a thousand times the normal amount of protein in my urine. The doctors couldn't believe it, it was just an astronomical number.

This led to my second problem. Because I lost all of that protein, the protein level in my blood was very low. That, in turn, left my blood pressure very low. That's why I was so exhausted and why it was dangerous for me to play basketball—I could have collapsed on the court at any time. The other thing that happened is my cholesterol went off the charts. I had cholesterol counts of 600, 800. Anything over 240 is considered high. In fact, a number of doctors couldn't figure out how I was even walking around.

Considering how extreme the numbers were—toxins building up, my blood protein very low, and low blood pressure—it made sense that many doctors thought I couldn't be treated. Going by the numbers alone, it looked like my kidney filters were too far gone to be saved. I was in trouble. These kidneys were shot. I needed a new one. I was practically dead on my feet.

But Dr. Appel didn't stop at the chemistries. He looked closely at the biopsy of the kidney, and when he did, the proper conclusion became "Maybe." I'm a yes-and-no guy, black and white. But this was the most uplifting "Maybe" of my life.

The biopsy showed a kidney whose filters actually weren't ruined. In fact, they weren't all that badly damaged at all. Despite the chemistry, I didn't have a lot of scarring. This disease was just starting. Dr. Appel thought there was still a lot of time to work with here. After all, I'd had a full physical in July with USA Basketball and my numbers then were fine. That biopsy meant I still had a chance, that somehow I wasn't too far gone.

This is why patients should get as many opinions as possible. I think people stand in awe of doctors—which, in a way, we should—so we worry about questioning their judgment. But no doctor will tell you that he or she has all the answers. I know not everyone can get the best doctors in the world to gather around at a conference and analyze their charts. I know how lucky I am. But everyone should get another opinion from someone. Dr. Appel was actually a third opinion. Sometimes differing opinions are a good thing.

And that includes your own opinion. These days, with the Internet, a patient can educate himself by reading studies, medical journals, and opinion papers. It's long work, and it's confusing sometimes, but it is *your* life, your health. *Wait and hope, or go make it happen?* I'd sit at the computer so long my eyes crossed. Everything Dr. Appel talked about, I would go and try to research. He was holding out hope that there just might be a way to treat this without a transplant, and that left at least the *possibility* of playing again one day soon.

This was a very strange time and it illustrated the downside to being famous. Yes, I could get access to great medical attention, which was the first priority. But I also had to deal with the media. This was a very private thing for me, so I wasn't talking to anyone. That was partly because it was a very fluid situation. We had very few answers. When we did get answers, I figured I would talk to the media. But once the media got wind that I might be sick, they went looking for concrete facts.

Was I going to play? Was I going to get a transplant? Was I going to die? No one knew, but that didn't stop them from trying to claim they did. You'd turn on the radio and actually hear people debating it. I'd come downstairs and see Tracy leaning over the newspaper all upset saying, "That's not true."

"Tracy, stop reading the paper."

"But they have it all wrong."

"You can't let other people tell you what's happening in your own house. Especially when we don't even know what's happening. You've got a degree in broadcast journalism, so it shouldn't surprise you how they think." We both laughed.

But other people *were* reading. Our friends and family were getting inaccurate news, hearsay, all this speculation. Then they'd call in a panic. We'd have to talk them down, tell them no one knew anything. It just made the entire ordeal more stressful.

I mentioned much earlier that we held a meeting at my house in Coral Gables, with David Falk, John Thompson, Pat Riley, Jeff, and Tracy, along with Dr. Appel, of course. These were the people who undoubtedly had my best interests in mind. Throughout my life they had proven they would tell me what I needed to hear, not what I wanted to hear.

Before the meeting, Dr. Appel gave me a checkup right there in the house. This was my first face-to-face meeting with him. All he knew about me until this point had come from medical records and lab results. The first thing that surprised him was the amount of excess fluid I was carrying around in my muscles, maybe as much as twenty-six pounds' worth. He could not believe I had just recently been standing on a gold medal stand.

One of the bits of good news was that my pre-Olympics physical, which included a urinalysis, showed I had almost no protein in my urine at the time. Although it was not unusual for the disease to come on quickly, it was good that it was still in the early stages. Basically, I had suffered a very sudden and very massive leakage of protein from all of those millions of filters. I had deteriorated so quickly I was a mess.

During the examination, Dr. Appel asked me some questions. His chief concern was whether I had been or still was on any drugs at all, whether steroids or street drugs. I told him I wasn't and never had been on drugs and that every test would show that. He said that was a good thing. Later he also ruled out the anti-inflammatory pills I used as being the cause. He came to the conclusion that it was a genetic disorder.

As we gathered around a big table in our dining room, everyone was very anxious. You could feel it in the room. Tracy joked that it felt like a NATO summit, which was just the perfect line to break the intensity. This was a powerful group, a lot of important, self-made people, giants in their industry. But there was no doubt who was in charge. Dr. Appel stands only five foot six, and he was surrounded by some very large people, but with his intellect he projected a commanding presence.

Dr. Appel opened by saying there was a 50 percent chance that we could get me better without dialysis or a transplant. That alone got everyone's attention. He said it would take a lot of medication, a lot of immunosuppressant medicines, and while he couldn't give any guarantees he thought we should try that route. He felt, on the basis of my biopsy, that time was on my side and we should use that time to try to beat the focal sclerosis. We could hold off on dialysis or transplant until after we had exhausted the other options, or until I was done with my playing days.

The thing was, in the interim, I needed to retire. I had to focus on dealing with my disease, and no matter what we tried, it was still a long shot that I would return to play. Somebody asked, "Well, Doctor, what are the odds of this happening?" And I remember Dr. Appel turned very serious.

"I'm a doctor, not God. I can do my best in terms of this, but a lot of things are not in our hands. A lot of this is totally guesswork as to what happens." It was a very humble answer. A very honest answer, from an expert in his field. That's why they call it medical practice.

Dr. Appel then brought up Reggie Lewis, a great player for the Boston Celtics, who in 1993 was being treated for a heart ailment, was cleared to play, and then died on the court. The doctor was sued for malpractice, and while he was eventually cleared by a jury, just the mention of Reggie hung in the air that night at my house and said plenty. We knew this was serious business and we knew Dr. Appel was going to be humble. He wasn't going to sit there and guarantee anything; he wasn't going to guarantee that he was correct and the other doctors were wrong. No promises. All he could do was work with me. If everything went right and we received a great deal of luck, then maybe. That was all he could offer—maybe.

That was actually very reassuring. Everyone recognized that we had just found the doctor who would tell me what I needed to hear, not what I wanted to hear.

The next day we held a press conference to announce my retirement. Dr. Appel, Dr. Richards, Pat Riley, and I all attended. It was a tough day because as an athlete, getting seriously ill isn't the way you expect to go out. It was a very emotional conclusion to a difficult week and a half. I had worked very hard to be the best basketball player I could be and I

Early school years

First time on a merry-go-round

With my mother and grandmother

At Indian River High School

Mrs. Threet

Just after I announced my intention to attend Georgetown

High school graduation with my parents

Mrs. Threet and me in Chesapeake

Tracy and I visit the Threet home

*Tracy and me in New York
before we were married*

Playing for Charlotte
Jonathan Daniel/Getty Images Sport/Getty Images

Facing off against Mount Mutombo

Andrew D. Bernstein/
National Basketball
Association/Getty Images

*Hitting a twenty-foot shot at the buzzer to close out Boston,
104–103, in the play-offs*

Nathaniel S. Butler/National Baketball Association/Getty Images

Battling Shaq
Tony Ranze/AFP/Getty Images

Receiving the trophy for NBA Defensive Player of the Year from Bill Russell
Rhona Wise/AFP/Getty Images

Nana relates another story to Mr. Cosby.

Booth photos with Tracy

At our wedding: Bud, me, Dikembe, and Patrick

The family

Moving into the future together

Tracy, with her mom and sister, at our wedding

Our first Christmas with Trey

Nana and Trey

Mrs. Threet with Trey

Sydney gold—I had no idea how sick I was at the time.
Andrew D. Bernstein/National Basketball Association/Getty Images

Grabbing a rebound
Andrew D. Bernstein/National Basketball Association/Getty Images

On the podium
Darren McNamara/Getty Images Sport/Getty Images

Patrick, Coach Thompson (with Trey), and me

Trey . . . not so happy at the hospital

Happy times in Miami

Patrick and I faced each other a lot in the play-offs.
Stan Honda/AFP/Getty Images

Announcing my retirement, October 16, 2000, with Dr. Appel and Dr. Richards
Marc Serota/National Basketball Association/Getty Images

Myka comes into the picture.

Our first Christmas with Myka

Tracy, Trey, and Myka

Myka puts on a big smile.

My dad and me, presurgery

With my mother

With Jason Kidd

Coach Riley stops in to check on me

Spending time with kids from the Thompson Children's Home back when I was in Charlotte

Feeding time
Jo Winstead/Alonzo Mourning Charities

Five kidney transplant survivors get to play with a dolphin.
Jo Winstead/Alonzo Mourning Charities

Finally!

Andrew D. Bernstein/National Basketball
Association/Getty Images

With my doctors and Jason Cooper, the man who would save my life

had made great sacrifices to make the Miami Heat a championship contender. I was only thirty and in the prime of my career, with my eyes on an MVP and an NBA Title. This, I thought, was the year we had the team that could not only get past the Knicks, but win it all (instead, Shaq and the Lakers did). And now, for the first time since I was a little kid, I didn't have a basketball season to prepare for.

The one thing I wanted to get across to the media, and in turn the fans, was that despite this setback I fully understood how lucky I was. Right away, I was dedicating my charity and humanitarian work to kidney research and treatment. I didn't want people thinking that I was feeling sorry for myself. Yes, I was down about it, but I knew that in the grand scheme of things, I was fine.

"I've always said this, I'm a blessed individual" is what I said that day. "I have a great deal to be thankful for. Throughout the years, God has blessed me with a great deal, and I know this, and I know there are a whole lot of other people out there that are a whole lot worse off than me right now."

I'm a big believer that positive thinking will produce positive results—Tracy and I both share that view of life—so the last thing I wanted to do was sit around and think, *Woe is me.* That was the first thing, the very first thing, I had decided. I would not allow myself to fall into that trap. *Wait and hope, or go make it happen.*

I did not want anybody to feel sorry for me because I always knew there was somebody out there who had it a whole lot worse than I did. Someone was sicker; someone had fewer options. I had been able to get the best specialist in the country to look at my case. Not only did I have the finances to get the best health care in the world, I had an NBA health care plan that paid for all of it.

The cost really hit home when I went to pick up a prescription of cyclosporine from Walgreens and I asked the pharmacist how much the prescription would cost without health insurance.

"Like a thousand dollars," she said.

I couldn't believe it. *A thousand dollars?* All I could think about was all the people who are working nine to five and don't have the medical insurance I did to get this stuff. The ones working two jobs and their kid is sick and he needs this medicine. I actually had the money to afford it without insurance, yet the NBA paid for it anyway. That's the cruel irony of health care. The people who can afford care also have the best health insurance. The ones that can't afford it might not have any. A thousand dollars on top of all the other costs will break them. They might not be able to take the medicine they need.

That day at Walgreens was like, *Boom.* That just hit me hard. It made me look at things from a different perspective. I was doubly fortunate when so many others weren't at all.

Dr. Appel's initial treatment was a combination of different drugs, none of which would have worked for me on their own. That was the problem that a lot of doctors saw—they looked at my situation and determined that if they gave me, say, an immunosuppressant medicine to block the body's protein loss through the urine, it would cause my kidney to get worse. On the other hand, if they gave me, say, a certain blood pressure medicine to block the protein loss in the urine, that would lower my blood pressure further, and I couldn't afford for my blood pressure to go lower. So you couldn't do just one thing at a time—you had to juggle all of them.

So Dr. Appel flipped it around. Rather than give one treatment at a time, in the traditional way, he wanted to use a combination of drugs. The key was to give me a little bit of one medicine *and* a little bit of the other and then slowly raise the dosage of each one, in steplike fashion, until there was success.

Dr. Appel said with this method he had found 50 percent of people have their illness go into remission. With me, it slowly lowered the protein in my urine, which in turn raised the protein in my blood, which in turn brought my blood pressure up so I felt a lot better.

This was a cutting-edge treatment plan. Dr. Appel says that many doctors still don't know about it.

There was one issue that even Dr. Appel's experience hadn't prepared him for: my size. He had never worked with anybody six foot ten and 260 pounds. It was kind of funny. At times I felt like a test rat, since they didn't really know what direction to go in. They were so accustomed to writing set prescriptions for average-size people; with me, they were using a hypothesis, an educated guess, on how I should be treated. They had to keep checking my blood every week to see how my body chemistry held up. I turned into a pincushion. I went from being a guy who was very uncomfortable with needles to someone who was getting stuck every day.

Slowly they figured out the science and I began to feel the progress. I grew obsessed with it; these were my new stat lines. Forget points and rebounds, it was creatinine levels and protein counts. I even started to feel good again. At the beginning I had been getting light-headed and dizzy just walking around. Now that problem had gone away.

I didn't just wait around for my chemistry to drop, either. Without basketball to play, I had a lot of free time and I didn't want to spend it sitting around the house getting depressed. I poured myself into my charities and tried to make the most of the opportunity that freedom from work can provide.

Physically I tried to get out every day. I live in south Florida and the sunshine is a powerful thing. Since I couldn't lift weights or run the way I was accustomed to, I got into yoga, which made a tremendous difference in my recovery. When Dr. Appel gave me clearance to try, I walked into Prana Yoga in downtown Coral Gables and went at it full force. Yoga made me feel better and stronger, not just physically but mentally and spiritually. I began to combine that with a holistic approach to health, including eating better and just trying to be well.

My focus was to attack this thing from as many different angles as possible. I even used to talk to my disease. I'd verbalize my intentions, trash-talk it a little bit, even.

"I know you're in there, but you're not going to stop me from doing what I want to do," I'd walk around saying. "I'm going to make it happen, regardless. You're not going to stop me. I walk by faith, not by sight. You will not stop me."

It was kind of a mind-over-matter thing. Your mind is so powerful. More than we realize. If you put your mind to doing something, you do it. Just as we make it a priority to go to work and provide for our families, use that approach to everything in life.

One day in December 2000, Dr. Appel called me from New York. He had looked over my latest blood work and wanted to tell me the news immediately.

"Your protein is now almost normal in the blood. Your protein's way down in the urine. Your kidney function is actually significantly improved from what it was, based on your chemistry.

"You can start working out again."

It had only taken a few months. This was one of the greatest things I had ever heard. I promised Dr. Appel I'd take my recovery slowly, and I did. My trainer at the time was Brian Bratton. We worked out at the University of Miami and in private gyms, and I did sprints in Peacock Park in Coconut Grove. We kept it simple. I used to push myself to levels that frightened even my professional teammates. Now I was content doing small stuff. At first, it wasn't about becoming the strongest person, just a strong person.

It actually didn't take that long for me to get back into reasonable shape, and by February and March I was eyeing a return to the Heat. I kept pestering Dr. Appel for the latest info, the odds I would be able to return. He finally gave me clearance in mid-March. That day I rejoined the team and began practicing and working out at the Heat's facility. I would continue practicing with them until I received permission to play in an actual game. It felt like I was beating the focal sclerosis. I was ecstatic.

Each day after practice Dr. Appel would have blood drawn for a chemical analysis. While he was supportive of my desire to make a comeback, he was also very nervous about me playing again. It was one thing for the medicines to even out my numbers so I could walk around without being light-headed, but how would my body react when I was exerting myself full force?

Playing basketball at the NBA level takes a lot out of you even if you're in top physical condition. The exertion is incredible and the physical wear and tear unavoidable. That's why so many of us are health fiends and worry about everything we put into our body—it is very easy for your system to get thrown out of whack. It's like owning a Bentley or a Ferrari and putting regular unleaded gas in it. It won't run at its optimum level.

No one really knew what would happen. There was no way to accurately predict; there is no guidebook. Sean Elliott of the San Antonio Spurs had played after a kidney transplant in 2000, so that was the best case to study. Dr. Appel talked to Sean's doctor a number of times. But each body is different, and I was trying to play on my old kidneys, not on a new one that would presumably operate better.

Dr. Appel's other concern was dehydration. He declared I simply could not be allowed to dehydrate, and he called all the people at the Heat to tell them so. At the first break of my first practice of my return, I sat down and had five different people hand me a Gatorade bottle. It was comical. I actually got sick a couple of times from overhydration. But my numbers steadied as we got into March, and my return became inevitable.

Finally, just before a March 27, 2001, game against the Toronto Raptors, I was cleared to play.

Dr. Appel told the media that there were no guarantees, but that if

I were his son, he would let me play now. That was what I wanted to hear. By then, he and I had developed a relationship that went beyond just doctor-patient. I knew he had my best interests in mind and I knew this was about me returning to the court safely, not about Dr. Appel getting the glory of returning me to the court. There's a big difference. (To this day, we talk at least once every two weeks about my condition. No matter where he is, even on vacation, he gets my monthly lab work sent to him. We are constantly adjusting the medicines and discussing everything.)

Dr. Appel understood that this wasn't about money—I had all the money I needed. But I was a competitor. I had spent my life focused on achieving a single goal, winning an NBA championship. Once you've made your money to assure the security of your family, why else would you play basketball? It's for the love of the game, yes, but the ultimate goal is to win a championship.

A passion for our work and a love for our chosen fields is what Dr. Appel and I share. I know that if he was given $100 million today he'd be right back at work tomorrow anyway. He has such a love for nephrology, it's not a matter of money; it's what he wants to do with his life. I wanted to play basketball. I couldn't shake that. I didn't even need to explain that to Dr. Appel, just as he wouldn't have to explain it to me. When you meet people that passionate about something, it's obvious.

I didn't start against the Raptors that first night, because Pat Riley was very concerned about my health and wanted to keep my minutes down. But late in the first quarter he put me in, and the sellout crowd in Miami gave me a long standing ovation. I missed my first shot but I made a couple of blocks right away and pretty soon I felt like myself again. I played nineteen minutes and had 9 points and 6 rebounds. We lost, but I felt great. I felt like I had won.

That night Dr. Appel had the Heat trainer, Ron Culp, draw blood at halftime. Then he called me after the game to see how it went. For the rest of the season, he called me before and after every game. The numbers kept coming back fine and I was feeling pretty good.

But there were all sorts of small hurdles. One was simple aches and pains. Basketball is a physical game; you are going to get some bumps and bruises. Because of the disease, I couldn't take a nonsteroidal agent like Advil, Motrin, or Aleve, which would have been the obvious cure. I couldn't take a potent narcotic, either. Dr. Appel had to find the right medications to deal with the pain. The good news was I've always had a high pain tolerance, so most nights I wouldn't request anything.

Fatigue was really my biggest hurdle. I just couldn't keep my energy up the way I had before. I didn't know what the issue was, and neither did Dr. Appel. But his wife, Alice, did. She's a Ph.D. in biochemistry and on the Columbia University faculty. One night the Appels were watching a Heat game on television and I looked sluggish down the stretch. Alice suggested that they raise my red blood count above normal levels. My numbers were fine for a person with a regular job, someone who is sitting at a desk, but not for a professional athlete. This was something no one else had thought of.

We had to get clearance from the NBA because raising your red blood cell count is the kind of thing that gets track athletes and cyclists banned from their sport. It's blood doping. But for a basketball player, a higher red count wasn't as big an advantage. Besides, I was being up front about it and I was doing it with the best of intentions. The NBA agreed and we got my blood count up, which helped immensely. I even became the national spokesman for Orthobiotech, the company that made the drug Procrit, which helped my anemia so much. Once I got on it, and my red blood cell count increased to normal levels, the change was dramatic. I had the late-game energy to compete.

The new worry was my potassium. Dr. Appel was concerned because the harder I exercised, the higher my potassium went. Potassium is a chemical in the body that's very closely regulated and there is little room for fluctuation. If your potassium goes too high, the heart just stops beating. It can kill you instantly. I could have just been running down the court and collapsed and died. With potassium, you're allowed only one mistake. He was constantly looking at that, too.

I returned for the final thirteen games of the 2000–2001 season; I even started three games, though I was just getting back into game shape. We finished the season with fifty victories but then got swept in the first round of the playoffs by Charlotte. It was a disappointing end to a long, emotional season.

The 2001–2002 season was better for me, but worse for the Heat. We were a lousy club that season, going 36–46 and not even making the playoffs. But I was back to almost full strength, starting all but one of the seventy-five games I played.

I had regained my strength, my stamina, and my fire. I was back to challenging players defensively, banging them underneath the glass and getting out full speed in the open court. I was just playing again. I averaged 15.7 points and 8.4 rebounds a game.

My career wasn't over after all — just the talk about it was. I felt like God had come down and touched me. I was doing some charity work to give back, and I thought I was healed. I thought I had done just what I told the disease I would. I had beaten it rather than it beating me. I thought I had kicked the disease into remission and never would hear from it again.

But all the positive thinking and bold talk in the world didn't mean a damn thing to focal sclerosis. It wasn't done with me. Not by a long shot.

8

THE SEARCH FOR A DONOR

"The disease doesn't just affect the afflicted" is one of Alonzo Mourning's sayings. Danny Meyer only knew Alonzo from watching basketball—mostly old Georgetown games against his beloved Syracuse Orangemen—when that truth about kidney disease came to mean something to him.

His son Simon had total renal failure at age nine, went through four months of dialysis, and then got a kidney from his mother, Susan, in a transplant. The disease had been bad enough. The cure was worse. The kid was weak and the medications strong. Nothing seemed to go right.

"He had every complication imaginable," Danny said. "Every last one."

Eventually the immunosuppressants reacted in the worst possible way, giving Simon lymphoma. The cure was killing him. He began chemotherapy on top of everything else and life for the boy was not only immensely difficult, but impossible to explain.

His mother and father were hit with that gut punch of parental pain, the *feeling of not being able to protect or comfort their child. They felt frustrated, at times even worthless.*

"My son was depressed; he was having a tough time," Danny said. "My mission was to put a smile on his face. I couldn't cure all the diseases, I couldn't make him well. It was hard for me to give him advice because I didn't go through this.

"But maybe I could put a smile on his face, do something to help keep him going."

He knew Alonzo had undergone a transplant of his own. Through a connection from his days as a student at Syracuse with Danny Schayes, a long-time NBA player, he got word to Alonzo. Simon and his family lived in the Bay Area; a brief meeting was set up between the transplant survivors after a Golden State Warriors game.

"Around the corner came Alonzo, immaculately dressed, tall, handsome," said Danny. "He strides over to us like he knew us, bent right over to my son, and said, 'Man, you're looking good today, Simon.' "

Simon beamed.

"The world changed," Danny said. *A friendship was born.*

Simon was understandably wary of doctors and he distrusted medicine. It had given him cancer, after all. He wasn't doing all he needed to help his kidney. He was at a tipping point. Alonzo instinctively knew all about that.

They talked about how important the medicine is, about working with doctors, and mostly about how Simon needed to keep his mind strong so his body could follow along.

"If I can do it, Simon, you can do it," Alonzo said.

The team bus was leaving. Alonzo gave Simon a pair of autographed sneakers, his cell number, an e-mail address, and a promise to stay in touch. Simon was in awe. His parents were in tears. "A genuine moment," Danny said.

They thought that would be it. "Alonzo had already done more for us than I could have dreamed. I kept thinking though, This can't be the end of the relationship. But how much can you ask of someone?"

Then Simon decided to take Alonzo up on his offer and send an e-mail. And a surprising thing happened: Alonzo e-mailed back. Then he called.

Then they kept talking. Right in the middle of his NBA season and an impossibly busy life, Alonzo kept finding time for this little boy he barely knew.

"He's reminded all of us about the good in people," Danny said.

They talked about little things, big things, and things that had nothing to do with being sick. Just guy things, friends things.

Simon's mood changed. He became more trusting, less scared. The illness was still troublesome; there is likely the need for another transplant. But the smiles were more frequent.

One day, about a year later, Danny and Simon went to watch Alonzo and the Heat play the Sacramento Kings. During the course of the game, one of the King players committed a hard foul on Alonzo, knocking him violently to the court.

Simon is just a kid, and a small one at that. But he was so outraged by the rough play, he stood up, his head barely visible over the people seated in front of him, and with fists clenched screamed: "Hey, don't touch my friend!"

I n the summer of 2002, I considered myself to be a person with an uncommon amount of resilience. I was unbreakable, even indestructible, unstoppable. Of course, this is how you have to think when you are a professional athlete. There is no room for doubt, no place in your psyche to consider weakness. That serves no purpose, so you just shut it out completely. Contemplating such a thing isn't going to help you dunk on Tim Duncan, it's going to hurt you.

So I was invincible. And when I considered all the things that had been thrown at me, on the court and off, only for me to plow right through them, I had good reason to feel invincible at that point in my life.

Dr. Appel thought otherwise, mainly because he was growing increasingly concerned about my chemistries. I'd had a relapse. My body was no longer responding to the medications the way we wanted it to. The numbers weren't just rising, they were rising dramatically. By September, my creatinine count came in at 7.5, almost five times what it should be. Dr. Appel told me he couldn't let me play.

I was devastated. This made no sense. What had changed? Why? No one knew. I felt good, but the numbers didn't lie. Dr. Appel was not going to put me out there unless it was safe. But he wasn't going to put me on dialysis, and he didn't think a transplant was necessary yet, either. He still thought we could get my disease into a dormant stage and get me back on the court. He gave me a lot of hope that this was a temporary setback. I just needed to take some time off and go back to square one, finding a new treatment combination that could get me back on the court. But at the same time, I had no clear timetable for a return.

I went to Pat Riley and broke the news. I was so down that I couldn't even bring myself to attend the press conference announcing that I was, once again, going to be out. Riley had to do it for me.

We started a new series of medications, trying to find the right mix. These attempts were more powerful and toxic than the previous ones. If the disease wasn't going to kill me, it seemed like the cure was. The side effects were brutal. My joints ached, I had headaches and mood swings, and my skin was changing, breaking out with a lot of acne. There were days I could barely move and days I just didn't want to. I was not a pleasant person to be around. I had gone from invincible to impossible in a few short weeks.

I continued to turn to holistic solutions, which I will detail later. I changed my diet and cut down on salt considerably, and I did a lot of yoga. That helped, not only in curbing the side effects, but in keeping my mind clear and my attitude positive. I knew that if I just sat around and took those medicines I was going to be in bad shape. But a lot of people do that. They think taking the medications is the only thing they should be doing, the only way to treat themselves physically. So they take the medicines and are couch potatoes. I believe you have to stay active and not mope and feel sorry about everything. Some would say that one of the reasons people lived to be hundreds of years old during Biblical days is because they stayed active. You need to go out and live. That's the entire point.

Dr. Appel worked all fall and couldn't get the chemistry right. Then he worked all winter. Then all spring. The season came and went. The playoffs came and went. I was still out. But he never gave up. He finally began getting my numbers in line, making me feel better, allowing me to work out again. The guy was relentless. He told me late in the spring of 2003 that I would, once again, be able to return to the NBA.

I wanted to return to the Miami Heat for the 2003–2004 season. It had been a terrible year without me—the Heat had won just twenty-five games—but even though we were so far from winning a championship this was still my franchise. Miami was my home now and I felt very comfortable and very loyal to everyone there. Plus we had picked up a young guard in the draft named Dwyane Wade. He had just led Marquette to the Final Four.

But it became a business matter. My original seven-year, $105 million contract had run out; I was an unrestricted free agent. If I was healthy, I could expect to return to my 2001–2002 level of play, which would make me one of the better centers in the NBA. I wasn't an All-NBA candidate anymore, but I was good. At worst, even if I was relegated to a backup role, I was one heck of a backup. In the NBA, the market for a very good backup center was about $5 million per year.

Jeff and I had a meeting with Pat Riley and he said the Heat couldn't offer me that kind of money. In fact, they offered significantly less: a one-year, $1 million deal. I was floored. That wasn't the kind of deal I could accept. Jeff and I agreed I needed to test the market. I went home and told Tracy, "We are going to have to leave Miami for a little while." Neither of us could really believe it. Being in the NBA is a nomadic existence. Very few players stick with the same team their entire career. Many bounce around each season. But after eight years in south Florida, we'd thought we'd never leave. This was home. We could maintain a home there and return when I was done playing, but just the thought of another city was depressing.

Jeff had Dr. Appel put together a packet of information offering me clearance to play and detailing my health. He sent it out to the other teams in the NBA.

"At the current time, his physical examination is entirely within normal limits. His blood pressure is normal and his cardiac, pulmonary, and the rest of the examination were normal," the document read. "While he still is only in partial remission of his kidney disease, I have no reason that he cannot play professional basketball at the same level he did prior to last summer. Of course, we will continue monitoring him closely as we did when he returned to his professional career several years ago."

That was enough for five teams to express interest in signing me—Denver, Dallas, Memphis, New Jersey, and San Antonio. This is when you need a great agent, and I had one in Jeff Wechsler. You can't just put yourself out there like you are applying for any job. You have to protect what you're trying to sell and work the system.

Jeff was worried about dealing with San Antonio because they had had Sean Elliott play for them after his kidney transplant. We thought that, if they passed on me after a physical, my market value would plummet because other teams would think the Spurs understood this disease very well. So we wanted to see what the other teams and their doctors would do before dealing with the Spurs.

This was a little like the college recruiting process, except that it wasn't clandestine, it was treated like what it was—a business transaction. Everything was very matter-of-fact. The teams were all willing to come to Miami to try to get me to sign. While there was some wining and dining, it was nothing like the college process. I was a grown man with professional representation, not a naïve teenager with no idea what was happening.

The first team was Memphis. We met with the owner, Michael Heisley, Coach Hubie Brown, and General Manager Jerry West, who was an NBA legend (he's the guy in the logo) and had just come from running the Lakers. They offered me a multi-year deal for what is called in the NBA the mid-level exemption, which is a way of describing how that kind of deal works under each team's salary cap. It was worth about $5 million a year. This was reassuring.

Denver came next with a group from the front office led by general manager Kiki Vandeweghe, another great former player. They rented this amazing two-story suite at the Shore Club on South Beach for the meeting and they offered a one-year deal worth $14 million. I said, "All right. We'll think about it." Then we went to dinner, where they spent time selling me on the potential of the team.

Mark Cuban, the owner of the Dallas Mavericks, is a young, self-made billionaire who is very active in all facets of his organization. He's a very interesting and charismatic guy. Rather than send a bunch of people to talk to me, Mark only sent one—himself. Mark offered a multi-year deal at the mid-level, about the same money as Memphis. But he also laid out his plan for the team, which including not only signing me, but getting point guard Jason Kidd out of New Jersey. He thought by adding the two of us to a team that had won sixty games the year before, we could win the NBA title.

That, of course, was what I wanted more than anything else. I would have been willing to stay in Miami and try to rebuild. I felt that kind of loyalty to the franchise, to Riley, and to the owner, Micky Arison. But I wouldn't do that anywhere else. Winning the NBA championship was my singular goal at that point. I had been an all-star, been a runner-up for MVP, been on the Dream Team, won the Olympic gold, and achieved financial security. I had done everything but win a championship and I was obsessed with rectifying that before I couldn't play anymore. I wanted to play for a contender and the Nets were a contender. Jason was such a great passer that everyone in the league wanted to play with him. He was a winner.

Mark asked me if I knew Jason well and since I did, he asked me if I could talk to him about trying to figure out a way to get him to Dallas. I said I would, and later I called Jason about it. But Jason spent most of the time recruiting me to come to New Jersey. Mark's plan backfired and in the end, when I didn't sign with the Mavericks, he came out in the newspapers and said I misled him. But I hadn't committed to any team and later we got it all worked out.

Rod Thorn, then the general manager of the Nets, came next. When he got to town I was playing basketball over at a local facility. He found out and showed up to watch me play in a high-level pickup game. Later we had a meeting and they offered the mid-level exemption and, of course, the chance to play with Jason Kidd. So I had three multi-year offers for about $5 million a year with a total worth of around $24 million, a single one-year offer for $14 million, and we still had the possibility of the Spurs.

This is where Jeff became invaluable. With this many offers on the table, he decided to make a counterproposal. Since I was essentially a mid-level exception guy at this stage of my career, and considering I had just lost an entire season to a kidney ailment, it was difficult to demand more money. I just wasn't going to get it. But Jeff figured we needed to protect these offers, so he told all four teams, "Okay, but here's the deal. We're going to do this without a physical."

Whenever you sign a contract there is a physical within forty-eight hours. They check everything from your blood work to your knees. If you fail the physical, the deal is off. Usually the physical is just a precaution, but I was a different case.

Jeff pushed the envelope. His fear was that I'd agree to terms with one of the teams, then fail my physical for some reason, maybe something not even related to my kidneys. Then not only would I have no contract with that team, but the whole market would disappear. My career would be over, my worst nightmare. No one would sign me to a mid-level after that, so that physical contained so much risk for me.

Of course, it was also risky for the teams. They could sign me for all this money and then find out I couldn't honor the contract. Jeff was honest with everybody, saying, "Look, Alonzo's in remission now. The doctors tell us this remission could last a week, two weeks, three weeks, a year. They don't know. So you're signing him understanding that you don't know what could happen."

We were adamant that everyone knew what they were getting into, that the situation was very clear. He thought, despite that, at least one team would agree. Actually two of them did, Memphis and New Jersey. The Nets were coming off back-to-back appearances in the NBA Finals and needed someone to help push them over the cusp. From Rod Thorn to the owner to Jason Kidd, I was that guy.

So I said good-bye to Miami. We were off to Jersey.

•   •   •

I felt a lot of pressure when I joined the Nets. I wanted to live up to the expectations and help push the franchise to an NBA title. But I struggled. Getting back into top condition was very difficult and my kidneys weren't helping any. I kept getting fatigued and I knew recovery was going to be a long process. My mind kept thinking I was an elite player again, but my body couldn't keep up.

It was still early in the season and we were having an intense practice. One of my teammates was Kenyon Martin, a very tough but at times immature forward out of the University of Cincinnati. Kenyon had a world of potential, but he didn't always practice hard, and I had mentioned that to him. I said I thought he was supposed to be one of the leaders of the team but I wasn't seeing it, I wasn't seeing the leadership.

The Nets had a lot of little cliques and some of the players were really full of themselves because they had reached the Finals in consecutive years. But reaching the Finals wasn't the goal; winning it was. I was brought in to give them a little maturity and get them over the hump, so I said that to Kenyon.

We were running wind sprints at the end of practice and I was struggling to make it ahead of the other guys. My body was really giving me a hard time. So he made a crack about how could I be their center when I could hardly grab a rebound.

I went after him for that. I charged him in great anger. I was grabbed by some of the guys before I could get my hands on him, and eventually Coach Scott settled everyone down. Guys make mistakes, and Kenyon was young and immature, so I excused him. But I didn't forget.

The thing was, at the time that near fight happened, I felt like I was turning a corner. A couple of nights later I scored 15 points against the Toronto Raptors in what was my best game. Everybody was like, "Man, he's really coming back into form now." It was a confidence booster. I really had started to feel better and thought I was getting into game shape, regaining my strength and timing.

I was home packing for a long West Coast trip when Dr. Appel called. He had been analyzing my blood work every week with growing concern because my chemistry kept getting progressively worse. When I signed with the Nets, my creatinine count was 12.5, which is very high. My normal count used to be 1.7. For a normal person, a number such as 12.5 would prohibit them from playing basketball. Dr. Appel had figured out that, because of my size, I could have much higher than normal numbers and continue to play. But how high was too high? He didn't know.

The real trouble was my potassium level, which had begun to rise again. The only way the body excretes potassium is through the kidneys and if your kidney function is poor, eventually the potassium starts building up. As my level rose, he began to see the writing on the wall. This experiment was probably over. It was just a matter of time. In mid-November, as a precaution, he reserved a room at New York–Presbyterian Hospital for December 19 for me to have a kidney transplant. He just didn't tell me at the time.

That night while I was packing my bags, Dr. Appel asked me how I was feeling.

"You know, Doc, I'm a little tired." That was to be expected, but I was still excited about the Toronto game.

"Well, Alonzo, you know what? I cannot let you go on this road trip."

"Why not?"

"Your potassium level has increased to 4.8 and I'm afraid right now that if it goes over 5.0, if you run up and down the court, you could risk a cardiac arrest right out there on the court. You could die on the court."

Die on the court? I thought.

"We're going to need to start looking for transplant matches as soon as possible."

I had stopped packing by now. I felt the way I had the day I first heard about focal sclerosis back in Miami. It was as big a shock. I knew this was possible, but it was still difficult to hear. Death on the court was the greatest fear, obviously. I knew seemingly healthy basketball players, like Reggie Lewis of the Boston Celtics and Hank Gathers of Loyola Marymount University, had died on the court. One minute they were competing at the highest athletic level; the next minute, they were dead.

I understood the stakes. I just wasn't ready to immediately accept my fate.

"Doc, are you sure? Isn't there anything we can do?"

"There's something you could take, but I'm afraid of it because I'm not there to monitor you. I'm not going to be there for you on a road trip. I do have some colleagues in all the cities that you're going to, so I can get you in to get blood work done and maybe have them come over and listen to your heart before every game. But other than that, there is no way I can clear you to play without seeing the chemistry every day."

At this point, I knew it was over. That wasn't a real plan. It was too much work and too much risk. What was I doing here? What was the point? Was I going to risk dying at age thirty-three just to play basketball? I was devastated, but I wasn't going to be unrealistic.

It was a lot to decide, so I told Dr. Appel I would call him back in half an hour. I called Jeff up and he agreed that to go on the road trip would be ridiculous and dangerous. Like me, Jeff had become such an expert on the disease that he understood what Dr. Appel was saying. We both agreed it was time to move forward on a transplant. I called Dr. Appel back.

"I want to stop now. Get me a transplant. Then I'll get back and play again."

There was absolutely no doubt in my mind at that moment that I was going to come back, better than ever. My mentality was, *Let's do this as soon as possible so I can return as soon as possible.*

I won't say that, for a minute, I wasn't frustrated at the situation. I had just spent all this time and effort trying to get back to the NBA and now, twelve games into my return, it was over. How can you not be frustrated? I had been told that going back was possible, that we had plenty of time, that I had done all the right things. And yet here it was. Again. Only worse. Everyone was disappointed. Dr. Appel had wanted to succeed also.

"Look, we did all we could with the time that we had," he said. "You responded well to the medicines and we did all we could. This is the next step. This is what you have to do. And this is what we had been prepared for mentally all these years, for the past three years, this is what we've been prepared for."

I *was* prepared for it—Dr. Appel was right about that. I knew I was going to attack finding a donor and having the transplant the way I had attacked everything else. It was the only way. Sitting around feeling sorry for myself not only did nothing to get me better, it wasn't right. I had no reason to feel sorry for myself. When I told Tracy the news, we hugged and prayed, but neither of us shed one tear. We had developed a steel resolve by that point and we knew that as long as we stuck together and followed God's plan, the problem would resolve itself. She was very strong for me.

This was a disappointing development, Tracy said, but it wasn't bad news and it certainly wasn't the worst news. What if I had played one more game and that was one game too many? What if I had died? What would Reggie Lewis have given for a doctor to catch him, to be so cautious? It took me a few minutes to think of it in that way, but once I did I saw how lucky I was. I was alive. I had a great doctor. I had treatment options.

Getting sick is an obvious negative. But it lays out the truth in a stark way. I tell people the good thing about getting sick is you learn to appreciate that the positives overshadow the negatives.

"Well, Doc, what's the next step?" I asked.

"Right now, our next step should be trying to find a donor. Go ahead and have some of your family members come in, or whoever you have, friends or what have you, but we need people to come in who could be a donor."

How do you ask someone to donate their kidney? It's not like asking to borrow twenty dollars. You are asking for a part of their body. I hate asking people for *anything*; I've always considered myself self-sufficient, and I still like doing things for myself, taking care of my own chores, things like that. I come from a hardworking, independent family. Even as I became famous and could afford a lot of help, I still liked taking care of myself. I've never been the kind of star who wants to be waited on.

But now I needed to ask for a big favor of someone. Everyone has two kidneys and, if you are healthy, you can spare one. But asking someone for a kidney is asking them to undergo major surgery, take time off from work and family, go under anesthesia, and completely turn their life upside down. It is common for the person giving the kidney to have more post-op difficulties than the person receiving it. While death isn't common, there is a risk of it. All just for you. To make a request like that, to even hint about it—I had no idea how to even start with something like that.

I knew that if I wanted to live, though, I had to separate my pride from the fact that I was trying to survive. I am a prideful person, but I couldn't be stuck in my pride. I couldn't just pretend I didn't need anyone else to get me through life. The truth is, as self-sufficient as I thought I was, if I honestly looked at my whole life, I actually did rely on the contributions other people made to my development, both as a person and as a basketball player. My parents, my foster mom, coaches, teachers, agents, friends—I was the product of others. All of us are.

So now I needed more help, even if, as a grown man, I thought I was done with that. I thought I was forever in the role of providing assistance, not seeking it.

The challenge was to find someone with a kidney that would not just be a match in all the normal ways—which is always the challenge—but also to find one that would be physically big enough to work in my body. The normal protocol in transplants is to match two people who are about the same height and weight. At six ten and 260 pounds, I needed a big kidney. I couldn't have a pediatric or a normal-sized kidney. It just wouldn't handle the filtration.

But how many 6-10, 260 pound people are walking down the street?

The good news was, I had a lot of relatives, dozens of uncles, aunts, and cousins, all the people I used to play with as a kid back at my grandmother's house in Norfolk. My mom had five brothers, all of whom were over six feet and two hundred pounds. And as you might expect from someone who played basketball his entire life, I had a lot of tall friends, former teammates and opponents.

I decided to start with family members. I called up my uncles and asked them to come to New York and get tested. It was a difficult call to make. I told each one of them that they could say no at any point, that if they felt like not doing it, I understood completely. It would not affect what I thought of them in any way. I tried to get across that I knew how big a sacrifice this was. I was just asking. They didn't have to do it.

Four of my uncles said yes; a fifth was incarcerated at the time. I decided to bring the four to New York at the same time, along with my father. I was very humbled by their willingness to do this and I wanted to say thank you. It was actually a really fun time. It's rare to get all of them together. I took them out to dinner and we went to Times Square and had a picture taken of all of us there. It was cool.

I also had a couple of friends who stepped up to the plate, who called me out of the blue. Patrick Ewing, who is even bigger than me, volunteered. My barber in New Jersey, who was also a big guy, even offered. They all came to get tested for compatibility. Dr. Appel jokes that walking down the hall at the hospital with me and four of my potential donors was like being surrounded by a basketball team.

The problem was that everyone I brought to the hospital was the wrong blood type, except for Patrick. But he had high blood pressure, so he wasn't the best option. After that first wave, Dr. Appel told me that I needed to relax a little. I guess I was being too aggressive in finding a donor—the initial screening did not require them to come to New York. We could just ask their blood type over the phone. I got the point.

In 2003, the first hurdle for compatibility was matching blood type. To show you how quickly technology has advanced, that isn't the case anymore. They now have a procedure called plasmapheresis, which allows an organ from an individual with a different blood type to be successfully used in a transplant. I didn't have that available.

Throughout my time being sick, medical advances have amazed me. Not only because of how quickly what seems impossible becomes possible, but also because of how other things that seem possible never come to be.

I've grown extremely suspicious of the pharmaceutical industry in this country. If technology is advancing so quickly that things like plasmapheresis become possible, or we develop medicines that can stabilize a certain condition or help you live with a condition for the rest of your life, then why don't we ever develop any cures? The pharmaceutical industry is built on people needing to take pills, and the best way to keep business going is to develop pills that don't cure a disease and make someone well, but instead allow a patient to manage a disease as long as they keep buying the pills for the rest of their life. The fact that we never develop any pills that cure anything, that's what truly troubles me.

As we continued to work our way through my family and friends I also received hundreds and hundreds of calls, e-mails, and letters from people around the country volunteering to be tested. The outpouring from perfect strangers who read about my situation in the newspaper or heard about it on television was just incredible. For all those people to be willing to do that for someone they didn't know was very touching. I wrote all of them back thanking them and saying that tens of thousands of individuals are out there waiting for a transplant and if they wanted to be an organ donor they could still really help someone.

Of course, some of the e-mails were ridiculous, full of crazy stuff. People wanted money for their kidney, or they had other motives. One guy even said if I paid him a million dollars, he'd give me *both* his kidneys. I don't think he had done a lot of long-term thinking. Tracy and I would just laugh at offers like that.

Dr. Appel was focused on finding a match, but not too much of a match. Focal sclerosis comes back in about a third of patients who get a transplant, and it often comes back immediately. He felt that the better the donor match, the more likely the disease was to come back, because essentially the new kidney would be too much like the original. I needed a kidney that was different enough to resist the disease. But the less a kidney matched my own, the more likely I was to reject it. So he had to balance out the variables.

I needed someone who was big and who was related but not too closely related in terms of transplant genetics. There are six categories that are considered when rating a potential match, and in my case, a six out of six wouldn't be good. I needed something closer to two or three out of six, according to Dr. Appel. He thought cousins would be best, even second cousins.

We always called my paternal grandmother, Margaret, the Diana Ross of the family. Even though she was a grandmother, she was a stylish woman. She wasn't wealthy. In fact, she lived in public housing in the Tidewater Park area of Norfolk. But she was a very sharp dresser. And she never seemed to age. We'd be over at her apartment looking at old pictures and she looked exactly the same twenty years earlier as she did that day.

When I was growing up, my dad used to drop me off at Margaret's house on weekends and we used to spend a lot of holidays there. When you are young, you don't think about your grandmother living in low-income housing. You just love spending time there. I loved it especially because a lot of my cousins and friends were there to play with. One of those children was a second cousin, a few years younger than me, named Jason Cooper.

When I began searching for a donor, I hadn't seen Jason in twenty-five years. I used to hear bits of information about him, about how he had become a Marine, or how he was doing well, but we drifted apart. I didn't even know at the time I moved to New Jersey that he lived in the city, just over on Roosevelt Island.

When I became an NBA player, I built my father a house out in Chesapeake

My grandmother Margaret

that included a wing for Margaret. It was a way to get her out of public housing so she could have a better life. Margaret was a wonderful woman, but she smoked and she drank. Then she got cancer. In 2003, you could see it was really eating away at her.

She always loved the Atlantis Resort in the Bahamas—it was one of her favorite places. I had sent her there before and I decided in November of 2003 to send her and one of my aunts for a week. But Margaret was so sick she stayed only four days, returned to Virginia, and went directly to the hospital. When I heard about that I knew the end was near.

I believe in God's plan, not coincidences. The day Dr. Appel called me to tell me I needed to retire from the NBA and seek a kidney transplant, Jason, who was in Virginia visiting family, went over to the hospital to see Margaret and pray with her. The next day he was supposed to leave town, but his car broke down. He was told it would be ready the next day. With nothing to do, he returned to the hospital with one of his aunts to pray some more. When he walked into the hospital, there in the waiting room was my father. The three of them prayed together.

That was the day I announced my retirement from the Nets, explaining that I needed a transplant. They showed the news on the television in the hospital. My father knew what was going on; I had talked to him the night before.

"Junior is retiring from basketball today," he said (Junior is what everyone in my family calls me). Jason was stunned and felt terrible. He had followed my career, every twist and turn of it.

"Look, I know that Junior hasn't seen me in years, but let him know that I am in New York and if he needs me, give me a call," Jason said. "If he needs a kidney transplant, I'd be glad to help."

Shortly after that, my grandmother died. Soon after, I had exhausted my initial wave of potential donors. That's when my father told me, "You know, I talked to Jason Cooper, and he said he would be willing to get tested."

The number of things that had to happen for Jason's name to come to me cannot be brushed off as a coincidence. Simply put, God put me back in touch with my cousin. I called him up, made some small talk, got his blood type, and asked him if he would come over to the hospital to get tested. He never hesitated. He said *Absolutely*. I told him I'd send a car service for him, but he insisted that wasn't necessary. He'd get there himself. That was the thing about Jason; he never asked for anything.

The morning of his test I got to Presbyterian early and waited in the lobby for him. I had never seen him as an adult. But when he walked into the lobby, even though I couldn't recognize him physically, I knew it was him. I could sense the energy. It was just the way we looked at each other.

I shook his hand. We talked for a few seconds, then went up to the clinic and soon found out he was perfect for me. He was my second cousin, so he was related but not *too* related. We had the same blood type. He was a big, strong guy, six-foot-three former Marine. He was a two-out-of-six match, just what Dr. Appel was looking for. Jason never hesitated. "Let's do it," he said.

I just closed my eyes and thanked God. He had sent me the perfect donor.

9

THE SURGERY

Even before he got sick, Alonzo Mourning could have been described as a health freak. He often worked out for four or five hours at a time. He didn't just watch what he ate; he obsessed over it. He had a personal chef, chose organic food, and maintained a disciplined diet designed to help his body operate at the highest level athletically possible.

He made his living off his body. It wasn't a joke.

Then he got sick and took it to an even greater level. He thought about the ramifications of every single bite or swallow. Gone was red meat, almost all salt, even moderate amounts of alcohol. Eating was now about living. He took no chances. For four years, it is possible he didn't eat a single bad meal.

"He was adamant about it," Tracy Mourning said.

But now those failing kidneys were in the final hours of being his. It was the night before his transplant. Well before six the next morning, he would depart his home in Tenafly, New Jersey, drive down to the George Washing-

ton Bridge and roll into the Washington Heights section of Manhattan to New York–Presbyterian Hospital.

The kidneys were all but gone. He was already scheduled for surgery. What bad could happen now, right? If he did hurt his kidneys, what difference would it make?

So Alonzo Mourning decided to make an unexpected request. His personal chef was willing to make anything he wanted for his "last meal"—filet mignon, lobster, pasta, whatever.

"Two Wendy's hamburgers, cheese and everything, hold the mayo—and french fries, really hot," Alonzo proclaimed.

Everyone laughed. He said he was serious.

"I haven't eaten red meat in so long, and I used to love Wendy's, that's what I want for my last meal," he said.

And so it would be. Shari Rochester, his assistant, tried to find a nearby Wendy's. The closest one was about to close. She begged them to stay open, raced over, and returned with his burger and fries.

"You know what?" Alonzo said. "Sometimes simple is best."

I didn't want any tension at home the night before the transplant. There was nothing to gain from negative energy. Anxiety would only make things worse. This was not supposed to be a tense night, but a time of celebration. Everyone gathered at our house in Tenafly, a small suburb we had moved to when I signed with the Nets, and we practically had a party. It was very festive. My entire family was there, including Tracy, my mom, my dad, my mother-in-law, my son, Trey, my daughter, Myka, Shari our assistant and, of course, Jason. It was actually just a fun night. There was a lot of love in the air and people were telling old stories. It took my mind off things. The time would come to be serious, so this was a chance to not be serious.

There was hardly any way I could sleep the night before. Through the years, because of the transplant and all the basketball injuries, I've had nine surgeries. I've always had trouble sleeping the night before one of them. You just can't take your mind off what is about to happen. It's difficult to relax and sleep. That was especially true for this one.

This wasn't a knee scope. This was major surgery. This wasn't my career. This was my life. Not only that, I had brought my cousin into it. Jason was the best. I know God sent him to me, because I couldn't have had a better person to go through this experience with. He never got down, never showed any fear, never had any apprehension that I could sense. He made it very easy for me. I kept trying to give him an out.

"Look man, if you want to back out of this, I wouldn't hold it against you. I would totally understand."

He would just get mad at me.

"What, are you kidding me? What are you talking about? I made a commitment and I want to do this. We're going to go through with it. You know, I want to do it."

"Okay, all right. Thanks, man."

Then about ten minutes later I'd ask him again and we'd go through the entire debate again. Finally he begged me to stop because I was driving him crazy.

Jason didn't sleep any more than I did. We had to be at the hospital at six A.M., but we stayed up real late just talking. We joked that they were going to put us to sleep once we got there, so what did it matter? Eventually everyone else went to bed, but Jason and I sat up at my kitchen table. We have a TV in there and we just talked about a bunch of things, caught up on all the time we missed with each other and basically just kicked it. It was really the start of a great friendship. We eventually went to bed about four A.M., but we were up so soon it was like I just blinked my eyes.

New York–Presbyterian Hospital is a huge complex in Washington Heights, on the far Upper West Side of Manhattan. It is a historic place, the second oldest hospital in the United States, founded back in 1771. It was called Columbia Presbyterian until 1998. Its buildings sprawl out over a number of city blocks, from Broadway on the east all the way to Fort Washington Park on the west, and between 165th and 168th streets north to south. It's an incredible place with some of the most talented doctors in the entire world and all sorts of people hustling around.

The nephrology division is annually ranked among the best in the country, along with Brigham and Women's Hospital in Boston and the Mayo Clinic out in Minnesota. The division handles hundreds of consultations and does more than two hundred transplants per year.

While Dr. Appel was my primary doctor and would be at the hospital that day, the actual transplant would be handled by Dr. Mark Hardy, an expert at the procedure. There was no question as we fought through the early Manhattan traffic that December morning and pulled up to Admitting that Jason and I would be in the best hands possible.

I had grown very nervous in the days leading up to the surgery, and my doctors sensed it. It was a natural fear. I'm not a person who fears much of anything in life, certainly not on a basketball court, but kidney transplant surgery is a little bit more intimidating. Dr. Appel had done his best to calm my nerves as my surgery day got closer.

First, he had me meet with Michelle, a very young patient of his who had received a transplant from a friend of hers. Michelle told me how easy it was: she was out of the hospital in a matter of days. She showed me her scar, which wasn't that bad. Her friend was out of the hospital even before she was.

There was a difference, though—she'd had a laparoscopic surgery, which requires just a few tiny incisions and isn't as invasive as normal surgery. They were able to take Jason's kidney out that way, with just a few cuts by the belly button. They insert a camera and just pull the thing out. It's pretty incredible. It used to be that the donor had a tougher time than the receiver. The risk was greater and the recovery was tougher, but that's changed in the last decade.

But I wasn't going to be lucky enough for laparoscopy; they would have to do a major cut on me. Still, it was nice to hear that this woman had essentially the same procedure and walked out of the hospital four days later. The transplant had happened two and a half years before, but she looked so healthy that it gave me some confidence. If this petite woman could do it, shouldn't a professional athlete be able to?

Then Dr. Appel took me up to Dr. Hardy's office. Dr. Hardy is in his seventies and is now vice chairman of surgery at the hospital. He had been doing these surgeries since the 1960s. He had all the experience imaginable. There may not have been a doctor in the country who had performed more kidney transplants. He tried to calm me down by saying this procedure was an everyday thing for him, no different for him than it is for me to play a game of basketball.

"This operation is so easy I could do it with my eyes closed," he told me.

"Doc, could you keep one eye open for me?" I asked. Everyone laughed.

That might have been when I decided that this was going to go the way it was supposed to, so worrying about it wasn't going to help. I needed to just pray and leave it in the hands of God and these talented doctors.

So when we got to the hospital early that morning, neither Jason nor I was outwardly nervous. We were joking around and trying to have fun with it, even as they wheeled us into pre-op. Hospitals can be dreary places, serious places, and Presbyterian is no different. They do their best to make things comfortable, but it is still a hospital and hospitals just have that certain light, those long halls, the linoleum floors, the big doors. Life-and-death stuff happens there and you just can't change that fact.

It was late December, the darkest and coldest time of the year, but rather than let everything depress us, we just kept laughing. Maybe we were nervous or maybe it was just Jason's personality, but Tracy video-taped our entire pre-op and we were screwing around a lot at the beginning. I think we realized it was out of our hands now, so why not embrace it. Of course, Jason is such a positive person that he probably influenced me.

Then again, the truth is I was, deep down, nervous. I was just hiding it and fooling everyone, maybe even myself. When I first got to the hospital Dr. Appel did a cardiogram on me to check my heartbeat. This was a standard test that he had performed on me hundreds of times. But this time he heard all these extra beats. My heart was racing. He had never heard an extra beat in all the years of being my doctor and now here they were, unmistakable. He didn't tell me at the time, but he was worried; he immediately thought about Reggie Lewis. He left the

Trey with me at the hospital

room and called the cardiologist, who had given me a complete pre-op checkup a couple of days before.

"He's just nervous. Don't worry. The extra beats are nothing," the cardiologist said. Indeed, they were nothing, but as Dr. Appel said, between my nervous extra beats and his nervous extra beats, we had more than enough extra beats going around. I'm just glad I didn't know that the doctor who was trying to calm me down needed a doctor to calm *him* down, because that would have caused even more beats.

Eventually they wheeled Jason and me to the pre-op room. I kissed Tracy good-bye and promised to see her in a few hours. Jason and I were left alone and once again I told him that if he had any second thoughts, if he wanted to get up and leave, he could.

"You could just walk out that door," I said. "I won't blame you."

Jason shot me a knock-it-off look. He wasn't going anywhere.

"If I wasn't about to save your life, I'd kill you right now."

Jason went off first because they had to get his kidney out, of course. I sat in pre-op and prayed for him. That was always the hardest thing for me. I wanted God to know that if there was going to be any trouble that day, it should happen to me. Let Jason make it through fine, it wasn't his kidney that had failed. He was just doing the right thing, being generous. If someone was going to have complications, I prayed that it would be me.

While Jason's surgery was going on, they wheeled me into the operating room. The plan was to cut me open, make room for the new kidney, and then wait for Jason's. He was in the operating room right next to mine. When they got his kidney out, they would just walk it over in a little dish with ice underneath it and put into me. It sounded good. I nodded to the anesthesiologist that I was ready to go and that was that.

At least for me, the nervousness was over. Everyone else didn't have it so lucky. Tracy and my family were either in the hospital waiting room, leafing through magazines, or back home, trying to stay busy with some task or the other.

Dr. Appel was in his office pretending to work, waiting for news. He got a couple of calls from a doctor named Gerald Fischbach, who at the time was the dean of the Columbia University medical school, which is associated with New York–Presbyterian. He called to ask how the surgery was going, looking for updates, which Dr. Appel couldn't understand. Why was the dean, who wasn't even a basketball fan, suddenly so interested in Alonzo Mourning? Turns out he was trying to get insider info for the then chairman of the board of trustees at Columbia University, who just happened to be David Stern, who of course was also the commissioner of the NBA and very interested in my progress. That's David Stern for you, always figuring out a way to find out news before anyone else.

Dr. Appel also got a call from Dr. Hardy in the operating room, which made him nervous. In over three decades of having Dr. Hardy do umpteen transplants and all sorts of other surgeries, Dr. Appel had never, ever received a call from him during the operation. Down there Dr. Hardy always knew what to do. He was the expert. But now here was this call.

"What's wrong?" Dr. Appel asked.

"I can't get the kidney in," Dr. Hardy said. "There's no room. Can I cut the muscle underneath the kidney?"

To properly perform the surgery, Dr. Hardy needed to place Jason's donated kidney into my abdomen and then attach the kidney's blood vessels to my iliac artery and vein. My old kidneys were not removed from the body, because taking them out often leads to complications. The old kidneys stay, and they either stop operating or they continue to function (at about 15 percent of a healthy kidney's capacity). Either way, they don't do any harm. Meanwhile, the new one is just hooked up to the bloodstream and then its ureter, which is a three-millimeter duct that delivers urine, is attached to the bladder.

Because the old kidney is still in there, room can get tight. The new kidney has to find a new place. The old kidney is in the back quadrant, but the new kidney usually goes up front. Mine was going to go in the lower right side of my abdomen, just underneath my pelvic bone.

The problem was that I had built up a huge amount of muscle mass in my abdomen and my lower back. Normally, people are fat enough that a doctor can slip the new kidney right in and it's no problem. You just hook it up to the arteries and veins and sew the patient back up.

Dr. Hardy had performed many transplants, but he hadn't seen anything like this. I just had too much muscle and not enough free space; all those years of working out as hard as humanly possible were coming back to haunt me. To compound things, my old kidney was large, so it took up even more space than normal. Jason's kidney was smaller than mine were, but it was big enough. A kidney will actually grow to adapt to the body, even a kidney that's thirty or forty years old. But with my big kidneys staying, there was just no room.

The obvious solution was what Dr. Hardy was suggesting to Dr. Appel—cut the muscles under my old kidney to open up some space. But we had specifically hoped to avoid this because doing so would assuredly end any chance I had of returning to the NBA. One slice of that muscle and it was over. I knew it was a possibility, and if it had to happen, then it had to happen. But I had desperately hoped it wouldn't.

"Mark, you can't cut the muscle," Dr. Appel said. "He wants to play basketball afterward. Those are the muscles that go down to the legs. You've got to squeeze it in somehow. Don't cut that muscle."

Dr. Hardy went back to work and pulled my muscles even farther apart. Using clamps, he created a huge, gaping hole in my abdomen that was ten fingers wide. He got inside of me, moved my organs around a little, found some space, got the kidney in, and started hooking it up. It was an incredible effort. By giving it a second chance, he saved my career. You can't imagine how thankful I remain for that. Of course, at that moment my career was a secondary concern. Right away the question was whether the kidney would work.

My wife is crazy about photography and videos. She carries a camera around all the time. At games, around the house, on holidays—she is always taking pictures. We may have more photos than any family in America, boxes and boxes of them. In her next life she's going to be in the paparazzi. And she is the same way with video: she films everything. That's her thing, so before my transplant she asked one of the doctors if they would set up a camera and film it. I was so happy she did because I've watched the surgery since then and it's incredible. Just about everyone else I've shown it to cringes and runs at the sight of the blood, the clamps, and the sheer weirdness of watching a surgery on someone they know. Not me. I could cook up some popcorn and watch it all day. You ought to see it on my big-screen plasma.

The best part was when they were waiting to see if the kidney would work. The video shows that when Jason's kidney went into my body, it was a grayish-blue color. But when they attached it to the artery, it began turning bright pink as it filled up with blood. It's unbelievable to see. Then they attached the ureter and waited for my body to produce urine. If it did, they'd know the transplant had worked. If not, there was trouble. They had a bag on the floor. So they waited and waited. They wouldn't stitch me back up until it finally happened.

When I got out of the operation and was placed in post-op, Dr. Appel came over to take a look and when he saw a bag full of urine at the end of my catheter, he knew things were promising. Once I began to wake up, he sighed and thought, *We're out of the woods.*

A few minutes later, they brought me up from the recovery room to my regular room. It was there I shed my first tears in years. I don't even know why. It wasn't the pain; it was just a lot of emotions coming to the fore. So many things had built up heading into that transplant that when I woke up and Dr. Appel told me I was doing fine, the faucet just came on. I couldn't stop. I was like a little kid or something.

Actually, it was like being an infant, because I was in such a helpless state. I really was. I felt incapable of taking care of myself. I just felt so weak. I felt like every ounce of energy in my body had just been drained away from me. All I had the energy for was to open my eyes and talk, and even talking tired me out after a minute or so. I felt weak and helpless as a baby.

Then I looked down at myself. Lying in the bed, I had all these tubes coming out of my arms, wires coming off my chest for the heart-rate monitor, and I saw a catheter coming out of my private area. I could see all these tubes and wires everywhere. Then I looked out the window and it was snowing over the Hudson.

I decided to pray. "God, I'm humble right now. Truly humble." And I thanked him. That's all I could think to do. As bad as this was, I had to remind myself I was one of the lucky ones. I might not have been able to lift my head or roll over, I could hardly manage a smile, but I was still a lucky one.

"God, thank you for the life you have given me. You have given me an incredible life."

I told him that if he gave me an opportunity to get back on my feet, to get myself back, that I would do everything possible to use this experience to lift the lives of others and to help others.

I was in the room by myself at that point and I was actually talking out loud. Words are powerful. And the thing about God—and this is where my faith lies with him—is that I know he put me in that situation for a reason. Maybe it was because he felt that I could handle it. Maybe because he felt that I would do something with it, that I would use it for good. Maybe because I would create some type of change for others. I didn't know what God's plan was, but it pleased me to be in that position because I knew that this was just the beginning. It was a *new* beginning. By going through what I would have to go through, I would be doing God's work. I would help others get through what they would have to get through because I had gone through it, too.

It was fine that I had to endure a great deal of pain and discomfort so that I could enlighten others through my experience. That I was as helpless as an infant right then, so tired that blinking was a chore, was all part of the plan.

Tracy came in soon and we just hugged and I cried some more. It was a very powerful moment for me.

The transplant floor at New York–Presbyterian is an amazing place, with hallways shaped in a giant H and lots of rooms with views of the

Hudson River. Not that I spent much time admiring the scenery. In the days before Christmas, everyone in that hall just wanted to get discharged in time to go home for the holidays.

I was lying there, trying to recover the day after the surgery, when the doctor came in and told me that I had to get up and move. I was in a lot of pain, a lot of excruciating pain. And that was just while lying there. The thought of even sitting up seemed impossible. I have a high pain tolerance, but this was a whole new level. I had just woken up and I looked at him like he was crazy. Just the day before I had this massive hole in my stomach.

Yep, he was crazy.

"What do you want me to do?"

"You need to get out of bed and walk."

"Walk where? Man, I'm in pain."

"Well, you can't lie in bed all day. You have to get up and you have to promote some circulation. We've got to get you moving."

"Man, I am in pain," I said.

"That's all right. Walk slow. Just stand up and inch along."

So that's what I did. This guy wasn't going to let up, so I somehow hauled myself up on my feet, fought through the pain, and walked. Slowly. Very slowly. I had an IV in this arm, an IV in that arm. I had heart wires sticking out of me and I had this device connected to me with a transmitter into a machine in the hospital. It allowed the nurses to keep an eye on everyone who had a heart monitor on. You could see all of them on a screen and you could see the rooms that they were in. And then I had a catheter. All of this, and he's asking me to walk.

It turns out that walk just continued the change I was feeling in my life, because that walk gave me *perspective*. I got out into the hallway and was pushing all these poles along. I wasn't even really walking. I was just shuffling along like the little old man on the Benny Hill show. I was in so much pain all I could do was shuffle, shuffle, shuffle. Out in the hallway I kept telling everyone to stay away from me as I walked because I was scared someone was going to get caught up on one of my wires or, worse, the catheter.

So I pushed these poles and my IVs as I inched down the hall. I wasn't feeling very good about myself. In my mind this was unfair and difficult and Dr. Hardy was wrong to make me walk. I was allowing my-self to wallow in a little bit of pity.

Then I walked by a room, real slow, and I looked in and I saw this teenage boy in there with his parents. Right then my nurse, Mary Jane Samuels, mentioned to me that this fifteen-year-old boy hadn't just had a kidney transplant, but a heart transplant also.

"Both?"

"Yeah, both," she said.

I stopped. This hit me hard. A heart transplant *and* a kidney trans-plant. That changed my mood in a hurry. I knew that *Wow, I'm going to be okay. I'm going to be all right. But what about this kid?* I mean, I'm *so* fortunate. Why should I be worried about myself when there's so many other people out here that have it a whole lot worse than I do?

At worst, I was going to stay about five days. This kid was in for a lot longer than that, in these little rooms with snow falling outside and no chance to go home for the holidays. His parents were worried sick. The kid hadn't even got a chance to live yet. I thought back to when I was fifteen and then tried to imagine not having all of the experiences be-tween that point and now.

There were all these other individuals too, incredible people. There was a woman who was in there for two months for a lung transplant. Tracy had extended conversations with her. I met her and thought, *She's in this hospital for two months. I'm here for five days and I'm itch-ing to get out, feeling bad for myself. Two months?* I just couldn't imag-ine.

All of these people would gladly have switched places with me since I *only* had a kidney transplant. I just thanked God. My prognosis was good. My body hadn't rejected Jason's kidney. Things could be a whole lot worse.

In that hospital, in that transplant hall, there are just so many dif-ferent experiences. It's very emotional; the *range* of emotions is incred-ible. And those things strengthened my commitment to God, to Christ, and bringing him into my life.

It was very powerful and I don't believe it was an accident that Dr. Hardy made me get out and meet those other patients. If it was up to me, I wouldn't have left my room, but those slow shuffles through the transplant ward changed me.

I was also blessed in my nurse, Mary Jane Samuels. She's a middle-aged woman and a mother herself who projects a motherly demeanor to all her patients. She was very caring, concerned, professional, and knowledgeable about transplant patients and what was needed in order for them to get through and live their lives comfortably and productively. She knew pretty much everything the doctors knew. She was also very funny and kept me laughing as much as I could. There were times I thought my stitches would come out.

Sometimes progress was measured by the littlest thing. The doctors told me I couldn't leave the hospital until I had a bowel movement. I wanted out, but it wasn't happening. I sat there thinking, *I haven't gone in a couple of days.*

After surgery, the pain medicine makes you constipated. On top of all that, during the surgery they moved my organs around. But organs aren't made to be moved around. They're not made to be actually pulled up, picked up, and moved. They're in a place for a reason. Pushing my organs around like that affected my digestive system. It made me even more constipated.

Now they were telling me they wouldn't let me out of the hospital until I had a movement. This made me obsess about having one. Then Jason has his movement before me.

"Aw, man. You had it already?"

Coop just laughed. He was bragging about it and everything. I had to come up with a plan. I was so jealous. So then I talked to my mom about it and she gave me some advice. I was sure I was constipated as an infant, and my mom had needed to find a way to release the hounds. I asked my friend and security guy Tony Thompson, who was with me, to do me a favor.

"Tony, we've got to do something about this. My mom said I need to go and get some prune juice."

He just laughed. "Man, you ain't going to drink no prune juice!"

"My mom said that would do it—come on, go and get some prune juice, man."

My mom was back at our house in Tenafly and it was snowing out, so she couldn't bring any over. That's why Tony needed to go out and get it. It was freezing. He wasn't too happy, but he wandered around Manhattan until he found someone selling prune juice.

Now, I hate the taste of prune juice. I took one look at it and I couldn't do it, I couldn't stomach it. So I decided to avoid it for a second. I just set it on this radiator that I had blasting in my room. But I wasn't thinking. As the prune juice sat there it got real warm. When I finally decided to drink it, I was like, "Oh, this is even worse than normal, it's not even cold juice." So I just took it like a big shot, I just took it all down in one gulp. It was terrible. Warm prune juice.

Tony and I started to get into a real deep conversation about life. These are the things you talk about after a transplant—all of a sudden you can talk about anything to anyone. There are no barriers anymore. After you go through that, you don't worry about being politically correct or waiting for the polite time to start a conversation. You just go for it.

We were talking when I suddenly felt like somebody stuck me in the stomach with a cattle prod. I just stopped. This was an incredible amount of pressure. This was a couple of hours after the prune juice and I needed to get to the bathroom in a hurry. But I couldn't move that fast because I'd just had the surgery. When I tried to move too fast the pain was excruciating. I had to move very, very slowly. So I'm trying to get out of the bed and Tony is thinking something is really wrong. He's like, "What's wrong, you all right? You all right?"

"I've got to get to the bathroom."

When I finally made it in there, he started laughing; he's outside just cracking up. I got in there and it works and I scream to Tony, "Yay, I did it! In the bathroom!" Like it was the moment of a lifetime, like I had just won the NBA Championship. I had had my movement and I was excited. A couple days later, they let me out.

Not that I felt all that great. I was still so weak I could barely walk or even stand. I hurt and was very tired. There is nothing you can do but wait for your injuries to heal and for your body to get some rest. There are about 15,000 kidney transplants in America each year, which means a lot of people know of someone who has had one and survived—even if it is just someone like me that they know from the NBA. So in a way, the procedure doesn't seem like such a big deal; it is just a routine thing. Our doctors are so good they make it seem like nothing. Well, the doctors may do a transplant every day, but the patient only has one, and it isn't routine to us. It's a brutal procedure.

When we were finally released, Jason and I held a press conference in the downstairs level of the hospital. There was a lot of media there and I tried to use the time to thank my doctors and nurses, all the fans who had written and prayed for me and, of course, to promote awareness of kidney disease. In terms of my health, my recovery, and my possible return to the NBA, there wasn't much to say. There was no way to know what was possible. Jason's kidney was working well but he wasn't safe either. Complications could hit either of us.

We were leaving the hospital, but we weren't yet well. In a lot of ways, the hard part was still to come.

The lasting memory of that press conference came in the form of a great picture taken of Jason and me looking at each other that ran on the cover of the New York *Post*. I saved it and have it hanging in my house. It's a special memory for me.

I'm not sure I can ever express my gratitude to Jason. He's the reason I can function. That's the cold reality. People forget, but if it wasn't for that man I am not living the life I am living.

I wouldn't have become such great friends with him either.

He was so gracious to sacrifice to save my life. I cannot repay him. I just cannot. He never asks for anything, never says anything but that it was no big thing. But I know it was. I know the truth with that. Jason didn't just give me a kidney. He didn't just give me my life back, or the chance to play basketball again, or the ability to be healthy for my wife and children. He gave me a real lesson in the value of *giving*. His sacrifice saved my life and created a true, lifelong friendship. And by witnessing his sacrifice firsthand, I changed a little myself. I became a better person.

Much better.

10

SURVIVORSHIP

Pastor Willie Alfonso is a former homeless, illiterate drug addict from Brooklyn who found religion, turned his life around, and today is the team chaplain for the New Jersey Nets and the New York Yankees. When you've traveled out of that hole to find sobriety, meaningful employment, and a beautiful wife and family, you don't give up easily.

So Pastor Willie was undeterred the first time he met the new addition to the Nets, Alonzo Mourning. That was back in 2003.

"He wasn't a very talkative person unless he knew you," Alfonso said. "I would go over to him in the locker room and say hi and he'd kind of just look at me and kind of grunt a little bit. He wouldn't say very much.

"He wasn't being disrespectful. A lot of athletes are very private. They don't let anyone into their world. And I understand why: so many people are trying to get something from these guys. So I understand that and I respect that."

Even as Alonzo faced the transplant, the two remained distant. Then, the day after the surgery, Pastor Willie decided to drive over to New York–Presbyterian to visit. He wasn't sure he could even get in the door, and if he did, he anticipated another brief, hurried conversation.

Still, he tried. What he found was a smiling Alonzo, ready to pray with him. Then he found even more.

"As I was about to leave, I asked him this question. I said, 'Zo, what are you going to do with God? Where do you stand with God?' "

Alonzo paused and considered the question. He was a man of faith, a very spiritual person, and he had leaned on God so many times over the past few years. It wasn't that this was foreign to him, but, truth be told, here flat out on a hospital bed, there could be no glossing it over. He was close with God, but not nearly as close as he should have been. This was a moment to lay it all out there. This was a moment for clarity and honesty.

"You know Pastor Willie, I've done so many things, I don't know where I stand with God or whether God would even embrace me."

Pastor Willie decided to flip it around.

"Let me share with you what I've done and where I've been and let's see if that compares with what you've done."

He went on to tell Zo the story of his life, all the dirt, all the disappointment. If Pastor Willie could now walk with God, then who couldn't?

Alonzo agreed. The two prayed and there in that bed, one day after life-saving surgery, Alonzo reaffirmed his life's commitment to Christ. He wasn't officially "born again" but the result was similar.

"You know, the walk with God is a very tough walk," Alonzo said. "It really is. And the reason it is, is because there are so many obstacles and so many things that deter you from thinking about God's word that you sort of get off the path. It doesn't mean you suddenly become a bad person, but you aren't as close to God as you should be. You aren't consistent with it.

"To this day I have to work to be consistent with it. It isn't always easy. But I know I have to continue to try and to do certain things because I made that commitment to God in that hospital bed."

My body did not reject Jason's kidney. That was the good news. Everything appeared to be working and both of us were able to go home for the holidays. Technically, the transplant was a success. Technically, I was "well."

But in reality, the doctors reminded me there was a 30 percent chance of failure. Either my body could reject the kidney, or the focal sclerosis could return. That 30 percent chance of failure wasn't just hanging over me on the day I went home, or the day after, or the week after that—but every single day for the rest of my life.

Thirty percent?

It's considered fairly good to shoot 30 percent from a 3-point range in the NBA. Now doctors were telling me that those were my chances of rejecting the kidney and going back to square one. It's the devastating reality that every kidney transplant survivor deals with. Emotionally, it is very difficult to handle. We build this procedure up to be the one that will cure us and save our lives. Unlike chemotherapy or heart surgery, we even bring someone else in on it, often someone close to us, and alter their life forever.

But even if we do everything right, even if the doctors do all they can, there is no guarantee that a transplant will work. In fact, almost one out of three of us are just buying time, whether it is a week, a month, or a few years. And when something goes wrong, so many people can't understand why. I've seen so many people, especially little kids and their parents, crushed by this turn of events.

So no one who's had a transplant knows where they stand. Are we cured or are we sick? What do we tell people when they ask, people who understandably just want to hear something positive? When we were healthy, how would we have felt knowing there was a 30 percent chance today was the day we'd have major organ failure? That would have scared me to death; now it is my everyday reality.

How do you go on living like that? How do you plan? Do you risk being too far from hospitals? Can you really live your life the same old way? People say, carpe diem, seize the day, live like there is no tomorrow. But what does that mean? Does it mean you stop working, you give up on serious pursuits, you don't save or build for the future? None of that would make sense.

These are the questions every transplant survivor deals with. The doctors can explain every detail of what will happen when we are under anesthesia. But no one can tell us what will happen once we wake up.

The truth is, we shouldn't live our life the same old way. We should live life better, which isn't the same as living it frivolously. Every one of us has certain things we wish we could change about our behavior. Some of them are big things. Some of them are just little things. It could be eliminating alcohol from our life. It could be taking time to walk the dog. It doesn't matter what it is, we all have something. Many things even.

This, your second life so to speak, is the time to try to change your life for the better.

Your life is dictated by the actions and decisions you make. For me, the changes were focused on two main aspects: the physical and the spiritual. For both, the road was longer than I would have thought.

Coming home was difficult. I thought it would be a positive, a big step toward recovery. But the process is slow, and even a big step doesn't seem like much when you're so far down. Jason came to stay at my house and the two of us were miserable together.

When I got home I couldn't sleep. Not only did I struggle to nap during the day, I couldn't even sleep through the night, no matter how exhausted I was. I just couldn't get any rest at all, which quickly catches up to you. The medication they had me on made me so restless that I was getting up really early, around four in the morning, not falling back to sleep until late at night, and then repeating the cycle again the next day. Pretty soon the recovery made me feel as bad as the surgery.

One of the biggest struggles was the medications. The prednisone they had me on was something my body didn't handle well. And what my body was going through from the actual surgery was quite painful. I had a twelve-inch gash in my lower abdomen. Sitting, bending . . . just about anything involving movement made it feel like I was being stabbed with a big knife.

Then there were my internal injuries. I was grateful that Dr. Hardy had found a way to fit Jason's kidney in, but the process was not fun. He had had to move my organs around; the push and pull was just very unnatural. When they fit my new kidney in, they weren't able to put the muscles and organs back in their exact original positions before they closed me up. So they created a lot of open space that wasn't there before. When the body has open spaces inside of it, as I suddenly had in great quantities, it automatically sends fluid to those spaces to fill them up.

So now I had all this fluid filling up these new gaps. That made me incredibly bloated. I felt full all day long; I could never get rid of that feeling. The doctors took an MRI of my stomach and showed me what was happening to me. In an MRI the fluid-filled areas show up black. All those black spaces in my abdomen were one of the weirdest things I saw through the entire process.

The cure for the bloating was one of the most uncomfortable things imaginable. They ran a tube through my stomach to drain the fluid out into a bag. I had to walk around with that bag for about ten days.

On top of that, I was taking these medicines that were no joke. They were very toxic, very strong, and it took a while for my body to adapt to them. Eventually I did, and I think my high tolerance for pain helped in the recovery. The beginning was horrible, though. There were days when I struggled to do anything but lie there in discomfort. I didn't want to move at all, even though I knew it was essential to my recovery that I keep moving.

The one thing recovery did offer was time to contemplate life. And I spent a great deal of my recovery doing just that. I had always been a health nut and I had become somewhat fanatical after I was first diagnosed, but I knew that there had to be a way to be even more diligent. While drastic changes weren't necessary for me, since I'd been a professional athlete, I know that's not the case for so many of the kidney transplant survivors I've met through my work with the National Kidney Foundation.

I can't put it any simpler than the old saying, "You are what you eat." Whatever you put into your body, your body has to process it— and the worse the food is, the more difficult it can be to do so. Often we make our bodies work extra hard to process food that offers little nutrition and actually has long-term repercussions. So what tastes good isn't always good for you long-term.

Your mind and your taste buds often have different agendas. You have to ignore your taste buds even before you stick food into your mouth. Your taste buds are telling you why this is going to be really good. But you have to use your mind to think about your body processing the food, to think about your cholesterol and blood pressure going up, your arteries being clogged.

After the transplant, I wanted my body to conserve energy and only deal with the most important tasks, namely making sure my kidney worked and getting me back on the basketball court. So now I don't eat junk—I think *There is no way I'm putting that in my mouth. I know what effect it will have on my body.*

You can't just assume you'll avoid health troubles. You can't just pretend that you are able to eat junk and mistreat your body, that if you don't commit to exercise and good eating nothing bad will happen to you. When it comes to your health, you can't rely on being a good parent, or a good worker, or even a holy and moral servant of God. That isn't how it works. You have to become an active participant with your health. It doesn't just happen.

Sometimes the entire thing seems unfair, because you say, "Why me?" I understand those feelings very well. I see all these other people doing worse than I did—eating worse, acting worse—yet I got sick. As much as I tried to maintain a positive attitude toward my disease, and I think for the most part I did a pretty good job, I was like everyone else. There were days I got very low and asked God, *Why?*

One day a college teammate, Mark Tillman, called me up and recommended I read a book that reminded him of me, *Why Christians Get Sick*, by George Malkmus.

I went and got it and now I buy it by the dozens and give it out to everyone. It's about a pastor who had cancer. His illness led him to look into the health of his colleagues, other pastors, and he began to realize that some got sick while others lived long lives and died of natural causes. He tried to analyze why and realized it pretty much came down to their lifestyle, their nutritional lifestyle. God, he said, made the human body perfect—but we pollute it. I know this isn't always the case with illness, especially with sick children, but for most adults his views are very applicable.

What the pastor in the book did was totally revamp his nutritional regimen. And he healed himself. He got rid of his allergies. He had a body odor; he got rid of that. He got rid of the cancer itself. It's an eye-opening book. It shows how *you* can control your health. I wasn't going to go that drastic and adopt this huge, strict diet where I'm a vegetarian and everything. I couldn't do that because I've got to have some type of meat, some chicken or some fish. But if I scaled my bad eating habits down some and then incorporated a balance of physical fitness in my life, I knew that it would help me. And it *has* definitely helped me. I can feel the difference.

If nothing else, the days after a transplant are a time to reexamine every aspect of your life. It is a second chance, even with the 30 percent possibility of failure hanging out there, and we need to make the most of it.

Even Coop took an inventory of his life. The transplant enabled him to understand that, yeah, "I need to start doing a better job taking care of my body, too. I need to focus on my health." That's one of the things that happens in transplantation—it makes even the donors understand that they have to take better care of themselves.

Coop went so far as to refocus on his own future. Since the transplant he's gone back to school and gotten promoted at his job. He's found ways to make donating a kidney a life-altering experience too, improving not just my life but his own as well. He's realized that if you don't make something like that a positive, then it is a wasted opportunity in life.

Spiritually I faced an even more difficult and personal journey. In some ways, it was more painful than the physical recovery.

I'm a faith-based person and have been my entire life. Regardless of the scenario, I've always believed my faith in God would take me through whatever obstacle I was confronted with. That belief is what carried me through my illness.

Jason (top right) and I have grown into true friends. He is quite a character.

Faith is an invitation to honesty. To confront honesty in the presence of the Lord is to face it in a way that no other experience can provide. When you are humble enough to be completely honest with yourself and the Lord, it is a valuable opportunity to account for the difference between what you say and what you truly believe.

It is human nature to be inconsistent. It doesn't matter what it is you are trying to be consistent at; eventually, you veer off, or step back, even just a little. That is just how people are. You're going down one path and eventually, if only for a moment, you forget. You forget and you stop doing the things that are beneficial to you. Or maybe you don't forget but you decide that going in a different direction might be good for a while. You have to be reminded. You have to have people remind you.

A person's relationship with God is no different. It is easy to speak about doing God's work, but it is difficult to actually do it. In fact, many of the people who speak loudest about God are the ones doing the exact opposite of his will. Organized religion, or more specifically, some leaders of organized religion, have turned many people away from God. People see bad people misusing God's word and they have a negative reaction to it. I'm no different. Some faith-based people are the most evil people in the entire world. We have people waging wars based on faith. But who are we to judge that? There is only one judge. You can only pray for those people, ask God to forgive them, and move on. You can't allow them to keep you from having the best possible relationship with God. You can't let them stop you or cause harm to you. You can't let someone else dictate your life.

When I was in that hospital bed after surgery, as helpless and as humble and as exposed as a grown man possibly can be, I enjoyed a connection with God that was more personal and honest than ever before.

When Pastor Willie showed up in my hospital room and asked me what I was going to do about God, it hit me in a way that no question ever had. I don't believe in coincidences. I don't believe it was a coincidence that I signed with the New Jersey Nets and not some other team. I don't believe it was a coincidence that the team chaplain was Willie Alfonso. And I don't believe it was a coincidence that, even though he expected me to brush him off the day after my transplant, something drove him to go to the hospital and give me another chance.

I had been close with God for years. But there is close and there is *close*. It is one thing to walk with God and another to walk hand in hand with God. It wasn't that I was a bad person who needed a drastic change in my life or my lifestyle. It was like eating healthy. I could do a little better. I could be closer with God. I could be more honest with God. Sometimes just doing a little better makes all the difference.

Pastor Willie was a Hispanic man, fifty years old at the time of my operation. I knew almost nothing about him when I expressed some reservations about whether God would even want me to be close with Him. I had not been a perfect person. I was being as honest and as raw as I could. That's when he told me his story.

He grew up in Bed-Stuy, Brooklyn, one of the toughest neighborhoods in America. His parents abandoned him at the age of ten, and he was left homeless and working the streets for himself, scavenging for food and shelter. He didn't attend school and soon fell into drugs, becoming a degenerate addict. At the age of twenty-seven, he was illiterate, on drugs, and had no family, no real friends, and very little hope. He was the guy under the bridge, so far gone that when you look at him as you drive by you wonder how a person could get so low and if there is even a way to help him.

Pastor Willie eventually owed so many drug dealers so much money that staying in Brooklyn was no longer safe. They were all out to kill him. So in 1981 he fled to Staten Island, joking now that since there are so few Hispanics on Staten Island, no drug dealer would think to go to look for him there.

On Staten Island, Willie met a man named Arnold Lang. He was a white man who tried to talk to Willie and tell him about the power of God. Willie would have none of it. He'd say, "You're crazy" or "That's for white people" or "Where was your God when I was eating out of garbage cans? Where was your God when I had to live in abandoned buildings?"

But Arnold Lang was persistent and eventually he talked Willie into attending church. Something clicked once Willie got there. He kept going back. Soon a retired teacher who belonged to the church started tutoring him, teaching him how to read and write. Over time Willie got clean and sober, got a job, gave his life to God, and became an ordained minister. Today, besides being the chaplain of both the Nets and the Yankees, he is also an administrator for a program that reaches out to inner-city kids who are going through the same bad experiences that he did. He has chosen to go back into the depths of American society, where he works to save the kind of homeless drug addicts he once was.

Hearing this amazing man's journey, how could I feel bad about myself or my plight or the length of my recovery? How could I have doubts when he had returned from such a dark place to walk with God? Pastor Willie assured me that whatever I had done to cause me to question whether God would accept me was nothing compared to what he had done. And, really, none of that stuff even mattered. Because it wasn't a matter of God accepting me, but of me accepting God.

As Pastor Willie and I prayed together, it just refocused me. I hadn't been a bad person, but I just took too much for granted every day. At that point in my life, I wouldn't say I felt *entitlement,* because I was always grateful, but at the same time I had forgotten how blessed I was . . . regardless of the current scenario. I was *so* blessed. Despite being so sick that I couldn't sit up, I still had doctors around me, people around me who cared.

There are people who go through what I went through, who battle kidney disease, who wait on lists, who struggle with medications, who don't have the hope, don't have the strength, don't have the support that I did. When you think of that you gain an entirely new perspective.

I think it was faith that led me to the mind-set I needed to heal my body. Faith enabled me to get back to putting my priorities in order and overcoming my doubts. Putting Christ first gave me the strength to handle that situation.

Pastor Willie is a God-fearing man who walks with the Lord. Not only does he talk it, he *walks* it. Whatever he does in life, he walks it. Every person on the face of this earth has to realize there is a reason they are here. We all have an obligation to touch someone else's life in a positive way. You are supposed to do that. I believe God put me through some rough situations so that I could have a positive effect on people's lives.

I'm not some saint. I still make mistakes. It's not easy to walk as close to God as I promised I would in that hospital bed. But I understand there is always another chance to try better. I understand my purpose here, and I genuinely believe that God has blessed me to get through those particular scenarios and obstacles for a reason.

As Pastor Willie and I grew close, he started coming over to the house to visit Jason and me. One day, he said: "Zo, you've got a lot of work to do and it's not anything that has to do with basketball. God has such a plan for you, but you have to have faith and you have to put the ego down. I don't expect you to do what I do, I don't expect you to go out and preach and all of that, but I expect you to walk using the Lord's word as your strength."

So we laid out a plan for me to redouble my efforts to serve God and help people. I recommitted to my work with the National Kidney

Foundation, not just raising money and awareness, but personal, hands-on work. I recommitted to raising money through Zo's Fund for Life and using my charity work to have very personal relationships with sick children, the ones who don't have the adult perspective that makes understanding this entire circumstance easier.

And I recommitted myself to simply treating people better on an everyday basis. The truth was, I had again gotten too guarded, too protective, too callous. Whether it was a simple smile or a hello, there were ways I could brighten someone's day. It wasn't right for me to be the scowling Zo off the court. During the game was one thing, since that was business. But off the court, I needed to be a better person to all.

One day Pastor Willie and I were praying. I was still in a lot of pain and not physically active. "God, if you get me back on my feet, as long as I am breathing I am going to continue to do what I can to do your work and help as many people as possible whether it be through my philanthropic works or just by in general encouraging people to try to change their lives in a way that might help them," I said. "Either way, I am going to reach out."

Pastor Willie said it was during this time that I was able to transfer what I believed in my mind into what I believed in my heart. It isn't something you can see from the outside or even explain to others, but it is something you can feel. Every person can feel it when it happens. There is an eighteen-inch difference between your mind and your heart, but it can take a long, long time to make that transfer. God's word says that the first thing He looks at is a person's heart, because you can't fool anyone with what is in there. I had always believed in my mind I was accepting Christ in my life. And at a certain level I was. But the eighteen-inch change that happened for me really made a difference.

I can feel it each and every day, even when I feel I'm being inconsistent.

I spent those first weeks learning again about my relationship with God and recommitting myself to physical well-being and trying to make it through some very long, tough days. One of the blessings I had was Jason Cooper. He stayed at my house, where we were able to connect and bond. I looked at him and said, "Wow, this man saved my life. This person stepped up to the plate," and I say that to myself every time I see him.

Jason, of course, didn't want anything in return. He didn't want anyone to make a fuss over him. When we first got back to my house he kept saying he could leave.

"Look, I don't want to intrude. I can stay at my place in the city. I can get a friend of mine to come over and take care of me."

"What, are you kidding me?" I said. "C'mon, man. You're staying right here. And you're going to have home-cooked meals and all that stuff. So you don't have to worry about anything. You're not intruding. You just gave me a damn kidney. You just saved my life. What're you talking about intruding?"

He kept talking that way until I finally told him that he sounded like I had probably sounded when I kept asking him if he wanted to bail on the transplant. After that, he got the point and relaxed.

Coop is a special person and now that he was in my life again, I never wanted to loose touch with him. He was like a new brother for me. We did things that family members would do. We played a lot of competitive games of chess. We played Scrabble. We laughed as much as our scars would allow. And we tried to support each other.

The process of recovery was slow for both of us, but I started feeling a lot better sooner than he did, which is a tough thing to experience. It didn't seem fair. Jason had to go back to the hospital a couple of times for minor problems after the transplant. He eventually recovered, but I felt very guilty over every pang of pain he dealt with.

As the weeks rolled on though, the days got easier. My mind got clearer and my heart was filled. I tell people now that having a kidney transplant was one of the best things to ever happen to me, and they think I'm crazy. I tell them if I could go back in time and rewrite history I still wouldn't change a thing, and they think I'm delirious.

But God had a plan for me and, as strange as it may sound, I believe this plan included focal glomerulosclerosis. I didn't understand it at the time. I didn't recognize the plan when it first happened. It was the same as when He gave me the courage to stand in front of a judge and ask to be put in foster care. It was the same when He put me on that stand at the Rayful Edmond trial. It was the same when He touched me after my fight with Larry Johnson.

I grew from those difficult challenges, and I grew from my transplant. Not just spiritually and physically, not just with a new close friend in my second cousin, but in every way imaginable. Not only did I not reject that kidney, I did not reject the opportunity presented to me.

I am a far better person, a far more Christlike person now than I was before getting sick. Sure, I'm not perfect. There's always room for growth. But I am a better man for all these experiences. I am closer to God, and I am closer to being the man He wants me to be. How isn't that a blessing?

11

THE COMEBACK

Shuichi Take knew that taking Alonzo Mourning from a hospital bed to, perhaps, the NBA was going to be a long, slow process. He wasn't even sure it was possible. He knew Alonzo hadn't worked out for months before his transplant or for six weeks after it. He knew Alonzo had been through a physical ordeal, that he was on medication that fatigued him, and that even baby steps would be a big deal.

He knew it would be a challenge. But how much of a challenge?

Shuichi was twenty-five years old in early 2004, when he was hired to be Alonzo's full-time physical trainer during the most difficult of recoveries. He had packed up his life in Washington, D.C., moved to New Jersey, and was now going to spend each and every day of the week with Alonzo in the small Oxygen Fitness Club in Tenafly.

It was the opportunity of a lifetime and he was excited about it—at least, he was until he had Alonzo pull off his shirt and saw what had once been a picture of physical fitness looking like just a regular old body.

"He used to be ripped and shredded like the anatomy chart," Take said. "Now he had small arms, no abs. It was a surreal moment."

No more surreal then when Alonzo pulled himself up on a treadmill that first day and struggled to even walk, sweating and straining at the meager 3.5 speed. He could barely stand up straight.

Later they tried some weight lifting. Alonzo used to regularly work out with 250 pounds on the bench. This time Shuichi tried just using the bar. Actually, scratch that, a regular weight-lifting bar is forty-five pounds. That was too much. He had to use a bar for women, weak women at that, which weighed just twenty pounds.

Alonzo did twenty reps. Barely.

"He was struggling."

By that time of the morning, locals were coming in for their daily work-outs. Oxygen is a small suburban gym, essentially one room for both weight lifting and cardio. Alonzo might have lost his muscle, but he was still six ten. You weren't going to miss him.

So people looked at him in disbelief. That was Alonzo Mourning, right? They had heard about the kidney transplant—but still, wasn't it only a couple of months ago he was running up and down the court as a New Jersey Net? Can someone get this weak, this fast?

Apparently so. Here was Alonzo, after all, grunting as he tried to curl a twenty-pound dumbbell. Twenty pounds.

"Right then it crossed my mind," said Shuichi, "that this was going to take a while. This was not going to be like an athlete out with a knee injury. This was an entirely different level. This was going to be some serious stuff."

Shuichi almost felt bad about it. He almost wondered if it was going to work. He had faith in his own abilities and the Zo he knew wasn't one to give up, but what about now? Can a guy who used to be able to do everything stay positive when he can hardly do anything? How do you motivate someone in that situation?

But then Shuichi looked at Alonzo's face. After what was undoubtedly the most pathetic workout of his life, his face said it all.

Alonzo Mourning was smiling.

Basketball is a team game. One player cannot win a championship. There are some great players, Hall of Fame players, like Patrick Ewing, Charles Barkley, Karl Malone, and John Stockton, who never won an NBA Championship. I didn't want to join that list. I knew how those players carried around that single regret that no number of all-star appearances or big contracts could ever make go away.

Professionally, the championship became my single-minded pursuit. Not that I hadn't been driven to win a title before, but the transplant created a sense of urgency. I knew my time was limited. In February of 2004, just as I was finishing my initial recovery, I turned thirty-four. That isn't old in life, but it is getting old in basketball. I would have only a few seasons left, a few opportunities to win that championship. I knew, even in the best case, I would not return as the centerpiece of a team. I would have to be a rotation guy, a backup, a specialist. I would have to return to the Nets and give them that push over the hump.

The transplant had eliminated whatever slight bit of complacency I had. There had been too much pain and too much sacrifice for anything less than a championship. And it had to come as soon as possible. I could not wait for next year anymore. Time was too precious and, as I sat there recovering, it was ticking away.

The doctors said I could start working out again six weeks after my surgery. As much pain as I was in, I counted down the days. In week four I called Kevin Maselka, my old trainer with the Charlotte Hornets. He's a guru to athletes and when I was with the Hornets he had really put a lot of weight and muscle on me, a lot of strength. So I trusted him completely. I knew Kevin was too busy to come and personally train me, but I knew he'd recommend someone good.

I told him I was serious about coming back, but I needed a trainer to be just as serious. I needed someone to train me and only me. That person would have to move to New Jersey and work me out as much as seven days a week. I'd pay them well and get them an apartment to live in, but I need something structured.

Kevin sent me Shuichi Take, a Cuban-Japanese trainer whose name was so difficult to pronounce I just called him Squeegee. Shuichi is a great guy and a talented trainer, and I had worked out with him before. I had a lot of faith in him and I put him up in an apartment in Hackensack, got his car shipped up, and made him aware that I was very serious about this. Part of Shuichi's job was to motivate me, to get me up in the morning and drive me down to the gym. I had never needed much of a push before, but I wasn't sure how I would react after the surgery, so I wanted to have someone there waiting for me each morning just in case.

On February 10, 2004, two days after my birthday, Shuichi came by and picked me up. I kissed Tracy and the kids good-bye and said I was going to work. Just as we would every day after that, Shuichi and I went down to the Tenafly Diner for breakfast. I had a bowl of oatmeal. I was a bit nervous and didn't know what to expect. I had always been an elite athlete, and even though I had come back from injuries before, this was totally different.

Shuichi's had a saying he first shared with me that day: "Not back, but beyond." His goal was that when he was done with me, I would be

Myka and me during my recovery

in better shape than I had been when I was healthy and had never heard of creatinine levels. *Not back, but beyond.* He kept repeating it to motivate me. It was just what I needed to hear, I needed a goal, no matter how far off it seemed.

When we got to the gym, Shuichi weighed me and measured my body fat. I was 261 pounds, which wasn't far from my playing weight. And I had 13.2 percent body fat. That's what a normal man would have, somewhere between 12 and 15 percent body fat. But I had always had between 6 and 7 percent, so I had just totally deteriorated; my muscles had just fallen apart. That right there told me how far I had to go.

The next thing Shuichi did was stretch me out. Then I was going to get up on the treadmill and do a slow walk. That's it, just a real slow walk. But first we wanted to stretch out completely, because at this point even a slow walk was a lot. I got down on the floor and Shuichi started stretching me out—and it hurt. I couldn't even do *this* without pain.

Besides the normal pain of coming off a kidney transplant, I had the twelve-inch incision to deal with. Since Dr. Hardy had needed to pull apart my muscles to an almost inhuman distance, the recovery was going to be difficult and painful. Also, to get me back together, Dr. Hardy had used sutures. He warned me that when I started working out, I might feel like I was ripping my insides apart.

"You might feel like you're tearing," Dr. Hardy said. "You might feel like you've got a hernia or something like that, but that's just the sutures that are in you."

It felt like tearing, and it felt like a hernia; and sometimes the pain seemed even worse. No matter the reassurances from Dr. Hardy that I wasn't doing any long-term damage, it was extremely painful. Just lying down and trying to stretch was an incredible challenge. I was about as low as you can be.

This is a universal feeling during recovery, not just for people who have received a transplant, but for cancer survivors, accident victims, and just about anyone who has stared down that long road and wanted to turn around. The first step of the comeback is *so* daunting. You feel like you can't do anything, and you can't imagine ever feeling like your old self again. You wonder how you will ever get back to living a normal life. It is a test of faith. As bleak and as difficult as that moment was, I still had faith. I knew I wouldn't just get back to a normal life. I'd get back to *my* normal life. I was 100 percent convinced I would play in the NBA the following season. Even as I lay there in pain trying to do some light stretching for a slow walk, my faith never wavered.

"Lord," I kept saying to myself, "if I made it this far, I know you've got me the rest of the way."

I talked to God throughout my recovery and it helped. Pastor Willie had brought me very close to God at this point; I had become very spiritual and I did not believe He had given me this disease and put me through what He had put me through for no reason. I was going to spread the word about kidney disease and continue my philanthropic work in South Florida, and the best way to accomplish those things was by returning to the NBA. I believed that if I did the work, if I did my part and came down to Oxygen every day with Shuichi, then He would help me return to the league. To me, getting my mind right was the most important thing. I didn't think my body could get me back on the court unless I believed it would happen.

If you keep your mind strong, the body's going to follow. You have to fix your mind on a goal, do your best to eliminate negativity and distraction from your life, and then proceed. If you focus on that one thing you're trying to be successful at, then there's a strong possibility that it will occur for you. The mental will drag the physical along with it.

Then there is the law of attraction. Whatever you bring into your life is what you will use to generate the energy of your life. If you're a positive, fun-loving, and outgoing person, then you are going to attract those types of people. If you give up, if you surround yourself with doubt, then you will attract negative people, negative energy. Remaining positive, maintaining that faith, was paramount for me because it would help attract the positive people and positive energy to make my recovery happen. I believed God could push me along in my journey, but not if I hung an anchor of negativity around my own neck. I turned it all over to God. I kept on believing God had my back, God had a plan, and God would deliver me to the place He wanted me to get to.

• • •

None of which means it didn't hurt that first day. Bending, stretching, just little things hurt. At one point Shuichi stretched my toes and they hurt. Those first few weeks, any type of exercise would tighten me up and make it even more difficult the next day. It was *pain*, a taxing spasm of pain. But eventually it was like a toothache. You get a toothache and it hurts, but you get accustomed to it until you do something about it, until it gets better. I learned to expect and even covet that pain. Lance Armstrong's autobiography played an influential and inspiring role during my recovery. "Pain is temporary. Quitting lasts forever" was a quote he used that made perfect sense. The pain I was experiencing was there on borrowed time. Soon it would not be a factor, but that time could not come soon enough.

That first day I walked twelve minutes on the treadmill. The speed was 3.5, which is a slow walk, the kind I would've laughed at before my disease. Now I was sweating and struggling like it was the toughest workout ever. It was incredibly hard for me. I had gone from being a world-class athlete to just about dying on a slow treadmill walk. That's when doubt started to creep in. I started thinking, "Why are you doing this to yourself? You are so far from the NBA. It's just a dream that will never happen." But that's where the mental strength came into play. It's natural to doubt. It's natural to fear. But with mental toughness, you keep going anyway. Even though reaching your goal is tougher than you even thought it would be, as long as you remain tougher mentally, then you can do it. "Pain is temporary. Quitting lasts forever" echoed through my mind.

When we got done with the walk, Shuichi had me lift some light weights. I curled with a twenty-pound dumbbell. I used to work out with fifties and sixties. I barely benched anything, just a little more than the bar, which was only forty-five pounds. I used to bench three hundred easily and work out around 250. It was depressing. I was lifting weights like an eight-year-old. And struggling with it. And it hurt.

The whole workout lasted an hour. There were times I used to work out for five, six hours. Shuichi drove me home, and although it had been a very humbling workout, I just wouldn't let myself get down. I sat there and thought, "You know what? This is progress. Forget about what I used to do. Forget about how I used to be an NBA all-star. I didn't do this yesterday. I didn't walk on the treadmill. I didn't lift any weights. I didn't stretch. Today was progress." After a transplant, you have to adjust to a new normal.

Early the next morning, there was Shuichi, all ready to go. We went and had breakfast and then returned to the gym. We stretched every day. We walked every day. We lifted every day. And the gains were slow—really, really slow. But it was exhilarating when we made progress. I'll never forget the day we got the treadmill speed up to 4.0. It was still just a walk, but now it was cause for a big celebration. I felt like I was sprinting. You have to use those little things to motivate you, to keep you coming back to the gym and keep you believing progress is possible. Even the smallest of milestones adds up. Eventually you discover you have made a big gain from where you started.

Dr. Appel stayed in close contact with Shuichi. He told him not to let me run until a certain point, because he knew I would try to push it. My big thing with Shuichi was if he said do ten reps, I'd do eleven. If he said do twenty minutes, I'd do twenty-one. I always wanted to go one past the goal. Because Shuichi and Dr. Appel knew my personality, they worried that I wouldn't maintain a slow recovery. Every day Shuichi would measure my blood pressure before and after each workout. During the exercise he'd keep constant tabs on my heart rate through a monitor. Dr. Appel kept telling Shuichi to be vigilant.

"He might feel good and want to run, but don't let him run until this day right here," Dr. Appel would say. "He might want to walk faster, but keep him at a reduced speed for now. He has to go through stages. He might feel good enough today to want to do a whole lot, but don't let him do a whole lot."

So there was a limit. It was a slow process. But I wasn't in a rush. I was very persistent, but I wasn't in a rush.

I know most people reading this don't make their living with their body. They aren't trying to get back to the NBA, they can't afford a full-time personal trainer, and they may not have the time to not rush. I know I was blessed. In a lot of ways, I had it very easy. But I think everyone needs to look at a transplant or a recovery as a life-changing situation. When you look at a life-changing situation, it's your second opportunity to live. You should seek to do things differently than you did before.

Eat healthier. Eliminate smoking or alcohol. Incorporate an exercise regime. You have to sacrifice. Everyone can do something. You can walk. Just about anyone can walk. Try to walk for five minutes. Try to stretch. Try to make small gains. You don't need a personal trainer or a world-class workout facility to walk. And whatever you do, don't just sit on the couch and feel sorry for yourself. Don't sit and think that you are living on a transplant and you've got to take medications and there is just no chance to ever get back to the person you were before. The fact is, you can get better. On my website, I even had Shuichi detail a complete health and fitness plan for people recovering from a transplant.

You can actually prolong your life, and you can help your kidney function at a much higher level if you do all those things necessary to help yourself through the process. You can wind up healthier than you were before—*not back but beyond*, as Shuichi would say. The kidney can keep you alive, but you have to help it. You can't expect the kidney to do its job if you aren't willing to do your job. Every transplant survivor has had a moment, or many moments, where they said, "I'll do anything to get a new kidney." They may have even prayed about it, telling God they'd do anything for that second chance.

Seeking a better life, a healthier life, is the "anything" they should be doing. One of the hardest things for me to give up was cold beer. I used to love a nice, ice-cold Foster's in a can. I can still taste it. Down in Miami, with all the humidity, a nice cold beer was just great. But I had to give it up. Now I just have a little lemonade and really, I don't miss it. I couldn't expect the kidney to do its part if I wouldn't do mine.

And here is where the transplant can be a blessing. People want you to recover. Your friends and family will try to help you recover. They will be more sensitive to what you need, respectful of what you say. In the past, when my friends came over the house, we'd drink beer. Now I just told them I couldn't. And that was it. Not one of them said, "Oh, come on, man, just have one." The peer pressure is gone. Anyone who says otherwise really isn't your friend. They should be encouraging you to not drink or smoke, to eat right, and to exercise.

If you are surrounded by people who don't eat healthy, use the kidney as a reason to change. Say to them, "We can't order pizza. I need to eat a salad or some fish." Tell your family that you can't eat fast food anymore, that you all have to eat healthier, that you have to buy organic food and prepare healthy, low-fat meals. You have to make meal preparation and exercising a priority. Ask them not to smoke in front of you; try to eliminate that temptation. There is no choice. There is just no choice. You just had a transplant; this is your time to be selfish. You can *wait and hope, or you can go make it happen.* Rebounds and rebounding from illness aren't that different.

For all that you just went through, you can't let someone else dictate the rest of your life.

Every day Shuichi and I would go to the gym and every day I'd try to find something to call progress. It might not be much, but most days there was something to inspire and encourage—the first time I could do a real bench, or when I went up in weight, or just could stretch a little easier. It took almost three months before we were able to actually do some semblance of a real workout. In the beginning, it was about just moving. It was a pre-pre-workout of sorts. Eventually I was lifting a decent amount, doing yoga, and by May we were working out on a nearby track, running sprints. I was still nowhere near where I needed to be, but the progress was wonderful.

In June, we decided to move the operation back to Miami. Shuichi came with me. We left behind Oxygen in Tenafly and started going to a gym in Coconut Grove and another over in South Beach. Now was the time when I needed to get serious. Soon after I got back to Miami, Dr. Appel cleared me to really go for it.

I always wanted to come back and play, even though everyone thought I was crazy. Jeff, my agent, kept asking, "Why push yourself? You already have all the money you need." I talked to Coach Thompson and he said, "Make sure you live to see your children grow old." But deep down they all knew me and they all knew that if there was even a slim chance I could play again, if there was a chance to win an NBA Championship, then I would go for it. The problem was no one could believe that I would be able to expend the same amount of energy post-transplant as I did pre-transplant. It is one thing to live a "normal" life, it is another to run up and down the court and bang with 250- to 300-pound men.

One of the things that concerned the doctors was the possibility of a direct shot to my kidney. I might get back to good enough physical condition to play in the NBA, but the threat of a contusion to the area around my kidney was not a thing to take lightly. The kidney is protected by a lot of tissue—it's pretty deep in your body—but the guys who play in the NBA are big, strong guys. When you're playing in the NBA, you get kicked, kneed, elbowed. Most of it isn't on purpose. In the game of basketball, you are going to bump into each other, and when the person you bump into is seven feet tall and weighs 250–260 pounds, things happen. Any one shot might damage the kidney. I was going to wear a piece of protective equipment to help, but it wasn't foolproof. Who really knew what could happen? Was I really willing to risk a damaged kidney, maybe risk my life, to play basketball again?

If I was, it wasn't going to be without complete preparation. I told Shuichi, "I want to build a layer of armor around my kidney." So we went about building that armor. I wanted to make sure my abs were as strong as possible to help withstand that inevitable elbow. I did so many different ab exercises. I was limited to certain exercises and how many reps of each I could do because we had to be so careful of that kidney. Shuichi had me start off real slow, but as the summer went on we kept going and going. We'd work out multiple times a day. I couldn't get enough. Sometimes, late at night, Shuichi and I would go down to Peacock Park, where he would use a long tape measure to mark off the length of a basketball court and I'd run sprints end-to-end with the Florida moon shining down upon me.

By August and September, I was getting back to where I had been before the transplant. Shuichi is a workout fiend too. He is in very good condition and for a long time he worked out right alongside me. Whatever I did, he did. But as we got into the late summer, I was able to leave him behind. I was beginning to work out like an elite athlete again.

The entire eight months was just incredible, a series of small steps that built into a complete transformation of my body. When I informed the Nets that I was going to be in training camp, everyone was excited. Just before I left for New Jersey, Shuichi weighed me and tested my body fat. I was 266 pounds and had only 6 percent body fat. I had lost thirty-five pounds of fat and replaced it with forty pounds of muscle. I was in the best shape of my life—not game shape yet, but the best shape going into any training camp of my career. My diet was better, I didn't drink alcohol, and I was getting a lot of rest.

Eight months after that first morning, what Shuichi had told me was true. I was not back, but beyond.

12

HOLISTIC MEDICINE

Alec and Ryan O'Toole had just attended a Miami Heat playoff game, gotten a tour of the locker room, and hung out with a star player, so, yes, they wanted to be Alonzo Mourning when they grew up.

As they flew with their mother and stepdad back to their home in Cleveland, the question Alec and Ryan asked each other was how they could be like him right now.

Alec, eight, had a kidney disorder. Ryan, twelve, was his protective older brother. This was May 2005. They had gotten to know Alonzo the previous November, when Alec was facing his second major surgery. The first surgery was supposed to have a 90 percent success rate. Alec was in the other 10 percent. So his mother, Christine, in a fit of desperation and in search of anything positive, decided to e-mail Alonzo care of the New Jersey Nets, where he was still playing.

"I never thought anything would come of it," she said. "I was just being a mother. I was crying while I was writing the e-mail, just trying anything."

Within twenty-four hours, Alonzo's assistant, Shari Rochester, called. Alec's surgery was scheduled for December 8, 2004. The Nets were supposed to play the Cleveland Cavaliers on December 7. Christine hoped maybe Alonzo could wave to Alec on the TV before the game. Instead, he got the family tickets, took Alec into the locker room, and had a private conversation with the little boy over confronting the fear of the next day.

Then he called the hospital after surgery. Then the next day, too, taking time to coach Alec on sitting up in bed and walking to the door and back. "He went over things, step by step," Christine said. "Here was this NBA All-Star motivating my little boy."

It went on and on from there. There were e-mails, calls, advice over issues big and small—what to expect from a doctor, what to say to the kids making fun of his scars.

"It was just so personal," Christine said through tears years later. "It wasn't just 'Get well soon,' which was more than we could have asked. They really talked."

So now, in the spring of 2005, Alonzo had brought the family to Miami for a playoff game and a few days of not thinking about medical charts and blood work. Now these two starstruck boys, seated side by side on the plane, decided they would be like Zo and give something back.

"I saw what Alonzo had done," Alec said a few years later, when he was twelve. "I wanted to do that, too."

If they couldn't play like Zo (yet, they hoped), they could give like him. Alec and Ryan decided to raise money for Zo's Fund for Life by holding a yard sale. The family didn't have enough stuff, of course, but maybe they could ask their neighbors in Cleveland's Westpark neighborhood and people at their church, Our Lady of the Angels.

"They had the entire thing concocted by the time we landed in Cleveland," Christine said.

The boys wrote letters and sent them out. They put a flyer into the church bulletin. They made phone calls, arranged drop-offs and pickups, and publicized the sale. Christine and her husband, John, said they helped only by addressing letters and driving the boys to the post office. "The two of them did this."

The big day came, and so did the crowds. Even local TV covered the

event. They sold everything. These two boys, these two brothers had just be-
come Alonzo Mourning, if not on the court, then off of it.

A couple of days later, the family returned to Miami for the annual Zo's
Summer Groove, a weekend about fun and fund-raising. There the boys from
Ohio walked up to the famous basketball player and handed him a check for
$1,500.

"I can't begin to explain the great things Alonzo Mourning has done for
my family, the genuine kindness he has displayed," Christine said. "But the
greatest gift of all is that he gave my two boys the appreciation of giving
back. That's the greatest gift anyone will ever give my sons."

From the moment I was told I had focal glomerulosclerosis, I became a medical student. Everyone who gets a disease is like that.
One minute, you've never heard of the thing—Tracy used to joke
it wasn't even in spell-check—the next minute, you're poring through
obscure medical papers on the Internet. My intense interest in focal
glomerulosclerosis had expanded into an equal interest in kidney transplants, recovery, and everything else associated with my condition. I almost fell asleep at the computer more times than I can count. It got to
the point where I could have a pretty fair conversation with Dr. Appel
concerning my treatment, which is something I think is very important
for patients of any kind. The doctors will always know more than you,
but there is no rule against trying to catch up.

I was a true believer in the power of modern medicine and Dr.
Appel, and I was convinced that the only way I was ever returning to
the NBA was by following his treatment plan. However, my wife had
some other ideas, too. Practically every night Tracy would tell me
about holistic medicine. I had no idea what she was talking about and
had no interest in finding out. I let her talk, but I wasn't listening. However, Tracy had been seeing a holistic doctor named Kirby Hotchner in
Miami, and she was sure that his approach could help me, too.

Tracy had always been into alternative health care and natural products and the like for her skin and her body. She liked organic food and favored environmentally friendly products. One of her friends had taken her to see Dr. Hotchner and eventually she became a believer. She even brought the kids over there for various ailments.

But, like so many people, I was very, very skeptical. I thought a lot of those people were scam artists, trying to get your money and trying to get you to buy into something that really doesn't have an effect on your body. If this stuff worked, why wouldn't Dr. Appel use it?

In truth, I didn't know anything about it. I was like a lot of people who have been brainwashed to think that the mainstream medical world is the only way. I think my background as an athlete closed my mind even further. We were always treating injuries, so I had a lot of medical experience and, of course, there is this macho mentality of "Just rub some dirt on it" and "No pain, no gain." Besides, since I was already spending all my time trying to learn about traditional approaches to dealing with my disease, I certainly didn't think looking for a new way of treatment was such a bright idea.

So I kept telling Tracy no.

"C'mon," I would tell her. "This is serious stuff. This is life and death."

But if you know my wife, you know that was never going to work. When she sets her mind to something, it is going to happen. So Tracy kept hounding me until finally, just to get her off my back, I agreed to go visit Dr. Hotchner.

I drove over to his office with absolutely no faith that anything he suggested would work. I doubt anyone has ever walked into his office more skeptical of holistic medicine than I did that day. I wasn't going there to achieve wellness, I was going to achieve peace and quiet from my wife. But a couple of things started to make me reconsider. First off, Dr. Hotchner is very serious about what he does. He attended a great school at Washington University in St. Louis. He's very knowledgeable about western medicine but he also studied holistic and natural approaches and, armed with all of the information, chose that route. That eased my fears a little.

Meeting Dr. Hotchner helped also. He is a small man, with a slight build and big glasses, who projects an incredible amount of knowledge. You meet him for one minute and you know he is a wise man, someone with complete command of the subject and confidence in his abilities. So that was intriguing. Then the first thing we did was pray. That Dr. Hotchner was a very spiritual person, a faith-based person, touched me also.

I began to warm up to the idea—at least, until he started the examination. Then I didn't know what to think.

He had an assistant there, and he told me to hold her hand. Then he had the assistant extend her other arm straight out and he placed his hand on her arm. We were a human chain. The assistant's arm was going to serve as some kind of barometer for what was going on. Dr. Hotchner explained the way the examination would work, saying that he would ask me yes-or-no questions about my condition and my subconscious would answer them by sending energy through my body and into the assistant, which he would then be able to read. If there was no resistance on the assistant's arm, then that was a no. And if there was resistance, it was a yes.

It was the weirdest thing I had ever seen. I just looked at this thing like, "How soon can I leave?" But he swore it worked.

He would ask something like, "Should Alonzo take this dosage of this drug." And then he'd claim he got the answer from the assistant's arm. A traditional medical doctor might consult tests and charts and things like that to make a determination and then say, "Hey, you need to be taking X amount of pills." Dr. Hotchner's approach would be to just ask my body. He would ask how much I should take, giving various options and then at the end he'd say, "You know what? Your body only needs one and a half of these pills."

He just kept asking questions and—this was pretty incredible—the answers started to seem accurate. I don't know how to explain why, but they just did. Of course, I was still a little skeptical, but I had come in not believing any of it, and after a little while I started thinking I could see becoming a believer—perhaps because his findings, though strange, were fairly accurate.

Dr. Hotchner was not a big basketball fan before I became a patient. He had been to two Heat games in person and watched maybe parts of a couple more games on television. That was it. He knew my name and nothing else. Living in Miami, he had heard the initial news of my illness and thought, *I could help him with what's going on.* He was very confident that he could assist me, but he had no contact with me and wasn't going to try anything direct. Instead, he said, he "put it out in the universe that I could help him. If it's meant to be, then he'll come and I'll help him." And then every so often, although he didn't know me personally or as a player, he said I would pop into his thoughts and he would send out another message.

"The universe has a way of connecting things," Dr. Hotchner said.

Since I'm someone who does not believe in coincidences and does believe in God's plan, this story made an impact on me. I started to think maybe it was God's plan for me to come here and meet this man and see this crazy arm test happen. I began to think that there had to be some truth in it. I didn't think my wife was just going to bring me to some witch doctor. And Tracy is very intelligent and very in tune with this kind of stuff.

So, I know this sounds crazy, but I began to believe enough to follow what Dr. Hotchner said. I only had one request of him: if I was going to be a patient, he had to become a Heat fan.

Dr. Hotchner started with my blood pressure medications. He thought some of my doses were too high, so he prescribed some alternative medicines to help adjust my blood pressure. If those worked, then I would be able to lower the doses of my regular blood pressure medicine. I decided to give it a try. I was willing to take a chance, take a leap of faith.

I don't believe any one doctor has all the answers. Not Dr. Appel, not Dr. Hotchner. I believe in second and third opinions, multiple consultations, and educating yourself as much as possible. To see a holistic doctor is to get another opinion, only an opinion based on a different perspective and knowledge base. I wanted all the brain power I could get on my case. I can't see how this is anything but positive for a patient. Not all doctors agree with each other.

I told Dr. Appel that I was also seeing Dr. Hotchner. It was critical to be honest with both of them. One reason why Dr. Appel was the perfect doctor for me was that he wasn't threatened by Dr. Hotchner. The same went for Dr. Hotchner. Dr. Appel even went to Dr. Hotchner's office and the two met and discussed my case for a few hours. They do not agree on everything, but Dr. Appel's main feeling was that as long was what Dr. Hotchner prescribed wasn't dangerous, then it was fine.

Dr. Appel believes the FDA should study the treatments of holistic doctors. It's the only way to gain a better understanding of what really works in holistic treatments. In terms of trying some of Dr. Hotchner's suggestions, Dr. Appel was supportive. I was fortunate to have Dr. Appel willing to work under these conditions. I actually think both doctors valued the experience of being able to work with each other.

The holistic approach is very different from traditional medicine. After the transplant, I knew that what I was doing traditionally wasn't necessarily helping me in the long term. I was on high doses of steroids and several prescription medications and I seemed to be getting worse and worse. Subconsciously, that is probably what helped drive me to see Dr. Hotchner in the first place.

When I first started treatment with Dr. Hotchner, I would see him once a week. I never missed a meeting, and it didn't take long before I was really into it. At the start, I was more traditionally indoctrinated about my condition and I had a little trouble with some of the initial procedures and tactics. We had to debate back and forth for a while until he gained my confidence.

In short time—maybe after three visits—I really started to believe in what Dr. Hotchner was doing with me. His treatments were totally nontoxic and compatible with everything that Dr. Appel had me doing. I started feeling better after only a few sessions. Little by little I was able to wean off the "toxic" medicines, and eventually the only prescription medicines I was on were the immunosuppressants and some natural thyroid and natural hormones. I was able to scale back almost all of the prescription medicine, and that was largely due, I believe, to the work of Dr. Hotchner.

Eventually, Dr. Hotchner weaned me off both my blood pressure and cholesterol medicines. I was still taking kidney medicines, but those other drugs had been causing me physical problems. My joints ached because of the blood pressure medicine, but once I replaced the traditional medicine with the natural substances, they felt fine. Now, I felt fine. And Tracy felt fine reminding me I should have listened to her sooner.

Dr. Hotchner gave me a lot of information, and it was overwhelming at first. There were many books and papers to read. But what he was doing—and I don't think I knew it—was training me to "treat" myself.

That's the opposite of traditional medicine, where doctors expect you to just go by what they say. But Dr. Hotchner not only told me what he was going to do, he let me understand the reasons why he was doing it and how it would help me. He wanted me to learn why I was eating the way I was, why I was exercising. He wanted me to be responsible for my own health. This is the mentality all of us should have.

There is a difference between being healthy and masking your symptoms. Too many traditional approaches focus on the latter. Dr. Hotchner is about the former. The solution doesn't come in a pill or a vitamin. That doesn't happen. You can't just open a vitamin bottle or take a drug and become healthy. To really become healthy, you have to change the way you think, what you believe in, your lifestyle, all those things. And that's a process for each of us.

I've been through a tremendous transformation in the five years I've been under Dr. Hotchner's care. Just tremendous. I have a whole new attitude to life. It's like a whole universe opened up to me.

One of my biggest problems was the fact that with my condition, I was *always* tired. Even when I had strength to work out and play basketball, I would get winded so quickly. Dr. Hotchner discovered that a big part of my fatigue was high cholesterol, which was a symptom of low thyroid function. He got me on to some natural thyroid supplements that dramatically boosted my energy. I'm not sure a traditional doctor would have found and solved the problem, rather than just treating the symptom.

It's that kind of thing that really helped build my confidence in the holistic approach and in Dr. Hotchner as a person. I call him at all hours of the day—I've even called him at halftime in a game or during a practice when I had a question. It could be anything from how much of a certain supplement I need to take, to how he would treat an ankle injury that I just sustained. Anything about my body, I like to get his input on.

The same thing goes for my wife and kids—I'll just call Dr. Hotchner to see what he'd do for a cold one of the kids has, or if Tracy is feeling under the weather. I've sent him my mother-in-law, my uncle, friends, and even teammates. Getting an NBA player to go is difficult because a lot of those guys are as closed-minded as I once was. But I've tried anyway. A lot of the guys are doing so much damage with the anti-inflammatories they take. But they don't know they're abusing their bodies, they are just dealing with the symptom of pain. I was the same way. I used to pop anti-inflammatories all day long. But there are alternatives, and if I had been aware of those alternatives when I was younger, I might have been healthier all along.

The American Holistic Health Association explains: "Holistic Health is actually an approach to life. Rather than focusing on illness or specific parts of the body, this ancient approach to health considers the whole person and how he or she interacts with his or her environment. It emphasizes the connection of mind, body, and spirit. The goal is to achieve maximum well-being, where everything is functioning at the highest level possible. With Holistic Health people accept responsibility for their own level of well-being, and everyday choices are used to take charge of one's own health."

I had always been extremely health-conscious. I watched what I ate, I employed a personal chef to cook me proper meals, I mostly avoided red meat, and I obviously worked out a great deal. And after the transplant I was becoming disillusioned with conventional medicine's reliance on the pharmaceutical industry to answer every complication and the continual push of more and more drugs to treat my condition.

I also got into energetic techniques that Dr. Hotchner guided me through in order to balance my flow of energy. Yoga was a part of that practice. It's funny, there is a stigma about yoga—when I tell other players about it, they brush it off. It isn't macho. It isn't a traditional basketball exercise. But yoga is something every player should be doing. It helps with strength, flexibility, and the reduction of injuries. There aren't many sports where yoga makes more sense than basketball. Every team in the NBA and major college basketball should have a yoga instructor on staff. If we are going to have strength coaches, then we should have yoga instructors also. Yoga is the perfect way for players to train and I think in the years to come you will see a great movement toward it with professional basketball players. The stigma will be gone.

The same motivation I have and the same devotion I display toward basketball is the same approach and belief I took in my holistic treatment. I'm an avid learner and now I'm at the point where I can even help others who are taking a similar holistic approach to their recovery. I went from being the most skeptical patient to being an ardent spokesman.

Dr. Hotchner emphasized something I truly believe: God can heal anything, but you've got to believe it. It's your belief that's going make the difference.

He also believes in some basic lifestyle approaches that can pay big dividends. Dr. Hotchner is a proponent of sleep. He demands seven to nine hours a night. People are constantly shortchanging themselves on sleep; in America, it is a badge of honor to not sleep much. But sleep is very important in healing. Dr. Hotchner also talks about "temperance" which means avoiding toxic products: toxic drugs, fluoride in water and toothpaste, chlorine, pesticides. Many of us encounter these by the thousands within the environment. We can't avoid them totally, but we can change to natural products, natural soaps, natural toothpaste.

We can use natural pesticides in our house. We can get rid of the artificial sweeteners and chemicals in our food by eating organic. Even something as simple as getting sunshine into your life can make a difference. I'm able to get a lot of it in Miami, but wherever you are, if you can just get a little bit of sunshine early in the morning or later in the

day you will see benefits. Just fifteen, twenty minutes of sunshine pro-
duces vitamin D. Scientific studies have documented that almost every
single American is low on vitamin D. Doctors have frightened people
so much about getting too much sun that they aren't getting any. But in
small doses, early in the day and late in the day, the sun is beneficial.

Dr. Hotchner is a man of great sense. He focuses patients on doing
the small, everyday things to make them better. A lot of the changes
aren't flashy—a change in diet, exercising, drinking enough water, getting enough sleep, working on stress control—but they make sense.
They are all things that we know we should do, but usually don't have
the time or attention span necessary to do. As he says all the time, "It's
really what the patient does that determines whether they get better or
not."

I had to go in fully, or the treatment wouldn't work. I put my full
faith in Dr. Hotchner and I know that's why I got the results I did.

Not surprisingly, Dr. Hotchner is a very busy man. His practice in
Miami is overwhelmed with patients, and people from all over the
world fly in to see him. He is a genius. I know that I was blessed to have
become his patient; it is one of the benefits of being a famous basketball player with financial resources. I've had the opportunity to get the
best health care in the world. But kidney disease does not care about
your socioeconomic status; it strikes people everywhere, including
places where finding a holistic doctor is not so easy.

So while I encourage everyone to find their own doctor, I asked Dr.
Hotchner to provide a basic rundown of how he would treat a regular
patient walking in off the street. I asked him to go through the whole
process, be as specific as possible, and hopefully offer a different opinion to consider.

"The first thing my patients need to know is that I am a licensed
physician. I went to undergrad at Washington University and then to
the College of Osteopathic Medicine and Surgery in Des Moines,
Iowa. At an early age, around sixteen or so, I picked up a book that my
parents had. It was on yoga, and it talked about yoga and meditation
and a vegetarian diet. The next day, I started doing yoga myself, I became a vegetarian, and I started meditating. I became a certified yoga

instructor. I became a certified meditation instructor. Ever since then, I've continued all those things. I started developing a strong interest in nutrition, the natural therapies.

"When I was twelve years old, I decided I wanted to become a doctor, and I knew well before I went to medical school that I was going to do natural therapies. When I was in medical school, I spent time on my electives training in homeopathy, manipulation, nutrition.

"When I started in the early 1980s, there was almost nobody doing this. There were a handful of people around, but basically, they were being ridiculed by everybody. I was ridiculed by my classmates in medical school and even when I moved to Miami and I was a professor at a local university, for about seven, eight years, I had the same problems. Other faculty didn't like the way I practiced medicine. It was a very conservative group. That's why eventually, in 1998, I went into full-time private practice, so I could do my own thing.

"The fact is, I'm going to help people. And people get better and feel better, and there's a huge demand for this. I'm not going to go back to the conventional way because I know it doesn't help people. Very few people are helped by conventional doctors in cases of chronic, degenerative diseases. Conventional medicine has so little to offer people with those afflictions. Its forte is in acute disease care—with infectious disease, or in cases of severe trauma or surgery. Medicine really shines in those areas. But in the areas of prevention and the treatment of chronic disease, it has very little to offer. So I had to learn all these things that I was most interested in on my own, outside of medical school.

"I spend at least an hour with every patient during our initial appointment. I do a really complete history and a physical exam, and I ask a lot of background questions. Then we do something that's pretty unusual. I have a way of checking energetically through muscle testing, which is a way of sort of tuning in to the patient's body. It's a lie detector test of sorts. Over the years, I've developed a way to do the same kind of thing by asking yes-or-no questions, and I have an assistant who is trained in the method. A patient holds the arm of my assistant, who then holds out her arm. The patient's muscles control the autonomic nervous system, just as in a lie detector test. And by putting a true-or-false query to a person, I can get a change in the muscle strength depending on the answer. We've developed it to quite an art, where it's somewhere between 90 and 94 percent accurate. So I tune in to the person's system and just ask what's going on, what does the person need, what's going to be best for them, what kind of therapies? There's just all kinds of things that we can do that I've learned to do over the last twenty-seven years.

"Now, specifically for a patient with a kidney condition, a degenerative kidney condition, I will first start off by recommending a book on nutrition that I suggest to all my patients, it's the absolutely best book on nutrition. It's called *Eat to Live,* by Dr. Joel Fuhrman. His diet is so amazing that it will help almost anybody with any medical condition to start reversing their condition. Particularly, it's an incredible diet for people with kidney disease. It's a nearly vegetarian diet that has high amounts of fruits, vegetables, beans, legumes, and whole grains, and dramatically reduces the salt, the oils, the processed carbohydrates, and the animal products. The typical American diet is 93 percent processed food and animal products. It's a disaster in the making. So what Dr. Fuhrman says and what we teach people is that we need to reverse those ratios.

"There's another doctor named Dr. Lorraine Day. I recommend her books and DVDs to people. She's an orthopedic surgeon who healed herself of invasive breast cancer when she was dying. And she's put together a program in one of her DVDs, *Cancer Doesn't Scare Me Anymore.* She's developed a ten-step program which anybody can follow, ten basic steps which I share with all my patients to help them to heal. The first item on the list is diet; the second one, exercise. She says the most important thing—and I try to teach this to my patients too—is that you absolutely have to believe and remember that it's God's will to heal anything and everything. Without that belief, you're not going very far.

"Mainly what I try to make people aware of is that they need to be in tune with the whole mind-body consciousness—that's who you are and you need to remember that. Who you are isn't really diseased or broken. And the more you can remember that, the quicker you're going to heal. So that's the message I really try to get at with patients. And while we're remembering who we are, at the same time we're going to do natural things that help our system to balance it out, that are nontoxic. So the most important thing, the most important message I always have for people is we're not treating your disease, we're seeking the disharmony in your body and to get rid of the disharmony. We're seeking to remember the harmony that's programmed into us by God, our creator. So I change their focus from a disease-oriented system to a health-oriented system, and tell them, 'That's your natural gift of spirit, or God. That's who you are, and you've forgotten that.'

"Then I teach them how to remember that. I teach them certain laws of nature. I tell them to watch what animals do in the wild. Animals always eat a very specific diet, a healthy diet for their species type. They drink pure water, they exercise and move around, they're in tune with the cycles of nature. So I try to get people more in tune with those natural cycles, and get them aware, spiritually, of who they are.

"I'm also a licensed minister, so part of the treatment is based in spiritual healing as well. I'll do prayer with the patients. We pray every time they come in. And Alonzo can tell you this. Every single time I'll do prayer and open it up to the power of spirit in the person so that life force and energy can be released. We use nutritional supplements, other natural supplements, all kinds of different natural remedies we have at our disposal.

"What I try to do then is tailor a program for each individual based on history, physical examination, the information I'm getting from the energetic testing. I do extensive laboratory testing. I order a lot of tests that regular doctors don't do, from hormone tests to nutritional tests, heart risk factors. By putting all this together, I get a pretty good idea what's going on with the patient, and then I basically ask their body, based on this, what they need, how much they need. And each time they come in, we sort of go through this and fine-tune it."

13

OVERTOWN

Marty Margulies was in his sixties, a successful real estate developer, an art collector, a philanthropist, and a Miami Heat season ticket holder when one day, around 1999, he called Alonzo Mourning to invite him over to his penthouse on top of the Ritz-Carlton on Key Biscayne.

The two knew each other casually from Heat games and charity work. Margulies had been a loyal supporter of Mourning's annual Zo's Summer Groove festival and through the years had become impressed with Mourning's dedication to charity.

"Alonzo is a highly intelligent person," Margulies said. "He had come a long way from the person I used to watch on television when he was in college, where he appeared so angry."

After showing off his museum-quality art collection and breathtaking views, Margulies sat Mourning down and made a proposal. He wanted to build a youth center in an impoverished Miami neighborhood—maybe

Overtown, maybe Opa-Locka, maybe Carroll City. Somewhere where the need was great.

He was willing to donate $2.5 million to start the project. But he needed some hands-on help. For a youth center to succeed, it needed the credibility and energy that Mourning and his organization could bring.

"I felt it would be very important to have a name celebrity attached, and I knew Alonzo was committed to youth," Margulies said. "I don't see a lot of other athletes with that commitment. He gives his time, he gives his talent, and he's hands-on. It's not just, 'Here's a check, have a good time.' "

Mourning was floored at the proposal. He was still in his late twenties, with a young family, and he was trying to win an NBA Championship with the Heat. He already had minimal free time. This would be a major undertaking, one that would require concentrated effort and focus to succeed. He would have to hire a staff, and provide daily management, additional fundraising, oversight, planning, and on and on and on.

But, then again, he had gotten to know Overtown through the years. Standing in downtown Miami, you can look east or west. Almost everyone looks east, to Miami Beach, where the famous clubs, restaurants, and luxury condos are.

Alonzo always used to look west, to Overtown, one of the most blighted and hopeless communities in the country. He even used to drive through it on the way to games, a final reminder of how fortunate he was to be making millions playing ball. The community so touched him that each Thanksgiving he went door-to-door handing out free turkeys.

But that was just one or two days a year. That was just one meal. This kind of project could change everything.

"I just looked at Marty and said, 'Wow,' " Alonzo said. "Then I thought for a second and said, 'Okay, I'll do it.' "

Muhammad Ali said, "Service to others is the rent you pay for your room here on earth." That remark always stuck with me, because as soon as you start losing perspective on that, you start losing perspective on God's original plan for us to be here.

We are on this earth to help each other out so we can all live a peaceful life. That's why the earth was created, for all of us to live together. Slowly but surely, though, we're destroying it with the things that we do, whether damaging the environment or damaging each other. Slowly but surely, we are forgetting about the rent we owe. Slowly but surely, we are forgetting about God.

We are all products of someone else's service to us. None of us got to where we are all by ourselves; no one walks this earth alone. When I think about my life and all the obstacles I've had to deal with, both as a child and as an adult, I realize that my success was not just the result of my hard work, but the product of a lot of people's hard work. It is easy for me to say, "I made the NBA," but it wouldn't be accurate. I didn't do it by myself. Without individuals surrounding and supporting me through the years, I wouldn't be in this situation.

My life isn't what it is just because of me. My life is what it is because of so many other people. When you're a professional basketball player, living a life where you receive so much adulation, that is easy to forget. Perhaps it is for someone with a regular job, also.

So I strive to pay my rent. Just as I wouldn't have developed without people believing in me, so others won't develop unless someone believes in them. Sometimes I need to be that someone.

I was easy for people to find. I had talents that were easy to identify. I was so tall; I was a great athlete at an early age; I was someone who had a very obvious future. I was also someone who could make money for others by playing basketball, whether it was a college or a professional team owner. If basketball wasn't a popular and profitable game, then I wouldn't have received the help I did. My value was obvious. But what about kids whose talents aren't so easy to spot, so easy to profit from?

Others invested in me because of my athletic ability. But there was so much more to me than that. Basketball was how I got to Georgetown,

but once I got there it turned out I was capable of excelling academically also. It turned out that, when exposed to and challenged by a great
academic environment, I could not only succeed initially but also develop a lifelong interest in education, philanthropy, politics, and many
other fields. It turned out my talents were not restricted to basketball. I
have paid my rent in more ways than just entertaining people by playing basketball.

But without basketball drawing the interest of others who could
help me, what might have become of the rest of my talents? Where
would I have been then?

What happens if no one invests in that kid who may be easy to miss
but has the cure for cancer in him, or who has a great business mind,
or who can be a great musician or teacher or community leader? I believe that our exposures and our experiences dictate our destiny. The
person who experiences Georgetown has a different view of the world's
possibilities than the person who never experienced anything outside
of their neighborhood. It's so important for us to, as a people, create
better experiences for our children. All of our children.

So right away, when I got to the NBA, I wanted to do something to
help out, to help organizations who help kids. I knew I was in a position
to do a lot of good things. Because of basketball, I had an opportunity
to get people to listen to me. I promised myself I would take advantage
of that. I simply would not allow myself to fail the people who helped
me; passing it forward, helping others, is the best way to honor those
people.

I always look for places to help, for things to do. When I pick up a
newspaper and read about a kid dealing with illness, or hear about our
broken educational system, or learn about the need for a gun buy-back
plan—whatever it is, that motivates me. I can't just sit there and turn
the page. One of the women who works for my charity, Lisa Joseph,
receives phone calls from me at all hours of the day, brainstorming
about this idea or that. I see so many problems, it fuels the fire to do
more.

•   •   •

When I got to Charlotte, my first passion was foster care, which obviously was dear to my heart. I was twenty-two years old, just four years out of a foster home myself, and I understood how difficult that could be. I would look at all those kids in the foster homes, in the group homes, and I'd say, "These kids have the same abilities I did; they just need someone to help them find and accomplish their dreams."

There was and still is a great organization in Charlotte, the Thompson Children's Home—now Thompson Child and Family Focus. It was founded in 1886 and in a variety of ways embraces children who are at risk for social and academic failure. It is a place that provides intensive treatment, protection, specialized education, and stabilized family environments. When I first learned about it, I immediately began to support it in any way I could. I was still young and trying to adjust to the NBA, so I only did so much—at least, compared to now—but it felt great to do what I could. But when I left the Hornets for Miami I felt like I had abandoned the Thompson Children's Home.

Soon after, I was invited by Magic Johnson to Los Angeles for a summer festival he threw to raise funds for his charities. He staged an all-star game with a weekend full of events. I decided I wanted to do something like that on the East Coast. I had started my own foundation, Alonzo Mourning Charities (AMC) and I wanted to hold a big party each summer that was a way to bring people of all races together, serve the community, and raise funds to provide enrichment and educational opportunities for kids. The creative minds at Nike came up with the name, Zo's Summer Groove, and we ran with it.

We did a lot of different things—a basketball game, a youth summit, concerts, and a block party, all of which were reasonably priced for the people in the community. I wanted regular working families to enjoy it also. Then there was a golf outing and a big charity dinner to help raise money. We'd hold the concerts at Miami Arena and I could keep ticket prices down because I got the artists to cut their fee since it was for charity.

Each year with the help of my good friend, Andre Napier, who served as my COO, we worked relentlessly to top the Groove of the year before. The first year we had Chris Rock host the concert, which included Hootie and the Blowfish and Adriana Evans. People were blown away at how big it was. I was just twenty-five and new in town, but this made an impression. Then the next year we had Gladys Knight, Brian McKnight, and the comedian George Wallace. Then Lenny Kravitz, Cedric the Entertainer, and Jamie Foxx. Then Bill Cosby. We were getting all these personalities to come down and people were saying, "This is serious."

We raised a lot of money for Alonzo Mourning Charities and we were turning the money over to two groups. There was the Children's Home Society for Abused and Neglected Children, which helps find homes for some of the country's most vulnerable kids. The other was 100 Black Men of America, which is a mentorship program for young men that strives toward the intellectual development of youth and the economic empowerment of the African-American community based on respect for family, spirituality, justice, and integrity.

I was honored to support those organizations because we didn't just provide money but also publicity for them, which allowed more and more individuals from the city, from the community, to become aware of them and embrace them.

The thing about the "100" is, I think for all children, but especially for black children, it is so important to find the proper, positive role model to help you make the right decisions and be a productive citizen. One of the young men who came through the "100" is a local teenager, Stanley Davis, who has so much talent and personality I expect he'll become president of the United States one day. He gave an incredible speech at our 2007 dinner in Miami.

"If a woman's best friend is diamonds," he said, "and man's best friend is a dog. Then a young man's best friend is a mentor."

We lack role models and mentors in so many of our communities, and as a result we let so much great talent just fall by the wayside.

I believe in preventative work, in being proactive in helping people. If you can mentor a young man to a productive life, then society no longer has to carry him along. Seventy-five percent of the prison population doesn't have a high school diploma or a GED. A lot of people look at that number one way, as a sad coincidence. I look at it as an opportunity.

People who have even just a high school diploma are less likely to wind up in prison. If you get a kid to graduate from high school, you greatly decrease the chances he will be a convicted felon. As a nation, if we invested in education up front, it could cut the crime rate, cut the money we spend on incarceration. We spend $35,000 a year on each prison inmate. It doesn't cost that much to get a kid through high school and send them to community college or even all but the most elite universities. The numbers don't add up. If we focused on education, we'd also be focusing on crime prevention, prison costs, and improving the economy. These are things people know—but it's not the kind of policy argument that wins debates, wins elections. This is why I could never be a politician.

The 100 Black Men takes kids who are at risk and gives them the tools, guidance, and support to excel. The benefits of that are incalculable. That's why I support it; that's why I see a group like that as so important for our country. The thing is, you never know how it will play out, what that work could mean down the road. One of these kids may have that cure for focal glomerulosclerosis. But we'll never know if we don't give them the chance, if we don't invest in them. The reason I am where I am is because of exposure. If you expose these kids to the right things, the synapses are going to fire.

Consider the opportunity that Bill Cosby gave to my wife. Consider the opportunity I received to go to Georgetown because of basketball. Without those things, it is possible neither of us would be in this position. Odds are, we wouldn't.

My wife now runs Honey Shine, a mentoring program for at-risk young girls in south Florida, girls like she once was herself. It provides positive experiences that nurture the mind, body, and soul of young women, that brighten their paths and create balance in their life. She's touched hundreds and hundreds of lives, helped so many young girls down here. Honey Shine wouldn't have been established had Tracy not gone to college, and, for that, she certainly owes a debt of gratitude to Bill Cosby.

So less than twenty years ago, Bill Cosby decided to help one girl in Las Vegas, for no reason other than admiration for her mother and a profound sense of generosity. Now he is indirectly helping hundreds of young girls in south Florida. It's like a pyramid scheme of good work. It expands out. He didn't know what would happen when he sent Tracy to college. For all he knew, it wouldn't accomplish anything. But look where it went. Look at all these girls who are benefiting from his investment, benefits he couldn't have fathomed all those years ago. So what will happen to the girls in Honey Shine, who will they impact, how many people will they be helping twenty years from now? Mr. Cosby's investment will continue for generations to come.

That's God's work. It's not just about giving money and material things. It can be just giving a smile, a hug, love, encouraging words. If everyone had that mentality, we wouldn't have the issues we have in the world. Even just a fraction of that and we could cut many of the problems.

Even as I got the Summer Groove going, I always knew I was in a position to do more and more. I was about twenty-eight years old when Marty Margulies called and set up the meeting that changed my life. This was a big undertaking. It is one thing to run a foundation and the Summer Groove, which takes place in the off-season, and then dole out the money to various charities. It is one thing to go to Overtown each Thanksgiving with a bunch of turkeys and hand them out. That was fun, going door-to-door in these poor apartment complexes and neighborhoods and seeing how shocked people were not only to see me there, but see me with a turkey under my arm. But that was only one or two days of the year.

To be involved at the grassroots level with something that operates year round is a different thing altogether. I was trying to win a championship with the Heat. I had a young family.

But the meeting, the idea for a real youth center, this man Marty Margulies—it all came out of nowhere. I just thought, "Okay, Lord, you gave me these physical gifts for a reason, and playing basketball was not supposed to just be it. So I have used the benefit of being an NBA player to give back. You helped me form this foundation, Alonzo Mourning Charities, for a reason; but running Zo's Summer Groove, as great as it is, was not supposed to just be it. Your plan was for Marty Margulies, a man with great resources, who sits behind our bench, to see what we did, understand we were honest and genuine, and then decide to take the work to even greater heights. This is the reason you keep blessing me. And I know a lot of good comes out of doing your work, out of giving. That is all Christ did on this earth. So I need to answer this call, I need to follow your plan."

If you believe in Christ, then you know that he was put on this earth to serve and not to be served. And if there was any man who deserved to be served, it was him. All he did was heal the sick, teach people, feed people, comfort them. All he did was improve mankind with his words and his actions. He never asked for anything in return, he was just a carpenter. He is the best example of how we should live.

So I looked at the situation and said, "I have to try. I can't turn my back on this opportunity." I looked at Marty and said, "Let's do it. Look, if you are willing to come out of your pocket for $2.5 million, then I want to help do it, I want to make sure this center is financially viable for years and years to come and this community is going to get everything it can out of it."

I was determined right there that this was going to work. I was willing to come out of my own pocket, I was willing to put my reputation on the line for this center, I was willing to put in time in Overtown, hiring the staff, meeting the kids, reaching out to the skeptical community, to the neighborhood. I was willing to provide credibility to the center, to help parents trust we were doing the right thing.

I immediately got in touch with a good friend of mine, Andre Napier, who was a frat brother of mine at Omega Psi Phi back in college. He helped me start Alonzo Mourning Charities and worked as an executive director.

"Andre, we're going to do this, but we have to make sure we have the very best program in the country, we can't make any mistakes."

He put some feelers out and learned that the best out-of-school organization in America is called Self Enhancement Incorporated (SEI). This is a facility in Portland, Oregon, that was founded in 1981 as a one-week camp for high school boys. Now it serves some 2,300 kids and their families year-round in a community somewhat similar to Overtown. It has a 98 percent high school graduation rate, with 85 percent of the kids moving on to college. It's amazing. Even some of the wealthiest suburban schools, even private high schools, can't match those numbers. So many people from that program have gone on to very productive lives and now they are back working at SEI. It has changed the entire neighborhood.

I contacted the founder and executive director of SEI, Tony Hopson, and flew him down to have him help us with the curriculum, the building, the planning, everything.

There are plenty of needy areas in Miami, but we settled on the Overtown section, one of the poorest neighborhoods in America. It is among Miami's oldest neighborhoods, just northwest of downtown and in the shadow, these days, of all the skyscraping condo developments that have sprung up there.

It has always been a predominantly minority neighborhood, but back in the mid–twentieth century, it was full of life, sort of like South Beach today. There were a bunch of clubs and concert venues where Count Basie, Cab Calloway, Ella Fitzgerald, Nat King Cole, and Aretha Franklin used to play. I first became aware of Overtown when I came to the Heat. Rather than just drive to the old Miami Arena via the highway, I used to take side streets because I wanted to be in touch with the city. I drove through Overtown often and was distressed by the decay and poverty. That's why I started giving away turkeys and groceries and things like that.

Overtown was the perfect place for a center, both in necessity and symbolism. You can see Overtown, look right down into it, from the balconies of some of the most expensive high-rises in Miami. And yet there it sits. The split between wealthy Miami and poor Miami is just so stark, a division between power and poverty.

We have kids at the center who have never been to the beach. They live in Miami, just a couple of miles across the bridge from Miami Beach, and they have never been to the ocean. They have no idea. It's

Thanksgiving in Overtown (Jo Winstead/ Alonzo Mourning Charities)

like there is an invisible fence up around their community. They don't go over there; no one takes them; they barely even know it exists. Since parts of the beach are public property, they could go for free. And while they were there, they could walk past the art deco hotels, the nightclubs, the mansions, the art galleries, everything. They could have their horizons expanded and their minds inspired. But they don't go. Things like that are just sickening to me.

That's why I want to provide as much exposure as I can for these kids so that they can grow and flourish and find their potential. If they can't see Miami Beach, they can't dream of moving there one day. In much of America, kids have the opportunity to try a lot of different things and find out their talents. Maybe someone's a great musician. Somewhere along the line, that person was handed an instrument and told to give it a try. But what if that had never happened?

My uncle told me one day, "You know what? God makes no mistakes. At all." And I've shared that with plenty of these kids. I've told them, "Look, each and every one of you here has a talent, and the only way for you to find out what that talent is, is for you to educate yourself. And that's why you were given the tools that you were given to use. You've got a good brain. You've got a good physical stature. You've got to use all that to your benefit to find out your purpose here. You have to ask yourself, What is my purpose here?"

It was hard work, but we got the Overtown Youth Center, this beautiful facility, opened in 2003. The staff at my charity, including Grace Castro and Lisa Joseph, worked tirelessly on this. We built on the corner of Northwest 14th Street and Northwest 3rd Avenue, right under where I-95 and I-395, the highway to South Beach, meet. We have classrooms, computer labs, basketball courts, and so much more. We've already had nearly three hundred kids come into the program, a great number considering the entire population of Overtown is only eight thousand.

We try to get kids who value an education, who respect themselves and each other. That is almost all we ask of the kids. As long as they value the opportunity, we don't care where they come from. We have kids coming into our program in the sixth grade who can't read or write. We'll take them. The only way we won't take them is if their attitude changes, if they won't buy into the culture. We won't let the good kids get dragged down.

We provide so many different things—not just after-school educational programs, but also dance, sports, computers, just a safe haven. We provide the basic medical and dental care that many of these kids would never get otherwise.

We also do a lot of things that are, for lack of a better word, just *simple*. People don't understand some of the obstacles that are faced in teaching kids. We try to get them some food. Some of these kids don't get breakfast in the morning, so their attention span isn't great at school. Just providing some food in the morning can make a huge difference.

We have locker rooms with showers, and we wash clothes. That sounds like nothing, but some of these kids come from families that are completely broken down. If there is no dad and their mom is out on the street, then there is no one to wash their clothes. They may not have the money for a coin machine. Or the water in their apartment is turned off. Some of these kids have real hygiene issues that affect their participation in school.

Think about how self-conscious you were in junior high school, think about how the littlest thing could get blown up and get in the way of concentrating on school. If you are in junior high and you don't have clean clothes or you can't shower and be clean, think about how you would have approached a day at school. Eventually you would stop going. Or if you did go to school, you'd sit in the back and not draw attention to yourself, hope no one noticed you and made fun of your situation. Some of these kids drop out or fall behind for reasons that are so basic, so simple. For some kids, just a hot shower and washing their clothes makes a world of difference—because we know that, if a kid can't compete in a classroom environment, then their first reaction is to rebel. And that's where the trouble starts. We lose kids in this country over little things like this.

We don't have a mountain of statistics to show our success yet, but we will. We're just getting started and we look forward to the day when we can point to numbers like the ones at SEI. We did send five kids off to college last year. That was our first group. It was very emotional for me, because I remember day one, just trying to get some legs under this organization and trying to establish this SEI culture. To be able to see five kids go to college reminded me what it is all about. Five kids, five families in Overtown, had their lives changed forever. It's just a start, but these are five kids who now have the opportunity to go to college. And you know, maybe they don't all become doctors and lawyers, because education wasn't always valued in their homes. But you know that they will value education when they have kids, and that next generation will strive further.

I want to create this culture in every impoverished area in south Florida, where, despite so much wealth, we have some of the worst schools in America. It really is God's work, because it wasn't my idea to open the Overtown Youth Center, it was Marty Margulies's. His vision has inspired me to want to set up these centers across south Florida, across the state, maybe even in the entire country.

I know that God's plan wasn't for me to just stop in Overtown, just as God's plan for me wasn't to stop with playing basketball or handing out a few Thanksgiving turkeys. God is always giving you more, always building on what you are capable of. His full plan has not been revealed.

I started by handing out dinner in Overtown; now we're trying to hand out dreams. You think I'm suddenly going to stop?

14

THE TITLE

Like the two biggest dogs on the block, Alonzo Mourning and Shaquille O'Neal had been staring each other down for years. They went 1 and 2 in the 1992 NBA Draft. They went 1 and 2 in Rookie of the Year voting a year later. They battled through the years in game after game, Shaq bigger, bolder, and more successful, reaching five NBA Finals and winning three championships.

"But he had better teams," Alonzo would point out.

And that was true. Alonzo never had a Penny Hardaway or a Kobe Bryant as his running mate. If he had, then perhaps Alonzo Mourning and Shaquille O'Neal would have had one of those legendary NBA rivalries, like Wilt Chamberlain and Bill Russell or Larry Bird and Magic Johnson.

"There was a constant rivalry between us. He won championships. I didn't," Alonzo said. "I always felt I worked harder than him at all times. I felt I put more time into my body and he was just fortunate to have better teams."

While the rivalry didn't play out in hotly contested playoff games, it was very real. These two were not friends even if they pretended to be while spending time together on all-star teams and extended tours with USA Basketball. They were pleasant, they laughed, they even went out at night together, but the underlying edge always remained.

"We had a lot of battles on the court," Shaq said. "Alonzo wanted to be the toughest guy in the league. But I was the toughest guy in the league, so he couldn't be."

Shaq said that with a smile. He always smiled. Did he mean it or did he not?

Alonzo Mourning? He never smiled. If he said it, he meant it.

"One thing you learn real quickly about Zo is he is not a phony," explains Pastor Willie Alfonso. "What you see is what you get. He is not going to try to be something he is not."

But when he was dealing with Shaq, too often he was phony. Just as Shaq was with him. And then, late in the 2004–2005 season, Alonzo returned to the Miami Heat. And who should be waiting for him but Shaquille O'Neal, who had arrived via a trade himself.

"I never even considered Shaq and I could ever be teammates," Alonzo said.

But a funny thing happened when the two distant adversaries shared the same NBA jersey, when the two aging centers united to accomplish a singular goal—bring a championship to south Florida.

"It turns out, we complement each other better than I ever thought," Alonzo said. "We became real friends."

The feeling was mutual. Whatever reservations O'Neal had about Zo, whatever ill will lingered from old battles, quickly faded as he got to know Alonzo Mourning the teammate, not the opponent.

"I was the biggest hypocrite in the world when it came to Zo," Shaq said. "I didn't like him. But I didn't know him. He's a principled man who cares about his family and his community and his teammates. That's what I found out.

"Alonzo Mourning is a great man. A great man."

I never should have left Miami. I signed with the Nets in 2003 because I thought it was a great opportunity to play with Jason Kidd and win an NBA Title. I was caught up in things like market value.

Leaving Miami did have a couple of benefits. I was closer to Dr. Appel, I met Pastor Willie, and in my absence Pat Riley added the pieces that he then was able to trade to Los Angeles in the summer of 2004 for Shaquille O'Neal. Shaq had won three NBA titles with the Los Angeles Lakers but had gotten into a feud with Kobe Bryant. The Lakers had to choose between the two and they went with the younger guy. Shaq wound up with my old position, starting center of the Miami Heat.

I wasn't sure how I felt about that. I was working out in Miami that summer with Shuichi, so when the Shaq deal was announced I was in town to see the excitement.

Shaq mobilized the fans immediately—I was amazed at the crowd that turned out to welcome him to Miami. I wasn't upset he was coming, but I was surprised that the Lakers had traded him. He and Kobe Bryant won three titles together—why break that up? They had their differences, but why not sit those two down, work it out, and keep putting good pieces around them?

Shaq and I had always been rivals, and through the years we measured ourselves against each other. But if he was now a member of the Miami Heat, then fine. I was a member of the New Jersey Nets. And my main focus in the summer of 2004 was just returning to that team and helping them win a championship. I couldn't worry about Shaq, the Heat, or, really, anyone but me. My mind was in Jersey.

Stepping back onto an NBA court became an obsession for me. Not only did I want to play the game I loved and not only did I want to win an NBA title, but I looked upon myself as a role model for people with kidney disease. I wanted people who might doubt they could get back on their feet and live a normal life to see me in the NBA and understand anything was possible. That motivation to show people how to turn a negative into a positive was profound. To have them realize that if you attack a challenge—*go make it happen*—then anything is possible.

My return concerned Dr. Appel. He wasn't so worried about my kidney failing, but rather about how the natural muscle breakdown from high-stress activity might damage it in the long term. Because I work out so much, I have naturally high muscle enzyme levels and those can lead to kidney breakdown. Hydration became the focus of my life because it can help reduce breakdown. Dr. Appel was even worried about me catching a simple cold or an infection because I was on so many immunosuppressants. Between Dr. Appel and Dr. Hotchner I was on so many medications and natural supplements, I was downing about forty pills a day. I carried around a small duffel bag full of pill bottles that rattled as I walked.

And of course my new kidney was in the front of my abdomen now, not the back, and in the NBA you never know where an inadvertent crash is going to happen. I got Nike to make a triangular plate with foam rubber wrapped around it, which fit into a pair of tights I would wear under my game shorts. This provided a shield that would defuse the pressure of a direct shot to the outside of the plate, away from the kidney. It was designed to protect the kidney, but no one knew whether it would work in an actual game.

There was a play later that season when Shaq knocked me down and fell on me as we both went for a rebound. The plate was well constructed but it wasn't built to withstand a 350-pound man falling on me. Dr. Appel was watching the game back in New York and he just cringed at the sight. He called me right after the game and I said, "Don't worry, Doc, I just lifted all three hundred and fifty pounds right off of me. It didn't hurt a bit." I think that was the day Dr. Appel realized I was truly back to normal.

My time with the Nets was one of slow but marked improvements. I wasn't the player I'd been before my disease, but I was coming along. I averaged 10.4 points and 7.1 rebounds a game. Not bad for a guy coming off a kidney transplant.

As excited as I was to be playing again, I wasn't thrilled with playing for the Nets. Right as the Heat were trading for Shaq in an effort to contend for an NBA title, the Nets made a deal with the Denver Nuggets to trade Kenyon Martin for three future draft choices. Kenyon and I weren't close friends, but he was our top big man and one of the core players who had led the franchise to two NBA Finals. Worse, we didn't get anything in return for that trade.

To me, this seemed like a cost-saving move. The Nets had a reputation for being a poorly run franchise. The team had just gotten a new owner in Bruce Ratner, a New York real estate developer with eyes on moving the team to Brooklyn. Ratner may have been new to the NBA, but I wasn't. I had been around long enough to see a rebuilding job, and that's what this was. If contending for a title was still a priority, they either would have kept Kenyon or traded him for quality players. To take draft choices was to save some money and build to the future.

I didn't have a future. I had no idea how long I could play. I had no idea if the next day was the day my illness returned or my body decided to reject Jason's kidney. Besides, I hadn't undergone a kidney transplant and then nine agonizing months with Shuichi to play for a team that wasn't committed to winning the championship. I wasn't risking enzyme levels damaging my new kidney or a stray elbow screwing everything up to play for an owner who wasn't being honest about the direction of the franchise. (The Nets haven't seriously contended for the title since.)

No one was going to determine the direction of my life but me. I had come too far. I wasn't going to *sit back and hope*. I was angry and frustrated at the entire situation and after eighteen games I decided I didn't want to play for the Nets anymore. It was a desperate time, and it called for desperate measures. If they couldn't trade me, then I would retire. But I wasn't going to play for an organization I didn't believe in. I decided to force the issue and in December of that year, I didn't go on a road trip with the team.

The Nets had no option but to try to trade me. They decided to send me to the Toronto Raptors in exchange for Vince Carter. This was going from bad to worse. The Raptors were 8–17 at the time and headed for the lottery. They said they wanted me to come in and be a veteran leader for their young guys. The Nets' GM, Rod Thorn, told them it was unlikely I would accept such a role, but they were so eager to get rid of Vince Carter, who fans had turned against, that they made the deal anyway.

There was no way I was going to go to Toronto. To join a team that wouldn't even make the playoffs would have meant I was playing solely for the money. There would be no other reason. And I wasn't about the money. I already had money.

I was always up front with Toronto. The Raptors' general manager, Rob Babcock, came to Miami and we had a face-to-face meeting at Jeff Wechsler's house. I said, "Look, I understand your position, but I didn't come back from transplant surgery to be some veteran leader to your young guys when you're rebuilding. I came back to win a champi-onship. So I am either going to retire, and you guys are going to be stuck paying me a lot of money, or I'm going to a contender."

The way my contract was structured, the Raptors were on the hook for nearly $15 million even if I decided to retire. Jeff said that might be best for my future, to take the money and preserve my health. But I wanted to win a championship. "Jeff," I said, "I see a great opportunity here and I want to seize it. Toronto is not going to dictate my career. I'm going to dictate my career."

After a prolonged battle that often got nasty in the newspapers, Toronto agreed to buy out my contract for $9 million. Before the surgery, I don't know that I would have given up $6 million to become a free agent, but that's what I did. Toronto released me on February 11, and on March 1, Jeff worked out a deal with my old team, the Heat. Miami only had to pay a prorated portion of the veterans' minimum, about $300,000.

I donated the entire amount to local organizations that promoted literacy for underprivileged youths and provided food and care to poor kidney dialysis patients. That was my way of telling the community that I was serious about coming back, that I was serious about making a change in the Miami area, and, basically, it was my way of apologizing for ever leaving in the first place.

•   •   •

We had the pieces in place to be successful and I had very high hopes. Dwyane Wade was in his second season and coming into his own as a great player. Eddie Jones was a terrific wing player who averaged 13 points per game. And obviously anytime you have Shaq, you have a chance to win it all.

In my return, I had to accept a different role on the team, and not just primarily as a backup to Shaquille. I also had to accept a secondary role in the locker room and with the fans. I used to be the face of the franchise, but now I was a backup joining a team that was well on its way to winning fifty-nine games and a division championship. The team had already found its identity. So it wasn't *my* team anymore, and I didn't want to step on anyone's toes. I just wanted to work hard and earn everyone's respect. I didn't do a whole lot of talking. I worked as hard as I could, and I competed. I just hoped my actions did the talking for me. And when I eventually settled in, I got my voice.

The media kept interviewing me like I was the star, though. And I think they were kind of waiting for something bad to happen. They would say, "Come on, Zo is used to being the man here." But they didn't understand my overall approach to the situation.

Winning a championship for myself and the franchise was my only motivation. I didn't care if I scored a single point. I just wanted to win. I knew it could not be done by two people. As good as Dwyane and Shaq could be, I've never seen two people win the championship. So I put forth a very sacrificial effort on and off the court to make sure we were successful, and everyone saw that. Each and every guy saw that, saw the work that I put in, the commitment I put in. Eventually I gained the trust of my teammates.

I never could've imagined playing with Shaq until we teamed up that first season. My first game in Miami was played two days after I signed, against my old team the Nets. We won, 106–90. I only played two minutes, grabbed two rebounds, and didn't score, but it felt good to be back. Shaq and I didn't play together on the court at all that night. We didn't play together much that first year. I'm actually not sure why we didn't explore that more often. Back in college I played alongside Dikembe Mutombo, who is seven foot two, and it was a fearsome combination.

But Pat Riley had moved to the front office and Stan Van Gundy was our coach at the time. Stan was Jeff Van Gundy's brother and this was his first head coaching job. Stan is a good guy, but at that point I thought he was overmatched and lacked the experience necessary to lead us to the championship. And I didn't have the time to wait for him to get it. I didn't have a lot of confidence in him because I didn't think he used the personnel correctly.

There was a game at Indiana that we lost in overtime. Stan played me only four minutes and in the fourth quarter, when we needed some defensive stops to win the game, he left me on the bench. I knew I could've really helped. He had the wrong lineup in the game and it cost us a victory. One of my teammates came up to me after and said, "Does Stan have something against you, did you do something to him?"

"No," I said,

"Well, he needs to put you in the game."

We swept the Nets in the first round of the playoffs. That felt good. I had a big Game 2 with 21 points and 9 rebounds on a night when Shaq was off his game. That was my focus, being ready to put up starter's numbers when Shaq struggled. The rest of the time I just wanted to play great defense and grab rebounds. I didn't pay attention to how many shots I took or anything like that. I knew my role.

Shaq is a unique player. He understands when he's lacking energy or is hampered by an injury, and he isn't afraid to admit it. A lot of guys will pretend that they're bringing their A-game night in and night out. Not Shaq. One night during the playoffs he came up to me on the bus and said, "Big Man, I don't have it tonight. You have to get me tonight." At that stage of his career, there were times Shaq could still be the most dominant player in the league and times when he just couldn't do it. I was glad he admitted that. It allowed me to prepare mentally.

I loved it when beat writers would come up to me before the game and say, "Shaq's not starting. What are you going to do?" I've been doing this my whole career. This isn't foreign territory. Things like that motivated me because the media still doubted my ability to impact the game after the transplant. I had to keep showing people I could still do it.

In the second round, we swept Washington, 4–0. I started Games 3 and 4 when Shaq was out with a thigh bruise. We were 7–0 in the play-offs going into the Eastern Conference Finals against the Detroit Pistons, the defending NBA champions. It was a heated series that wound up going seven games.

All through the series, the media was coming up to me asking, "Why doesn't Van Gundy play you and Shaq together? You can play some power forward." The Pistons would've had a matchup problem against us because their two big men were Rasheed Wallace, who wasn't a great post defender, and Ben Wallace, who was tough but un-dersized. When Shaq was in there alone, they could concentrate on him. But if we were both in there, they couldn't counter because Ben would've had to guard me, leaving 'Sheed alone on Shaq. In single coverage we should have been able to score at will.

But it never happened. I ran into the Pistons' coach, Larry Brown, two years later and he asked why Stan didn't put us both in there. He said he couldn't understand it: "If you guys had played Shaq and you together, I wouldn't have had an answer for that."

He said he had been concerned about that the entire series, expect-ing it to happen. He and his assistants had stayed up at night trying to figure out how to guard both of us at the same time. But we never ex-ploited that advantage. That goes back to the talent of a coach and the knowledge of a coach. It's like a chess game. Larry had it and Stan didn't. I was particularly angry after Game 7. We lost, 88–82. I should have been in there at the end to help with defense, when we needed a stop to win it. But I watched us lose from the bench. I came back to win a championship, and once again we fell short.

Despite my disappointment I wanted to re-sign with Miami that off-season. San Antonio, which had gone on to beat Detroit in the finals, called Jeff and offered me big money to join them. The Spurs offer and

the chance to play alongside Tim Duncan to win the title were tempt-
ing. But I turned the offer down to stay with the Heat. Miami was
home, I thought we were close to winning it all, and I didn't want to
play for anyone else.

Micky Arison is the owner of the Heat and I felt a great deal of loyalty to him. Micky's a class act. His wife, Madeleine, and my wife,
Tracy, are very close, and in 2000 when I rushed home from the
Olympics in Australia to see the birth of my daughter, Micky sent the
team plane to meet me in Los Angeles so I could make it to the hospital in Miami in time. As you know, I got there with twenty minutes to
spare. He made that happen. There is no way I can repay for him for
that. The only way I knew how to do so was with my loyalty.

Micky's a smart businessman, too. He's a billionaire, a cruise ship
mogul. And when it comes to basketball, he's smart enough to hire the
right people and leave it to them to make good decisions.

Some of those good decisions came that summer, when Riley
traded Eddie Jones to Memphis for Jason Williams, a good point guard,
and James Posey, a valuable forward. He also signed veterans Antoine
Walker and Gary Payton to join Dwyane, Shaq, and me as a nucleus to
win a championship. We started slow, though, losing ten of our first
twenty games, and Stan resigned soon after. Riley took over as the
coach, which pleased me because I knew we now had a coach who was
capable of delivering us to the championship.

We wound up winning the division again and matched up with
Chicago in the first round of the playoffs. We had struggled toward the
end of the season, I missed a number of games because of a torn calf
muscle, and a lot of people picked the Bulls to beat us.

We went up 2–0 that series with a couple of home wins in front of
what was becoming a really enthusiastic crowd. But then things started
to unravel in Chicago. We lost Game 3, 109–90. Then in Game 4 we
were locked in a close game when Gary Payton took a shot and in the
ensuing time-out he and D-Wade argued about it in the huddle. They
just exploded on each other. We were on the bench trying to get everyone calmed down. We lost the game, the series was suddenly 2–2, and
it looked like we were imploding.

That's when Riley pulled one of his classic motivational tricks. Pat is a Hall of Fame coach not just because he understands basketball but also because he knows how to motivate a group of talented players. He finds a way to get everyone on the same page. He gets all these millionaires to sacrifice individual glory for the team goal. *A team is most successful when individual glory is not the concern.*

Right there in the middle of the Chicago series, with the wheels about to fall off and a change in energy desperately needed, he had a giant tin pen built in the middle of our locker room. He told us we were going to place all that we knew and loved in the pen. It would serve as a symbol of what we're playing for and remind us to ignore everything else.

He printed up thousands of little cards that said "15 Strong" on one side—because that's how many players are on the team—and the other side of the cards had pictures of our wives, our families, and other things that mattered to us. He said that the contents of the pen would be our secret; it was our thing. Then he put a blanket over the pen when the media came into the locker room. No one knew what it was but us. It became a big topic to speculate about.

As the playoffs went along, we keep putting stuff in there. Before every game, Riles or one of the players would roll in a wheelbarrow and dump a hundred more cards in the bucket. He even had the managers pack it up and take it on the road and set it up in the visiting locker room.

It sounds stupid, but it worked. The way I looked at it, he was putting good, positive energy in there. If we put good, positive energy in there, right in the middle of our locker room, we could build off it.

What was in that pen signified everything that each and every player was about. It signified us. And it helped us beat the Bulls. We held home court in Game 5 to take a 3–2 lead and closed the series out in Game 6 in Chicago, 113–96. Shaq took us home that night. He had 30 points and 20 rebounds, just dominated. That was the difference. He was all over the place.

After Chicago, we played the Nets again in the Eastern Conference semifinals. We lost Game 1, 100–88, when Vince Carter and Jason

Kidd both nearly had triple-doubles. But we rebounded and swept the next four games. It was no contest. I enjoyed beating the Nets again.

D-Wade took his game to another level against New Jersey. He scored 30-plus in three consecutive games and averaged 28 points, 6 rebounds, and 7 assists in our wins. He was in the stratosphere as we prepared for a conference finals rematch against Detroit. It got to the point where we just sat back in close games and said, "Okay, D-Wade, save us. Do what you do. Make baskets, get boards, get steals. We'll do our thing, but save us." And he did.

The Pistons were a well-oiled machine. They probably had the best starting five in the league. Four of those guys were all-stars that year—Chauncey Billups, Rip Hamilton, and Ben and Rasheed Wallace—and after four consecutive trips to the Eastern Conference finals, they had their system down. Despite that, we should have beaten them the year before. We had them on the ropes in Game 7 and didn't take them out. But we were ready this time.

We won Game 1, 91–86, and they beat us by 4 in Game 2 to even the series. Game 3 was back in Miami and the crowd was great. But what really stood out was D-Wade. He scored 35 in Game 3, made 13 of 17 shots, and had the defensive play of the game when he blocked a dunk by Antonio McDyess that would have given the Pistons the lead. In Game 4, Wade was just as good. He had 31 more points. It was fun to watch him come into his own. He was securing his place in basketball history. We lost Game 5 in Detroit, but finally closed the Pistons out back in Miami.

Everyone contributed that game. Shaq had 28 points and 16 rebounds, Jason Williams scored 21 on 10 of 12 shooting, and Wade had 14 after spending part of the day in the hospital with the flu. There was an amazing sense of urgency to win that game. We didn't want to go back to Detroit for a Game 7. We even talked about it in the huddle, talking about how "we're closing this out." We were so focused on clearing that hurdle and eliminating all the doubters who thought we couldn't do it. We were 15 strong.

The victory advanced us to the NBA Finals for the first time in franchise history. A night later, the Dallas Mavericks beat the Phoenix

Suns in Game 6 of their Western Conference series, and the Finals were set.

I had read both of Lance Armstrong's books about dealing with cancer and returning to win the Tour de France when I was sick, and had gotten in touch with him. He was a great role model for me and we exchanged a lot of text messages during the Finals because he saw this as my Tour de France, my chance to climb the mountain and be a champion. He said even though he was a Texan and we were playing a Texas team, he wanted me to win.

It didn't matter to me who we played, and I don't think it mattered to my teammates. The important thing was just getting there, getting that monkey off the franchise's back. I'm the Heat's all-time leading scorer and rebounder, so while making the Finals would have been special on any team, I had deeper feelings about doing it with a franchise that meant so much to me.

Dallas had a good team. Very talented, very versatile and deep. They used their speed to get to the basket, but they were mainly jump shooters. Dirk Nowitzki was their star player and he is the prototype European player, a tall guy who plays outside. He was first-team all-NBA that year, averaged 26.6 points and 9 rebounds a game, but he doesn't like contact. I didn't guard him much until Game 6, but when I did I made sure to get up into him, bang him a little, and make him uncomfortable.

We lost Games 1 and 2 in Dallas by double digits. Jason Terry scored 32 in the opener and Dirk went for 26 and 16 three nights later. The national media basically declared the series over. Everyone claimed Shaq was done and we were too old. But we never felt that way. I thought we were just a little too relieved to be in the Finals.

Guys wondered why we were in this position after playing so well, but we never said, "This is over, we're going to lose." Our focus was on getting better so we could win the next game. That's Pat Riley to a T. Don't worry about the first two games because there isn't anything we can do about them. He has a saying he uses a lot, "A playoff series doesn't begin until someone loses on their home court." It's a way of keeping a team balanced whether they are up 2–0 or down 0–2. Since all that had happened was Dallas maintained home court advantage, he was saying that nothing had happened. We had the next three in Miami, there was plenty of time to come back. All we had to do was focus on getting better, improve on the things we could, and prepare.

In Game 3 we were down 13 with 6½ minutes to play, but Wade carried us to a 98–96 win. He scored 42 that game, 15 in the fourth quarter, and played the final 11 minutes with 5 fouls. Shaq made two big free throws in the final minutes, Udonis Haslem had a clutch steal, and Gary hit the go-ahead jumper with 9.3 seconds to play. It was a great victory.

The next night, the Mavs' owner, Mark Cuban, went on the *Late Show with David Letterman* almost like the series was over. You do the late-night shows after you win, not before, and Dallas was only up 2–1. Cuban might as well have poured kerosene on a campfire. He lit a real big fire under us. He had a parade planned. He knew he'd screwed up, but it was too late.

We won Game 4, 98–74, and Wade was great again. He scored 36 points; Shaq had 17 and 13 rebounds, and we got big contributions from our bench. Posey had a double-double in 26 minutes, I had 6 rebounds and 3 blocks, and the Mavs scored just 7 points, a Finals record low, in the fourth quarter. Our defense down the stretch was incredible. It felt like we wanted the title more than they did.

Their plan all series was to take away one of our stars, Shaq or D-Wade. They thought, *If we take Shaq out of it we have a chance.* Or, *If Shaq isn't in then we'll double D-Wade the moment he comes across halfcourt.*

But two things happened. First, there was so much space on the double team, D-Wade would cut right through the two defenders and score anyway. Second, they weren't counting on contributions from our bench, guys coming in and giving us a huge lift. That's what happened in Games 3 and 4. Everyone had his job and did it. Whether it was grabbing rebounds, playing defense, or knocking down some shots, the bench did its job. When we got in there, our level of play didn't fall off.

RESILIENCE   •   225

Shaq's contributions were still pivotal, even if his numbers weren't reminiscent of early in his career. Just his presence alone changed the game. Shaq played 47 minutes in Game 5, with 18 points and 12 rebounds, but D-Wade was the star again. He scored 43 and made two free throws with 1.9 seconds left in overtime to give us a 101–100 win.

Wade went to the line twenty-five times that game. Dallas fans were upset at some of the calls he got, but he deserved them. That's the way they want to call the game these days. So if you're supposed to call it that way, then that's what you do. That's what it's come to. Games are being called so you can't even arm-touch guys anymore. That wasn't how it used to be, and it's not how I like it, but the league changed. So he was going to the hole and drawing those calls. All I knew was we were 48 minutes from a world championship. But to win it, we'd have to win one of the next two games in Dallas.

We brought the "15 Strong" pen with us when we returned to Dallas for Game 6. To be a trainer on that team under Pat Riley and have to take that thing down and travel with it and bring the wheelbarrow and everything else must have been tedious. Those guys earned their pay.

But it inspired us that last game. Riles gave his pregame speech and at the end he took all his championship rings and held them up. He had five of them—one he won as a player alongside Wilt Chamberlain and Jerry West, and four he won coaching the Lakers. He had them strung together on some rosary beads. He made us look at them and then he threw them into the pen. All of them.

"I will give all five of those up to win this one," he said.

The room was silent. He always found a way to get you up and going and ready to run through a brick wall for him. We practically tore down the locker room door to get out on the court.

I've never been part of a team that played so well to close out a series on the road. In Game 6 we got contributions from everyone. Antoine Walker had a huge game, 14 points and 11 rebounds. Udonis Haslem had 17 and 10. I had 8 points, 6 rebounds, and 5 blocks. And of course D-Wade was D-Wade. He scored 36 that night to give him an

Even without the ball, you can help your team be better. (Andrew D. Bernstein/
National Basketball Association/Getty Images)

average of 39.2 over the last four games of the series. He just hit another
gear. You saw his game mature so fast in the pinnacle stage of professional basketball. I was so happy for him because he had worked incredibly hard as a young guy coming into the league. Everyone
questioned when the Heat drafted him, but he came in and made an
instant impact. And then to see him shine at this level was something.
I was just glad to be a part of it.

As the final seconds ticked off, I was standing there thinking, *God, all these years and now we're a minute away from winning the championship.*

When the Mavs' Jason Terry missed that last shot and our 95–92 win was complete, I just ran onto the court. I was jumping up and down, hugging people. Shaq and I shared a huge bear hug that just two years ago I would've said was impossible.

I saw my wife in the crowd, grabbed her and hugged her. We both cried.

"Thank you. Thank you for your patience," I told her.

I went up and grabbed Jason too—he'd come down to watch the game and see his old kidney win the NBA title. Later I called my kids, my parents, Bud and Mrs. Threet, John Thompson, Coach Lassiter, Dr. Appel, Dr. Hotchner, just about everyone I could think of to say thank you. I owed so many people so much.

Everything else is a blur. I missed Riley's postgame speech because I was out on the court doing a live TV interview, but I saw it later on the championship DVD. It was a short one, saying no one can ever, ever take that NBA Championship away from you. You are a world champion. Even Pat Riley was practically speechless.

The champagne was already popped when I got to the locker room, so I grabbed a couple of bottles. I hadn't had a sip of alcohol since that day in 2000 when Dr. Richards called to wake me up from a nap and introduce the words "focal glomerulosclerosis" into my vocabulary. But that wasn't going to stop me now, six years later. I took a big chug and then got doused with a bunch of beer. It was an incredible feeling.

Eventually we went back to the hotel in Dallas and spent a good four or five hours celebrating before taking the flight home. Shaq was on the mic all night in the ballroom, and everyone was drinking and eating and having a good time. Wives were even allowed on the flight home that night, for the first time, so I got to savor the moment with Tracy. It was great. I'd achieved something I'd been trying to accomplish my whole career, and I could finally exhale. A lot of guys out there played this game at a very high level and didn't do this, didn't win a championship. To be a part of a select group of guys, a very small percentage of all the people who played in the NBA, that's what you play for. All the blood, sweat, and tears had paid off.

In some ways, the most important moment of the night had come earlier in the celebration. While we were in the locker room spraying champagne and taking pictures, the NBA asked me to go to the media room to do a postgame interview. There was a big crowd of reporters there and when I took a seat at the podium I just let all my emotions out. I was asked to reflect on my darkest moment now that I was having my brightest one and my answer went on for almost seven minutes.

It wasn't even an answer as much as a speech. I talked about everything. Dr. Richards's call, my retirement announcement, my comebacks, my search for a donor, the transplant, the comeback, everything. I quoted Frederick Douglass. I thanked God. I thanked Jason Cooper. I thanked my doctors. I thanked my family. I talked about motivating others who are dealing with troubles, about the way reading Lance Armstrong's books motivated me when I was sick.

I think the reporters were stunned because during the early part of my career, they could barely get two sentences out of me. And here I was going on and on, talking about my emotions and pain and personal things like that. The speech was broadcast live on national television and moved a lot of people who were watching. Since then it has become a hit on YouTube. All I can say is that talk came truly from the heart, because I sure wasn't expecting to give it. I hadn't given one second of thought to what I was going to say in that situation.

But I guess I had been preparing my entire life for it.

EPILOGUE

I planned on celebrating December 19, 2007, the fourth anniversary of my transplant, by helping the Heat beat the Atlanta Hawks. I was trying to do just that by defending a fast break. The Hawks' Mario West was going in for a layup, and as I tried to jump to block the shot, my right knee buckled and I crumpled to the court.

I wound up in a seated position.

I turned over and started pounding the floor with my right fist. My knee felt like it was on fire. It was an instantaneous surge of pain too powerful even to describe.

My teammates started coming over to me and Pat Riley rushed out on the court and I just looked up to them and told the truth: "It's over. It's over."

I knew not only that my season was over, but maybe my career. I had debated returning for that season to begin with; I had only returned for the 2006–2007 season because I wanted us to defend our NBA title;

but age, injuries, and complacency caught up with us and we got swept in the first round of the playoffs.

After that sweep I had again considered retiring, but the season had been so disappointing; I didn't want to go out like that. I discussed it with Tracy and decided to play one more season. Then, I promised, I would retire.

This was not how I wanted my career to end, though. Our team wasn't very good. Shaq and Dwyane were dealing with injuries, we had a bunch of new guys trying to fit in, and when we eventually lost to Atlanta that night our record fell to 7–18. (We'd wind up trading Shaq and winning just fifteen games the entire season. It was a disaster.) As an athlete, you envision your final game ending in glory—your final exit off the court—and having my knee torn in half, with me pounding the hardwood in a half-empty Atlanta arena, in the middle of a forgettable season, was not the way I had pictured it happening.

I couldn't move. The doctors ordered a stretcher for me. I was in such pain that I was disoriented, and I got halfway onto the stretcher before coming to my senses. I barked:

"Oh, no. I'm not leaving the court on that."

Ron Culp, our head trainer, kept telling me to get on the stretcher.

"No. *No way.*"

I slid myself off the stretcher. There was simply no way I was being wheeled off the court. None. I was going to walk off even if my leg fell off in the process. They kept saying there was no other way, that I should just get on it. They said there was no shame in being carried off the court. But I wasn't going to listen to any of that. This knee injury was bad, but I had been through worse.

I yelled to my teammates at the other end of the court. Earl Barron and Dwyane Wade came running down and I told them to help me to my feet. If this was going to be my last time on the court in an NBA uniform, I was going to walk off. I thought, *what if ten years from now, twenty years from now, I'm watching TV and they show a clip of me leaving the court on a stretcher?* I would've been kicking myself.

Dwyane and Earl got me up, I put my arms around them, and we all walked off together. We walked off the court, down the hall, and into the locker room. I had help, but I was still on my feet. The Atlanta crowd gave me a standing ovation, not that I could hear it. I hurt so much I couldn't hear anything.

When I got to the locker room I called my son, Trey, who I knew would be watching at home and very worried. I told him I was going to be okay. Then I called Dr. Appel and Dr. Hotchner, Jeff, Tracy, and each of my parents. Afterward I spoke to the media, so the fans could hear from me also. They all wanted to know if this meant my career was over.

"Each of you here know I've been through a whole lot worse than this. It's disappointing to even think that my career would end this way, but there are so many other things that life has to offer for me. I have a great family and I have so many other opportunities out there."

At that point I just didn't know. I flew back home with my teammates, thinking the whole flight about my basketball future. It's funny as I think back on it: I was looking at the pocket schedule of the rest of the season, thinking about when I would come back, not realizing the severity of the injury.

I had surgery the next day, and it turned out my injury was one for the record books, the medical journals. Never before had doctors seen someone tear both the patellar tendon and the quad at the same time. When our team doctor, Harlan Selesnick, opened me up, he said my kneecap was just floating around in there like a computer mouse on a pad. He said he had to take a couple of looks at my patella just floating there to even believe it was true. He had seen people tear their patellar tendon; he had seen them tear their quad muscle. He had never seen both. No one had. What was expected to be a one-hour surgery wound up lasting two hours.

When I got out of surgery Dr. Selesnick told me my leg would be in a cast for four weeks. Then I'd be in a brace for six weeks. He told me he wasn't sure if I would ever walk normally again.

"Doc, you're crazy. I'm not going to be in this for six weeks."

I was already plotting my return. If I hadn't been injured, I would have retired. But once I did get injured, and once everyone started saying my career was over and that recovery from such a major injury was impossible, I started thinking about coming back. It was the challenge to prove everyone wrong, that old fire of doubt burning inside of me.

That was exactly what I needed to motivate me at rehab. I still don't know if I will return to the NBA, but I do know, rather than sitting around and seeing whether my knee will heal, I will put myself in a position physically to be able to return if I so choose.

Wait and hope, or go make it happen.

Two weeks after surgery I was out of that hard cast. Four weeks later I was out of the brace.

"I heal quick," I told Dr. Selesnick, who was dumbfounded by the speed of my recovery.

What he didn't know is I went over to see Dr. Hotchner, who gave me some tea to heal my knee. We brewed this big container of homeopathic tea and each night soaked a white cloth in it. Then I'd take the brace off, put the cloth around my knee, roll saran wrap around it, put the brace back on, and then sleep on it. Every morning I cut off the wrap. The tea soaked into my knee each night. It cut down the swelling, healed the soft tissue, bone, and cartilage, and improved my range of motion.

Does something like that really work? Six weeks after an historic knee injury I was rehabbing and working out again.

With the season off, I poured my attention into running my charities. I did more work with the National Kidney Foundation. I was a regular over at the Overtown Youth Center, where we prepared to watch another group of kids move on to college. And I worked on raising the capital to build another youth center in Miami Gardens, a city just north of Miami that's in great need. The mayor there was willing to provide us not only land but also $1 million in financing.

I rehabbed every day, slipped in a little golf, and spent a lot of time with my family. My son, Trey, is eleven now and turning into a great basketball player. The doctors predict he'll be seven feet tall, and he is already promising to break my records at Georgetown. I look forward to witnessing that.

I spent so much of my life battling against opponents. This was a year when I could relax a bit. I had my championship, I had my satisfaction, I had my health, and I had my happiness. Today my creatinine level is 1.5.

My goal is to continue that long walk with God. I want to use the gifts he has blessed me with to influence others in small ways—things like encouraging people to fill out an organ donor card—and I want to change the world in big ways, too, by continuing to build a foundation for children and families to succeed.

The power of influence is something that can't be forgotten or abandoned. Just as we ourselves are influenced, we can influence others, too. It is our purpose in this world God has given us. If you were the only person on earth, how would you learn? If you could only teach one person one thing, what would that lesson be?

Whether my playing career is over or not is something I will decide. Even if it is, if I determine that refusing that stretcher and hobbling off the court was actually the most symbolic way for my playing career to end, then I will retire without regret. My life will not be defined by 15,602 points, 7,802 rebounds, or 2,571 blocks. My lasting legacy will not be basketball. Playing basketball is how I earned my money on earth, but it is not how I paid my rent on earth.

There is so much more for me in life. I realized that when I fought for my future in front of that judge back in Virginia, when Georgetown opened my eyes and challenged my mind, when Magic Johnson inspired me to start a charity, when Marty Margulies dared me to take it further, when focal glomerulosclerosis changed everything, when all those kids, my kidney kids, sought inspiration, and when God, in so many ways, through so many people, reminded me of what was most important of all.

I think about all of that a lot now. I finally feel I have the time to reflect. My career might be ending, but my life might just be starting; God's plan for me is great. That I know. His plan is great for all of us.

One of the ways I spent my time while injured was to just sit on the back porch at my house. It has an incredible view of Biscayne Bay. You can see boats and birds, sunrises and sunsets. But the most powerful and profound time to sit out there and just look, to take in all of God's majestic creation, is when it rains.

ABOUT THE AUTHORS

ALONZO MOURNING is a seven-time NBA all-star and a two-time NBA Defensive Player of the Year. He won a gold medal for the United States at the 2000 Olympics and an NBA championship with the 2006 Miami Heat, where he is that franchise's all-time leading scorer. He was also a three-time All American at Georgetown, where he earned a degree in sociology. Mourning is a national spokesman for the National Kidney Foundation and operates Alonzo Mourning Charities, including Zo's Fund for Life. He, his wife, and their two children live in Coral Gables, Florida.

Named "America's Best Sports Writer" in 2006 by Salon.com, **DAN WETZEL** is an award-winning columnist for Yahoo! Sports, the most widely read sports site on the Web, and a regular guest on sports radio shows around the country. He is the co-author of three books, including *Glory Road* (with Don Haskins), which became a major motion picture.

ABOUT THE TYPE

This book was set in Electra, a type face designed for Linotype by W. A. Dwiggins, the renowned type designer (1880–1956). Electra is a fluid typeface, avoiding the contrasts of thick and thin strokes that are prevalent in most modern typefaces.